Royal Numismatic Society

The Rules of the Numismatic Society of London

Vol. I.

Royal Numismatic Society

The Rules of the Numismatic Society of London
Vol. I.

ISBN/EAN: 9783337172565

Printed in Europe, USA, Canada, Australia, Japan

Cover: Foto ©Lupo / pixelio.de

More available books at **www.hansebooks.com**

THE NUMISMATIC CHRONICLE,

AND

JOURNAL OF THE NUMISMATIC SOCIETY.

THE
NUMISMATIC CHRONICLE,

AND

JOURNAL

OF THE

NUMISMATIC SOCIETY.

EDITED BY

W. S. W. VAUX, M.A., F.S.A.,
JOHN EVANS, F.S.A., F.G.S.,
AND
FRED. W. MADDEN, M.R.S.L.

NEW SERIES.—VOL. I.

Factum abiit—monumenta manent.—Ov. Fast.

LONDON:
JOHN RUSSELL SMITH, 36, SOHO SQUARE.
PARIS: M. ROLLIN, RUE VIVIENNE, No. 12.
1861.

LONDON:
PRINTED BY JAMES S. VIRTUE,
CITY ROAD.

CONTENTS.

ANCIENT NUMISMATICS.

	Page
An account of a hoard of ancient British Coins discovered in the neighbourhood of Frome. By John Evans, Esq., F.S.A.	1
Silver Coin of Carausius. By John Evans, Esq., F.S.A.	36
On some Coins of Constans II. and his Sons, discovered in the Island of Cyprus. By the Hon. J. Leicester Warren, M.A.	42
An account of British Gold and Roman Silver Coins found at Lightcliffe, near Halifax, in the year 1827	79
On a Coin of Mallus in Cilicia. By R. S. Poole, Esq., M.R.S.L.	87
On some Unpublished Roman Coins. By Fred. W. Madden, Esq., M.R.S.L.	91
On some Remarkable Greek Coins lately acquired by the British Museum. By W. S. W. Vaux, Esq., M.A., F.S.A.	104
"The Three Valentinians." By Fred. W. Madden, Esq., M.R.S.L.	112
On a Copper Coin of the class struck after the death of Alexander the Great, by his Generals, before they assumed regal titles. By R. Stuart Poole, Esq., M.R.S.L.	137
Unpublished Coin of Carausius. By John Evans, Esq., F.S.A.	163
On a Legionary Coin of Carausius. By John Evans, Esq., F.S.A.	161
On two Cretan Coins in the British Museum. By Reginald Stuart Poole, Esq., M.R.S.L.	168
On the Coins of Theodosius I. and II., with some Remarks on the Mint-marks "Comob." and "Conob," and on the Coins of Placidia, the Wife of Constantius (Patricius). By Fred. W. Madden, Esq., M.R.S.L.	175
On a Coin from the Cyrenaïca, presented by the late F. H. Crowe, Esq., H.M. Consul at Cairo. By R. S. Poole, Esq., M.R.S.L.	201
A few words on Byzantine Numismatic Art. By the Hon. J. Leicester Warren, M.A.	211
A Coin of Helike. By Dr. Julius Friedlaender	216
Unpublished Greek Autonomous and Imperial Coins. By W. Webster, Esq.	218

	Page
A selection of inedited Coins of the Egyptian series. By the Rev. H. C. Reichardt	224
Notes on the ἘΝ ΤϒΤΟ ΝΙΚΑ and ΑΝΑΝΈΟΣΙΣ types of the Heraclian dynasty. By the Hon. J. Leicester Warren, M.A.	228
On the Imperial Consular "Dress." By Fred. W. Madden, Esq., M.R.S.L.	237

MEDIÆVAL AND MODERN NUMISMATICS.

Unpublished English and Anglo-Gallic Coins. By the Rev. Henry Christmas, F.R.S., F.S.A. 17

Jetton of Perkin Warbeck. By the Hon. J. Leicester Warren, M.A. 32

Modern Art and the New Bronze Coinage. By Sebastian Evans, Esq., M.A. 38

English and Foreign Sterlings found in Scotland . . . 56

On some Looped Coins found with Anglo-Saxon Ornaments in Kent. By J. F. W. de Salis, Esq. 53

An account of a find of Coins in the parish of Goldborough, Yorkshire. By W. S. W. Vaux, Esq., M.A., F.S.A. . . 65

On an Unpublished Variety of the Coins of Ethelstan, King of East Anglia. By Fred. W. Madden, Esq., M.R.S.L. . . 85

On an English Jetton, or Pattern-piece. By John Evans, Esq, F.S.A. 109

On a hoard of Coins discovered at Hounslow. By J. B. Bergne, Esq., F.S.A. 140

On the Anglo-Hanoverian Copper Coinage. By the Rev. Henry Christmas, F.R.S., F.S.A. 144

On the Half-crowns of Charles I. with the "W" under the horse on the field of the obverse. By the late Rev. T. F. Dymock 185

On an Unique and Unpublished Pattern for a Half-crown of the last year of the Reign of Queen Elizabeth. By R. Whitbourn, Esq., F.S.A. 189

Short-cross Pennies of Henry II. or III., by the Rev. A. Pownall, M.A. 207

ORIENTAL NUMISMATICS.

An account of a find of Coins in the parish of Goldborough, Yorkshire. By W. S. W. Vaux, Esq., M.A., F.S.A. . . 65

Observations on some Double-struck Coins of the Bactrian King, Azes or Azas. By E. C. Bayley, Esq., H.E.I.C.S. . . 72

Notice of three Chinese Silver Medals. By John Williams, Esq., F.S.A. 241

NOTICES OF RECENT NUMISMATIC PUBLICATIONS.

	Page
Revue Numismatique	60, 131, 193, 249
Revue Numismatique Belge	60, 132, 197, 250
Numismatische Zeitung	61
Handbook to Roman Numismatics. By Fred. W. Madden	128
Minnespenningar öfver enskilda Svenska Män och Quinnor beskrifna af Bror Emil Hildebrand	130
Description Générale des Médaillons Contorniates, par J. Sabatier	192
Celtic Inscriptions on Gaulish and British Coins. By Beale Poste	248
Ueber die so-genannten Regen-bogen-Schüsselchen. Erste Abtheilung, von Franz Streber	250

MISCELLANEA.

Proclamation of the New Copper Coinage	62
Statistics of the Coinage	63, 198
Sales of Coins	63, 133, 198
Finds of Coins	133, 246

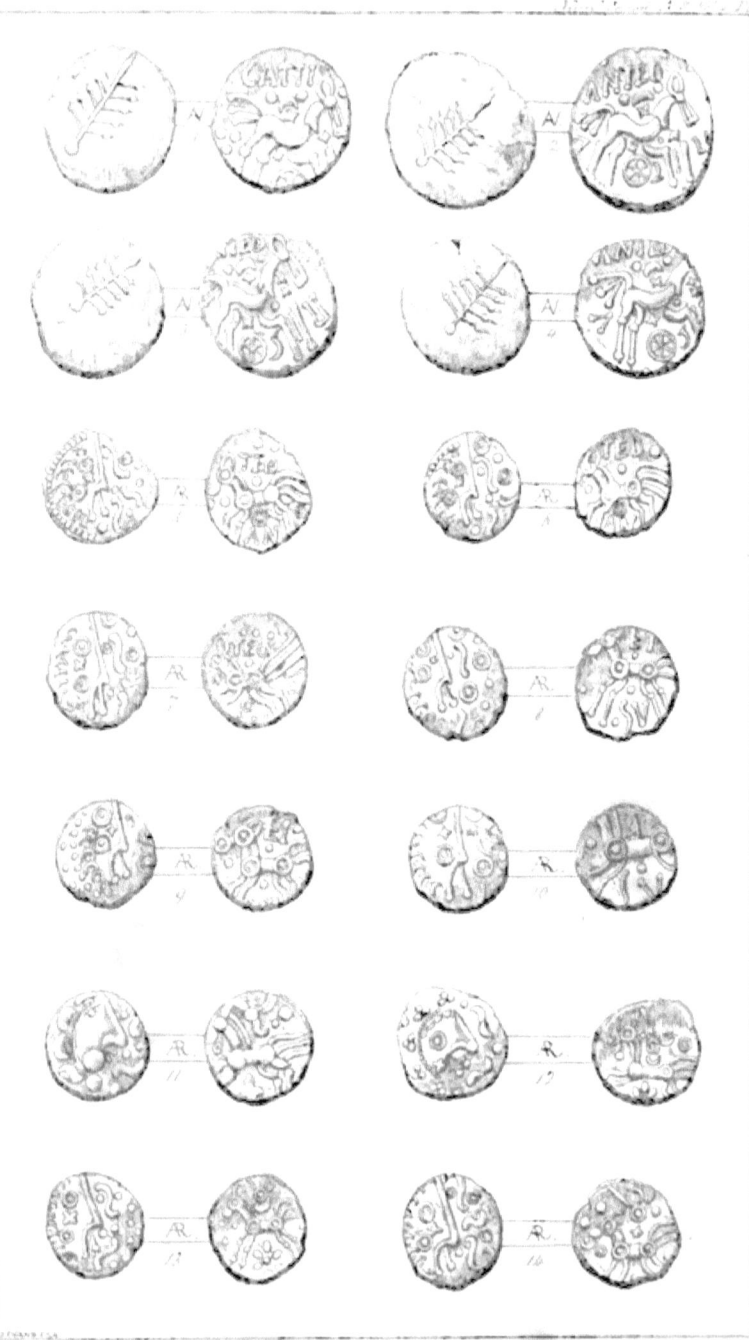

BRITISH COINS FOUND AT NUNNEY NEAR FROME. 1860.

NUMISMATIC CHRONICLE.

I.

AN ACCOUNT OF A HOARD OF ANCIENT BRITISH COINS DISCOVERED IN THE NEIGHBOURHOOD OF FROME.

[Read before the Numismatic Society, December 13th, 1860.]

By the kind co-operation of Captain **Murchison**, I am enabled to communicate to the Numismatic Society an account of one of the most interesting discoveries of ancient British coins that ever has been placed upon record. Although not in intrinsic value coming near some of the various hoards which have formerly been discovered, yet, so far as concerns the information to be derived from the coins themselves, and those of Roman mintage, with which they were found associated, the present find is entitled to take at least equal rank with the celebrated finds of Karn-Brê, High Wycombe, Farley Heath, Almondbury, Whaddon Chase, or Weston, if it is not even of more importance.

The neighbourhood of Frome, in Somersetshire, has long been well known to antiquaries as having from time to time produced many coins of the ancient British series, more especially of the class reading CATTI, COMVX, &c.; but the present discovery will materially add to the numismatic celebrity of that district.

It was on the 15th of October last that two men, ploughing in a field known as the Eleven Acres, and forming a portion of West Down Farm in the parish of Nunney, broke open a small urn, and thus brought to light the hoard of coins I am now about to describe. The village of Nunney is situated about three miles west of Frome, on the road between that town and Shepton Mallett; but the West Down Farm is close to the hamlets of Holwell and Leighton, the villages of the district lying very close together. The Eleven Acres field is rather higher than the surrounding country, forming indeed a summit level; and it was in the highest portion of the field that the urn was buried. The depth of soil above the solid rock is not more than from six inches to a foot, so that it is remarkable that the urn should have lain so long undiscovered. "Nature hath furnished one part of the earth and man another. The treasures of Time lie high in urns, coyns, and monuments, scarce below the roots of some vegetables," but still "that great antiquity America lay buried for a thousand years, and a great part of the earth is still in the urn to us." And so it had been with this hoard of coins, but for the chance stroke of the ploughshare. Whether its preservation hitherto has been due to an ancient yew-tree, which stood within five yards of it, and has only been lately cut down; and whether that yew-tree, or its predecessor on the spot, may by any possibility have been the landmark by which whoever deposited this hoard intended to recognise the place of its interment, are questions on which I need not speculate. However this may have been, the urn seems even now to have revealed its contents only by degrees, the first finders having discovered but one or two gold coins; the next man who searched upon the spot having found a large number of silver coins, all lying together, and without any gold coins among them; and another person, who searched subsequently and dug lower, having found several more gold coins and five or six Roman coins in silver and copper.

The coins of the hoard being thus dispersed, some of them were offered for sale to Mr. Walker of Bath, and Mr. Singer of Frome, both of whom at once proceeded to the spot, and collected them as far as was possible from the various owners into whose hands they had fallen. By dint of their efforts upwards of two hundred of the coins were recovered, by far the greater part of which eventually passed into Captain Murchison's possession, and some few into my own. Others were obtained by Mr. Glencross, the owner of the farm, who has kindly placed them in Captain Murchison's hands for examination, and who also allowed him to make a subsequent careful search upon the spot, through which six more of the silver coins were obtained.

The urn was so much shattered by the first finders, and the fragments so dispersed, that only a few small pieces could be recovered, and nothing can be now learned as to its form, except that it was circular, with the sides sloping outwards, and having an exterior diameter of about four and a half inches at its base. It was formed of clay very imperfectly burnt, and mixed, as is so frequently the case with British urns, with particles of calcareous matter, which in this instance appears to have been derived from the immediate neighbourhood, as a fossil shell—a *Rhynconella concinna*, from the great oolite—is imbedded in the bottom part of the urn.

A small bow-shaped fibula in bronze, of the type No. 11, Pl. xii., of Akerman's Archæological Index, was found upon the spot, but it is uncertain whether it formed part of the contents of the urn or no.

The number of coins it contained was, as far as I have been able to ascertain, 249, viz., 10 British coins in gold, 232 in silver; 3 Roman coins in silver, and 4 in second brass. These I will now proceed to describe.

No. 1.

> *Obv.*—An ornament somewhat resembling a fern-leaf (*Blechnum boreale*) or the backbone of a sole.
>
> *Rev.*—CATTI. A rude three-tailed horse, to the right; above, a crescent between two pellets and a small cross, like a heraldic caltrap; below, a wheel and pellet; behind the horse, three pellets; in front, a small cross. A^v. Pl. i. 1.

Of this type but two specimens were found, one of which is now, I believe, in the local Museum at Taunton. The weight of the other, which shows the legend very imperfectly, is 85½ grs. Another specimen is engraved in the Numismatic Journal, vol. i. pl. i. 8, which also was discovered in the neighbourhood of Frome, though now many years ago.

No. 2.

> *Obv.*—A similar ornament to that on the coin last described.
>
> *Rev.*—ANTEDRIGV, or ANTEΘRIGV. The three-tailed horse, to the right, with wheel, &c., in the field, as on the former coin. The concluding letters of the legend are scattered, the R being beneath the nose of the horse, the I between his fore-legs, the G in the space between the fore-legs and the wheel, and the V beneath the tail. The whole device is surrounded by a circle of pellets set at intervals of about an eighth of an inch. A^v. Pl. i. 2, 3, 4.

Of this type there were either seven or eight specimens found; the weight of those I have examined being as follows,—69, 71, 73, 77½, 79, 81, and 83 grs. They are of exceedingly base metal, in fact some of them appear to be only copper plated with gold. The type is engraved in the Numismatic Chronicle, vol. xvi. p. 80.

No. 3.

> *Obv.*—Rude head in profile; the outlines of the face portrayed by a thick crooked line, which bifurcates to form the mouth; the back of the head is defined by a beaded semicircle, while two ring-ornaments seem to represent the eye and the ear, with a small cross by way of decoration between them. The hair is rendered by a series of crescents with pellets in the centre of each. In front of the face are several curved or dolphin-shaped figures, ring-ornaments, and pellets, and the whole seems to be surrounded by a double ring of pellets placed alternately, and some little distance apart.
>
> *Rev.*—ANTED, or ANTEΘ. A horse, to the left, with a streaming triple tail, the head, shoulders, and hind quarters formed with ring-ornaments. There are several pellets and ring-ornaments in the field. The whole within a circle of pellets set at considerable distances apart. Pl. i. 5, 6. On one specimen, in which the "thrice-told" tail of the horse streams upward, the legend appears to be ANTEΘRI. Pl. i. 7.

There are several insignificant variations in the arrangement of the ring-ornaments and pellets on the field in various specimens. The metal is extremely base silver, so much alloyed with copper that many coins are coated with green oxide.

Of these coins sixteen at least were in the hoard, varying in weight from 13 to 21 grs., but mostly from 17 to 20 grs., the average weight of the 16 being 17¾ grs.

The type is engraved in the Numismatic Chronicle, vol. xx. p. 172, No. 11.

No. 4.
> *Obv.*—Head in profile similar to that on the coins last described, but occasionally of even ruder execution.
>
> *Rev.*—SVEI or EISV. Three-tailed horse, to the left, as on the former coins. In the field various pellets. On some there is a Y-shaped figure, or star of three points above the horse. Silver, like the last, excessively base.   Pl. i. 8, 9, 10.

Of this class 27 coins were found, the average weight being 17¾ grs., but individual specimens varying from 14¾ to 21½ grs. Unpublished.

No. 5.
> *Obv.*—An extremely stolid-looking head in profile, to the right; the workmanship very rude, but still there is a much closer approach to human features than on the coins of the two classes last described. The hair is represented by a number of crescent-shaped bosses placed alternately back to back, with occasionally three small pellets on each, and between the hair and the face is a beaded band, forming an arc of a circle. The chin is represented by a rounded projection below the beak-like lips. In front of the face are the curved objects and pellets.
>
> *Rev.*—Uninscribed. Three-tailed horse, to the left; below a sort of quatrefoil; above a kind of triquetra springing from a ring-ornament or pellet in the centre. In the field ring-ornaments and pellets.
>
>   Pl. i. 11.

The silver of these coins seems in general rather finer than that of the other coins of the find, and they are for the most part wider spread. They also seem to have been longer in circulation, being more worn. I have examined eight of them, and found the usual weight to be about 16 grs.

No. 6.

Obv.—Rude head in profile, very similar to that on the coins last described. It is, however, still more barbarous, the chin having disappeared, and the caltrap-like cross being inserted beneath the eye, which is now represented by a ring-ornament. The crescents which form the hair at the back of the head are converted into triangular groups of three pellets each, and the hair in front of the beaded band becomes more conspicuous. The same pellets, ring-ornaments, and crooked objects are in the field in front of the face, and there is a ring-ornament below the chin.

Rev.—Uninscribed. Very similar to the last, but the ornament above the horse loses its triquetra-like form, its principal feature being now a crescent below a ring-ornament. Silver. Five specimens; average weight, 18 grs. Pl. i. 12.

No. 7.

Obv.—A rude head, in profile, much resembling that on the last type described, but the lips no longer distinguished by separate strokes. The face is, in fact, the same as that on the coins reading ANTED and SVEI. (Types 3 and 4.) On some the face can hardly be recognised, and such was the case with the coin of this type engraved in Hawkins, pl. i. 15.

Rev.—Uninscribed. The same three-tailed horse, with various adjuncts in the field. There is usually the same quatrefoil below the horse, as on type 5; and above, a ring-ornament and small cross. The ring-ornament has a straight line like a handle projecting from it, and two crescents placed like ears above. On some we find the crescent instead of the cross, and on others there are small pellets, formed with an outer ring and small central boss, like those on the gold coins of Farley Heath and some of the silver coins from Sussex.[1]

Pl. i. 13, 14.

Like all the coins of this find, they are convex on the obverse, and concave on the reverse, but the coins that are

---

[1] Num. Chron., vol. ii. p. 231.

most dished belong to this class. It is likewise by far the most numerous, there having been at least 176 coins belonging to it in the hoard, varying in weight from 13 to 21½ grs., but the average weight being 18¼ grs. The silver of which they are composed is extremely base.

I now come to the Roman coins found with the British, seven in number, which are as follows:—

No. 1.—A denarius of the Æmilia family.
> *Obv.*—(ALEXANDREA.) Turreted female head, to the right.
> *Rev.*—M. LEPIDVS PONT. MAX. TVTOR REG. S.C. Lepidus crowning Ptolemy V. (Cohen, pl. i. 7; Riccio, pl. ii. 6.)

No. 2.—A denarius of the Julia family.
> *Obv.*—CAESAR. An elephant, to the right, trampling on a serpent.
> *Rev.*—Simpulum, aspergillum, &c. (Cohen, pl. xx. 10; Riccio, pl. xx. 12.)

No. 3.—A denarius of the Servilia and Junia family.
> *Obv.*—Laureated head of Apollo, to the right.
> *Rev.*—Q . CAEPIO . BRVTVS . IMP. Two captives seated at the foot of a trophy. (Cohen, pl. xxxviii. 8.)

No. 4.—A second-brass coin excessively decayed, possibly of Agrippa.

No. 5.
> *Obv.*—TI . CLAVDIVS CAESAR AVG..... Bare head of Claudius, to the left.
> *Rev.*—CERES AVGVSTA S.C. Ceres seated, to the left. Of genuine Roman work. Æ. 2. (Cohen, 72.)

No. 6.
> *Obv.*—ANTONIA AVGVSTA. Her head, to the right.
> *Rev.*—Portions of the legend—TI. CLAVDIVS CAESAR AVG. P.M. TR.P. IMP. S.C., which has

been double struck around a figure of Claudius standing, to the left. (Cohen, 6.) The drapery is treated much after the manner of that of SPES on coins of Claudius. This coin is of barbarous fabric, and has been struck twice, though possibly with the same dies. Æ. 2.

No. 7.—Also a second brass coin of ANTONIA; the same type, but still more barbarously rendered.

Having now described the different varieties of the coins of which the hoard discovered at Nunney consisted, I will proceed to an examination of the character of their types and legends, and of the features of novelty which those of British origin present; and I will next offer some suggestions as to the tribes or princes by whose authority they were struck, and the period to which they are to be referred.

With regard to the type of the gold coins, it is that which is already well known as belonging to the coins found principally in the counties of Somersetshire and Gloucestershire. The object upon the obverse, which bears considerable resemblance to the leaf of one of our indigenous ferns, has berry-like enlargements at the end of each spike, and it is hard to say what it is really intended to represent. There can, however, be but little doubt that there is in it a reminiscence of the wreath upon the head derived from the Macedonian staters, which appears in a more or less perfect state on nearly all the ancient British series in gold. Some of the links in the chain of successive copies of copies are still wanting, but one of them is certainly to be recognised in the coin found at Mount Batten, near Plymouth, engraved in Hawkins, pl. i. 6. There is, however, no difficulty in supposing that the wreath of Apollo, which on the coins of Cunobeline became converted into an ear of corn, and on those of

Dubnovellaunus, and others, merely left its trace in the shape of a raised band across the field, may have undergone the amount of transformation we find on the obverse of these coins. The three-tailed horse on the reverse is very similar to that on many of the uninscribed coins, both with plain obverses and with portions of the rude head upon them, which, after it had once become thus far degenerated, seems to have remained nearly unaltered in character.

There can be no doubt that the type of the inscribed silver coins, and that of most of the uninscribed, is derived from the class of coins of which No. 11 in the plate is a specimen; and in the description already given I have shown the various modifications of the original that were successively introduced. No. 11 has long been known as a British type, and is engraved, though from an imperfect specimen, in the Numismatic Chronicle, vol. ii. p. 89, No. 6. It is also given by Stukeley, pl. xxii. 8, though not to be found in Ruding or Hawkins. The type of No. 12 in the plate may be said to be now engraved for the first time, and the same is almost the case with Nos. 13 and 14, as the engravings in the Numismatic Journal, vol. i. pl. i. No. 13, Hawkins, pl. i. 15, and Ruding, pl. A. 86, do not convey the slightest impression of there being any attempt to represent a head upon the coin.

I am not at present prepared to say from whence we are to seek the original coin from which the head in profile on No. 11, with the dolphin-shaped objects in front, was derived. The dolphin-shaped objects are, however, to be found upon the coins of the Channel Islands' type, and upon many of the Gaulish series, and it is probable that they in turn derived them from some more classical prototypes. I may here remark that the small coin already mentioned as engraved in the Numismatic Journal, vol. i. pl. i. 13, was discovered at Mount Batten, near Plymouth, in company with a large number of coins of the Channel Islands' type, and the gold coin with the spike on the obverse previously cited. Among the minor details of the coins, the presence of the small cruciform ornament on nearly all the coins is well worthy of notice. It appears to be a frequent adjunct on the coins found in the western districts of England, and is to be observed upon those reading BODVOC and CORI (?), as well as upon the various types of the present find. It is also beneath the horse's head on the uninscribed coin already mentioned, which was found near Plymouth. (Hawkins, pl. i. 6.)

I now come to the consideration of the legends upon the coins, one at least of which is entirely novel; I mean that upon the coins Nos. 8, 9, and 10 of the plate, which from their analogy with the silver coins reading ANTED, with the AN below the horse, must in all probability be read SVEI, in preference to what might otherwise appear the more obvious reading—EISV. Finding, as we do, so many coins closely resembling each other in type, and apparently all belonging to nearly, though not quite, the same period, I am inclined to think that we must regard the legends upon them as representing the names of the princes by whom the coins were struck, rather than as giving the names of the tribes among whom they were current. I therefore consider that we have in the legend SVEI the first letters of the name of some British regulus, which possibly future discoveries may enable us to complete. There are not wanting examples of names with a very similar commencement among the princes of Gaul and Germany. In the inscription of Augustus at Ancyra mention is made of SVEBO, a prince of the Marcomanni; and SVTICVS, a prince of the Veliocasses, is known by his coins. The word SVICCA also occurs on tetradrachms, apparently of Pannonian origin. The Suardones, the Suessiones, the Suessitani, the Suevi, and the Suiones, are all instances of the names of tribes compounded with this prefix. An attribution of the coins to the Silures is tempting, but I am afraid hardly admissible.

The legend ANTED was already well known before the discovery of the present hoard, and some remarks upon it will be found in the twentieth volume of the Numismatic Chronicle, p. 178. It is satisfactory to me to find that my classification of the type in silver, then first described, with those in gold with the same legend, has been so fully and speedily corroborated. We are, however, now enabled to complete the name of the prince who struck these coins, and to add ANTEDRIGVS to the roll of British kings. I think that there can be no doubt of the correctness of the reading ANTEDRIGV; but whether the final S is omitted for want of space, or the termination is that of a genitive, I cannot say. On the coin of this type found at Banbury[2] the termination appears to be OV or QV, and both these letters are in the space between the hind legs and tail of the horse. I may remark that on the gold coin of Epaticcus the legend appears only to extend to EPATICCV; and that the rather peculiar arrangement of the legend Antedrigu is somewhat analogous to that on the gold coins of the Yorkshire type with DVMNO COVEROS, &c.

It is curious to observe how the form of the D varies upon different coins, being sometimes a perfect D, at others a barred D, like the Saxon Ð, and at others, again, a perfect Θ, thus affording a commentary on the

---

[2] Arch. Assoc. Journ., vol. ii. p. 24.

"Græcis literis utuntur" of Cæsar, when speaking of the Druids.³ The sickle-like form of the G on these coins is also remarkable, and entirely different from the shape of the same letter on the Yorkshire coins (Hawkins, pl. i. 9), which afford the only other instance of the letter G occurring on the ancient British series.

Whether the British name of Victory, Andate, enters into the composition of the name of Antedrigus, and whether by any chance the name of this prince is to be traced in the Arviragus mentioned by Juvenal—

—"aut de temone Britanno
Excidet Arviragus,"⁴—

are subjects for speculation. We shall presently see that so far as dates are concerned there is nothing to contradict the latter hypothesis.

In attempting to trace analogous names, that of Antebrogius, the ambassador of the Rhemi to Cæsar,⁵ is the first that presents itself; but it is not a little curious that the legend ANTED, or ANTEÐ (with the letters linked into a monogram), is found upon the coins of the Iceni. If the legend on the other coins of this hoard were to be read EISV instead of SVEI, we should have a further analogy in the Icenian coin reading AESV;⁶ but, as I said before, there are reasons for supposing SVEI to be the correct reading.

We must now consider to what period of history these coins are to be referred, and I must here confess that I am compelled by the circumstances of the present discovery to assign them a more recent date than I should otherwise have been disposed to fix. It is true that the extreme baseness of the metal, the great divergence of

³ De Bell. Gall., vi. 14. ⁴ Sat. iv. 127.
⁵ De Bell. Gall., ii. 3. ⁶ Num. Chron., vol. xvi. p. 80, No. 8.

the object or wreath upon the obverse from its original prototype, and last, not least, the comparatively light weight of the coins, all point to a late stage in the British coinage; yet the rude three-tailed horse on the gold coins, and their dished shape, bear closer analogy to those of the earlier and heavier coins than might have been expected, if, as is probable, there was a considerable lapse of time between the issue of the earliest and latest of the British series. The silver coins might from their type and character have been assigned to a rather later period than the gold, did not the inscription and their association together prove them to be contemporaneous.

We are not, however, left entirely to conjecture as to the date of these coins, as they could not by any possibility have been consigned to the keeping of the earth before the days of Claudius, one of whose coins it will be remembered was found with them. Like the other brass coins of Claudius, this has not the year of his tribunitian power upon it, so that an exact date cannot be assigned to it. The same absence of date occurs with the coins of Antonia, but these are merely barbarous imitations of those of Roman mintage, so that assuming the originals to have been struck in the first year of Claudius A.D. 41, I think that the deposit of this hoard could not have taken place at so early a period as the expedition of Plautius and Claudius to Britain, A.D. 43 and 44. It seems much more probable that the coins were buried at a somewhat later date, and it is by no means impossible that their original possessor may have perished during the wars with the Romans, when Ostorius Scapula was Proprætor in Britain, A.D. 50 to 55.

Now we learn from Tacitus that at that time the two most powerful tribes with whom Ostorius had to contend were, first, the Iceni, of whose position in the eastern part

of England, about Norfolk and Suffolk, there can be no
doubt; and, secondly, the Cangi, concerning the exact
situation of whose territories there has been much question.
It is, however, beyond dispute that the Cangi occupied a
tract of country at some distance from the Iceni, and that
after several skirmishes with them, the army of Ostorius
arrived not far from the sea which looks towards Ireland ("quod Hiberniam insulam aspectat"), and that one
of the main objects of Ostorius was to establish a chain of
forts in the western districts, between the Avon and the
Severn, which apparently had been attacked by the Cangi.
From these and other grounds Camden, Bishop Gibson,
and other writers, have fixed (and that with much show of
reason) the territory of the Cangi in Somersetshire.
When we consider how celebrated are the Mendip Hills
for their lead mines, and that the pigs[7] of lead inscribed
DE. CEANG., cast under Vespasian and Domitian, and
EX KIAN under Nero, have been discovered in various
parts of England, the former occupation by the Cangi of
a district including these hills, so abundant in mineral
wealth, appears all the more probable.

It is therefore possible that we have in this hoard the
coins of that tribe, and if so, the question arises, do the silver
coins attributed to the Iceni—the other powerful tribe with
which Ostorius had to cope—belong to the same period, or
is there any connection capable of being traced between
them? It is certainly very remarkable how closely the two
classes of coins correspond in weight, the average of twenty
Icenian coins in my collection being just 18 grs.; at the
same time the occurrence of the legend ANTED or ANTED
upon the coins of both classes is, to say the least of it, a

---

[7] Arch. Assoc. Journ., vol. v. p. 226.

very curious coincidence. It will be remembered, too, that some Roman consular denarii were included in the Weston find, as well as in this at Nunney, though, I believe, that at Weston there were no imperial coins discovered.

It is not, however, safe to enter further into the region of speculation, so that classing, as we must do, the coins reading BODVOC, CORI (?), COMVX, CATTI, ANTEDRIGV, and SVEI together, I cannot venture to suggest at present in what chronological order they are to be arranged, though the coins of the two latter classes must, I think, be regarded as the most recent.

Taking the weight alone of the small silver coins into consideration, it would appear that they were to be current as three to the denarius; but taking into account the different degrees of fineness of the silver of which the Roman denarii and the British coins were composed, this can hardly have been the case in reality, so that we cannot from this discovery determine the relation, if any, which subsisted between the Roman and British coinage. It is also impossible to say what were at that time the relative values of gold and silver, if the metals of which these coins are composed are worthy of those names rather than of pinchbeck and Britannia metal.

But though there is so much left for future discovery, and much in connection with the ancient British coinage that in all probability never will be accurately ascertained, yet it will be found, on reviewing the main features of the hoard I have been describing, that the new facts, for which we are indebted to it, are neither few nor unimportant. In addition to one or two hitherto unpublished types of uninscribed silver coins, we have those with the entirely new legend SVEI, the verification of the legend ANTED on the silver coins, and the completion of the name of ANTE-

DRIGVS on those in gold. But beyond all this, there is the association of all these coins together, proving that they belong to the same district, if not indeed to the same tribe, and showing the same simultaneous currency of inscribed and uninscribed coins together in the west of England, which had already been remarked of the coins of the Iceni in the east; and, farther still, we have the fact established of the native British coinage having survived till, **at** all **events,** some years after the accession of Claudius, not only among the Brigantes and Iceni, **as had** hitherto been conjectured, but also among one of **the** tribes of the west of England, and that possibly the long sought for Cangi.

JOHN EVANS.

II.

UNPUBLISHED ENGLISH AND ANGLO-GALLIC COINS.

BY THE REV. HENRY CHRISTMAS, M.A., F.R.S., F.S.A.

[In a Letter to C. Roach Smith, Esq., F.S.A.]

MY DEAR SIR,

IT has often occurred to me that if collectors of coins would from time to time take notes of the peculiarities of such as may fall into their hands, and when these have arrived at a certain bulk, communicate them to the archæological world, they would be doing no inconsiderable service to numismatic science.

I acted some years ago in this way, and, under the title of "Numismatic Scraps," furnished a few such notes. I now venture to trouble you with a more extensive series.

They comprise, as you will see, varieties of type and mint-mark from the period of the Heptarchy to that of William III. Some of the lacunæ thus filled up have been long looked upon as hopelessly blank—others are of trifling importance; but all will have their value when a new edition of Mr. Hawkins' excellent work on "The Silver Coins of England" shall be called for.

I trust that none of my remarks will be understood as derogatory to that book, the very faults of which add to its value, as they tend to show how scrupulous has been the care with which it has been compiled. A writer on coins, such as Mr. Hawkins, somewhat sceptical as to pieces which he has not seen, not prone to place reliance on any evidence save that of his own eyes, and disinclined to theorize, is of all others the one most fitted for the task which he undertook; and to add to his lists a far greater number of unpublished coins than I am able to do, would be no reproach to the diligence and research exhibited in that invaluable manual.

I might have extended this letter had I desired to notice American and colonial coins and tokens; but these fall rather out of my province; nor should I have touched on the Anglo-Gallic series, had it not been for the extreme interest attaching to the coins of Henry, Earl of Lancaster, of which I became the possessor by a fortunate accident.

As years pass, new types will occasionally occur, new mint-marks, dates, and other peculiarities will be observed, but this will take place less frequently. Vast quantities of worn coins are constantly committed to the crucible; collectors, at least in this country, are becoming more and more fastidious as to the preservation of those which they place in their cabinets, and a coin which merely exhibits a different date or a different mint-mark from those already known, is rarely on that account alone thought worthy of retention. On this ground, such a record as I here offer may have its value; some of the trifles it notices may never occur again, and at all events they should be "made a note of."

No. 1.—The first coin which I shall mention is one of Coenwlf, so far as I can find, unpublished; it is in very fine condition, and weighs 21 grs.

> *Obv.*—An extremely rude head. COENWLF REX. ⵙ.
> *Rev.*—A circle inclosing a pellet. From four points in the circumference of the inner circle straight lines are drawn to the circumference of the coin, thus dividing the space appropriated to the legend into four parts. DO . Đ . E . L.

There is a moneyer of Offa, named OEĐELRES. He may possibly be the same as the artist who engraved this coin. Several coins occur with well-known Saxon names of moneyers with the additional letters RES.

This coin gives a new moneyer as well as a new type to Coenwlf, unless DODEL, given by Mr. Lindsay, be the same. I think, however, that the name is OĐELD, for the reason given above, and because the letters are different—D and ð.

No. 2.—The next coin is one of Eric of Northumbria,—at least I see every reason to assign it to that prince. It was presented to me, in the year 1858, by William Gibbs, Esq., of Faversham, Kent, and it was found with several others—EADWIG, EADGAR, and EADRED—all of which were presented to me at the same time.

The coin is in good preservation, and weighs 18 grs.

Obv.—A small cross. ERNOBAEREX.

Rev.—In two lines, with three crosses between ·ENRO·
+ + +
ƎNRIƎ.

This reverse is, I suppose, blundered; but I read the obverse, ER(*IC*) . NO(*RTHVM*)B(*RI*)AE . REX. There is no blunder and no abbreviations but such as are highly probable. The silver is considerably alloyed.

No. 3.—Another coin has since fallen into my hands, which may possibly belong to Eric. It reads :—

Obv.—EREI . EPEHI · IRE. In three lines.

Rev.—EII I . + . . ERE. In three lines.

This coin weighs 22½ grs., is of fine silver, and well preserved.

No. 4.—The next coin is a penny of St. Eadmund—an ecclesiastical coin, only remarkable for the excellence of the work, and for its bearing the title of martyr as well as king. It weighs 20¾ grs.

Obv.—+SCE . EADMVNDE . REX . MAR.

Rev.—+DECEMVND . MONETA.

No. 5.—A penny of Eadgar, struck at St. Edmundsbury.

Obv.—A rosette. EADGAR . REX.

Rev.—A rosette. ZIC . EADMONIT.

No. 6.

Obv.—Harold II., without sceptre.

Rev.—Retrograde. WVLFWVRD . ON . DO.

No. 7.—A London penny of Henry I. Moneyer ESTMVND. (type Hk. 255.)

No. 8.—York halfpenny of Edward I. Mr. Hawkins states that he had not seen this coin. I believe there is now one in the British Museum.

No. 9.—York penny of Henry IV., weighing full 18 grs.

No. 10.—London light penny of Henry IV. Roman N on reverse, no other peculiarity.

Nos. 11-18.—These are unpublished varieties of the light groats of Henry VI. Those reading HENRICV' have been the only instances, with one exception, hitherto noticed; but there are many which bear the common reading, HENRIC. I have the undermentioned :—

LONDON.	HERICV'.	Differing in no other respect.
	HENRIC'.	MM. a cross patée.
	HENRIC.+.	Lis after DEVM.
	HENRICV'.	MM. *Obv.* Cross. *Rev.* Lis.
EBORACI.	HENRIC.	Differing in no other respect.
BRISTOW.	HENRICV'.	MM. Cross, *Obv.* and *Rev.*
——	——	MM. *Obv.* Trefoil. *Rev.* Cross.

We come next to—

Coins of Edward IV.

Nos. 19-32.—Of these I have some unnoticed groats.

No. 19.
   MM. Rose. Small annulet on each side of the head. Weight 60 grs.

No. 20.
   MM. Cross. Differs from that described by Hawkins in having no dots beside the crown, and no lis on the breast. Weight $59\frac{1}{2}$ grs.

No. 21.
   MM. Rose. Like the first described by Hawkins, but having no annulet before legend. Weight 60 grs.

No. 22.
A light groat. MM. Rose. Reads DEI GRATIA. Weight 44 grs.

This was shown to me by Mr. Lincoln, dealer in coins. It belongs to a collector in the country.

HALF GROATS. In Mr. Loscombe's collection was one of Coventry.

Rev.—CIVITAS COVETRE.

No. 23.
York. MM. Sun.

No. 24.
London. MM. Cross passing through a circle, somewhat resembling the cross of Malta. Weight 20 grs.

It is of much better workmanship than the generality of the coins of this prince. Very fine in preservation.

No. 25.—Penny of the same workmanship. Very fine.
MM. Rose. Weight 10 grs.

PENNIES.

No. 26.
London. First coinage; much clipped; must have lost at least 3 grs. Now weighs 12 grs.

No. 27.
MM. Cross. Reads DEI GRA.

This coin is struck on a larger piece than the pennies of the second, or lighter coinage.[1]

No. 28.
York. Very fine condition, but no quatrefoil on reverse. Weight 12 grs.

---

[1] It seems to have been a usual thing with clippers to cut the heavier coinages down to the weight of the lighter.

No. 29.—I have a London penny, *with* the quatrefoil, which *seems* to bear the name of Richard.

MM. Cross. Weight 8½ **grs**.

No. 30.

A much clipped penny of York, without the quatrefoil (of Edward IV.). Must be the first coinage, as in its clipped state it weighs 11½ grs.

No. 31.

Halfpenny. **Durham.** Lis on each side the head.

No. 32.

Farthing. London. EDWARD . REX . ANGLI.

Rev.—CIVITAS . LONDON. Weight 3½ grs.

This coin, from its weight, is probably of **the first, or** heavy coinage. **It is** in fine condition.

Coins of Richard III.

No. 33.

Penny. York. **MM. Lis.**

I have noticed **a London coin which** seems **to read Richard, but it is** uncertain **and** blundered, perhaps **a** contemporaneous forgery. **It is** only remarkable as bearing in the centre of the reverse a quatrefoil.

Coins of Henry VII.

Open Crown Groats. In addition to those **mentioned** by Hawkins.

No. 34.

MM. Rose. Rose on neck. Small cross **at each** side of neck.

No. 35.

MM. Rose. **Rose** on breast.

No. 36.

No MM. on the obverse.

Rev.—MM. Small cross. Small cross at sides of neck.

No. 37.—I have also a side-faced groat of very curious workmanship, which belongs either to this king or to his successor. MM. Rose. Weight 31 grs. It has not lost much by wear or clipping.

Obv.—ҺEDRIC ᔕII ⚹ ƉE + G + R + AGLIE ⚹ Ƨ ⚹ FRA✢

Rev.—POSVI . ƉEVM . A ƉIV✝OREM ⚹ MEVM.

It is in fair preservation, but the features have been a little rubbed, so as to make it impossible to tell whether the portrait be of Henry VII. or his son. The numerals read ᔕII.

The M . E . I . V. are particularly Roman, and very different from those usually seen on the groats of either Henry VII. or Henry VIII. The G is G, and the D is Ɖ. The A is neither Roman nor Saxon. It is not A nor ᴀ; but A. The N is the old English Ɖ. The first letter of the king's name is Һ.

Coins of Edward VI.

The base side-faced halfpenny of Edward VI. is now known. There are four specimens in well-known cabinets, three of which were in my own, and one remains there still.

There are two varieties—one of London and one of Bristol.

No. 38.—That of London is very base. It reads—

Obv.—E . 6 . D. G. ROSA . SINE SPINA.

Rev.—CIVITAS . LONDON. Cross and pellets. All Roman letters.

No. 39.—That of Bristol, same type, but old English letters. The London coin is unique. It was in my **cabinet**, and was transferred by me **to** that of **Mr. Bergne, F.S.A. It is in** poor preservation. **Of the** Bristol coin there are three specimens, one very fine, **in my own** cabinet; one not quite so fine, transferred **by me to the** cabinet **of Captain** Murchison; and a third, **in the** possession **of Mr. J.** Evans, F.S.A. That in my possession seems to be of tolerably good silver. Its weight is 5½ grs.

Coins of Mary.

No. 40.—Of Mary's penny, before her marriage, I have an extremely fine specimen. The reading is somewhat different from that of any yet published.

Obv.—The Queen's bust.   MM. **Lis.   MAR. D . G.**
ROSA . SINE . SPINA.

Rev.—Arms.   CIVITAS . **LONDON.**

Those hitherto known read M . D . G., &c. **&c.**

Coins of Elizabeth.

It has long been a **theory** of mine, **that from** A.D. 1561 to A.D. 1582 there were struck in each year all the divisions of the sixpence, as well as the sixpence itself, viz., the 3*d*., the 1½*d*. piece, and **the** ¾*d*. piece. I have **therefore** carefully watched for the occurrence of such **pieces,** and have been fortunate enough to find the **following not** mentioned **by** Hawkins:—

Nos. 40 to 68.

3*d*., or quarter shilling.   Pheon.   1563.
Lion.   1566.
Do.   1567.
Coronet.   1570.

3d., or quarter shilling.	Ermine.	1573.
	Acorn.	1574.
	Cinquefoil.	1577.
Three-halfpenny pieces.	Coronet.	1567.
	Castle.	1570.
	Acorn.	1574.
	Cinquefoil.	1577.
	Cross.	1581.
	Sword.	1582.
Three-farthing pieces.	Ermine.	1572.
	Cross.	1581.

Of the sixpences I have a variety of the Pheon, 1561, with a larger shield than usual.

Key. 1596. No MM. on reverse.

Cinquefoil. 1573.

Of half-groats I have found MM. lion, castle, anchor. Of Pennies: rose, portcullis, castle, ermine, cinquefoil. Halfpenny: crescent.

I have noticed that coins of the year 1571, MM. ermine, have the date generally altered to 1572, and are rare. Those with MM. cross, and date 1577, have the date generally altered to 1578, and are also rare. I have not found the smaller pieces with these dates and MM.

No. 68.—I have also the milled shilling with the MM. martlet. It is not fine, but has not hitherto been noticed. I presume mine to be unique.

Coins of James I. 1603—1625.

In addition to those tabulated by Mr. Hawkins, I have in my cabinet:—

No. 69.
  Crown   MM. Grapes.

No. 70.
  —   — Rose.

No. 71.
  Crown   MM. Scallop.

No. 72.
  —   — Lis. **Arms** surmounted by a plume.

No. 73.
  Half-crown. — Rose.

No. 74.
  Shilling.   — Cross.

No. **75.**
  Sixpence.   — Scallop. 1607. Noticed by Hawkins on Snelling's authority.

No. 76.
  Half-groat. — Coronet.

Nos. 77, 78.
  Penny.   — Coronet. Key.

Nos. 79—81.
  Halfpenny. — Bell, mullet, cinquefoil.

I would observe, **that Mr.** Hawkins seems to me unnecessarily to doubt the correctness of Snelling; so much so, indeed, as frequently to query **the** existence of coins which he had not seen himself, but which he found published by Snelling. **I** have, in almost all these cases, found the **coins** themselves.

Coins of Charles I. 1625—1648.

No. 82.—Twenty-shilling piece. Described **by Mr.** Hawkins on p. 167, No. iv.; but the description altered from Snelling. Mr. Hawkins had never seen the coin, and imagined that Snelling was mistaken. I have the coin, and find Snelling's description perfectly correct.

No. 83.—The Oxford penny. The specimen which I have is not fine, and is slightly double struck. It reads CAROL . D . G. &c. &c. That in the British Museum, figured by Mr. Hawkins, reads CAROLVS, &c. I have seen no other, but believe there are two or three more.

Coins of the Commonwealth. 1648—1660.

No. 84.—I have the shilling and sixpence of the year 1659. MM. Anchor.

No. 85.—Mr. Cuff appears to have had the half-crown of the same year, and with the same mint-mark. Mr. Hawkins mentions this with a query, and at the sale the coin did not appear.

The half-crown of 1655 is in the collection of Mr. Wigan, as also the shilling of 1657. Of this last, Mr. Lindsay has another specimen.

Coins of William III. 1694—1702.

No. 86.—I have a coin which I suppose to be a trial piece for a sixpence. It presents nothing extraordinary save the weight, which is 76 grs., 33 grs. over the average weight of the coin. The date is 1696.

ANGLO-GALLIC COINS.

Henry, Earl, and subsequently Duke, of Lancaster.

Nos. 87—89.—At the sale of Mr. Dymock's coins I purchased several groats (so described) of Edward III. When I came to examine them, I found them to belong to Henry, Earl of Lancaster. If the coins described in

Ainslie's catalogue are the same as those which **I** purchased in June, 1858, there must have been **some little** inaccuracy in the description.

Lot 356 was a groat bought **by the** late Mr. Cureton. It fetched £10.

Lot 357. Half-groat (Mr. Wigan), £5 **12s. 6**d.

Lot 358. Half-groat (Mr. Till), £2 **12s. 0**d.

It seems possible to me that **I may have now Nos. 356** and **358**. The coins **in** my possession **are—**

No. 1.—A groat; the usual castle type.

Obv.—+HENR . COM . **LANCAST.** Outer legend, **BEN**. &c. &c. &c.

Rev.—DNS. BERGERACE.

This coin is in bad preservation. Very base. **Weight** 33¾ grs.

No. **2.—Groat ;** lion type; **within** a circle of strawberry leaves a lion couchant, gardant, crowned. + LANCAIIE. **DVX.**

Rev.—EN . DNS . BRAGIIE. Outer legend, BEN., **&c.** &c. &c. A cross, the lower limb extending through the inner circle to the legend of the outer **one.**

This coin **is in fair preservation. Very base.** Weight 20 **grs.**

No. 3.—Half-groat ; castle type.

Obv.— + **HEN** . COM . LANC. Outer legend, BEN., &c. &c. &c.

***Rev.*—** + DNS . BRAGERACIE. Castle in **the usual** circle of strawberry leaves. Very base. **Weight** 18 grs.

Coins of Edward III.—Anglo-Gallic.

At the same sale (that of Mr. Dymock's collection), I purchased two groats of Edward III., which are so far as I can find, unpublished.

Nos. 90, 91.—One is of good silver. Weight 50 grs. It is considerably clipped.

> *Obv.*—A cross extending through the whole field of the coin. Outer circle, + BENEDICTVM . SIT . NOMEN . DOMINI. Inner circle, + ED . REX . ANGLIE. The quarters quite plain.
>
> *Rev.*— + DVX. AGITANIE. The usual castle type within a circle of strawberry leaves.

No. 91.—Billon. Much clipped but fairly preserved. Weight 45 grs.

> *Obv.*—A plain cross reaching through the inner circle only. Outer circle, + BENEDICT., &c. &c. Inner circle, EDOVARDOS . REX.
>
> *Rev.*—A lion rampant. MONETA . BVRD., in a circle of leaves.

Nos. 92, 93.—Of that very rare coin, the sterling of Aquitaine, struck by this king, I have two specimens, both differing from any yet published. In one the difference is slight, and consists simply in the spelling of the word Aquitaine; instead of being as usual AGITANIE, it reads AGITAINIE. The other presents a remarkable variety.

> *Obv.*— + EDWAR . DE . GRA . REX . ANGLIE. Half-length bust as usual.
>
> *Rev.*— + DNS . AGITANIE . B. Cross and pellets.

The B is probably for Bordeaux. In the word DE. for DEI. the letter E is a monogram, looking like ET or TE, and might be supposed to form part of the king's name, and to mean taken together EDWAR TE for EDWAR TERTIUS, but the presence of the word GRA. prohibits this. The other E's are formed as usual. In Ainslie's work this coin, the sterling, is said to be the only Anglo-Gallic coin upon which a monogram occurs. Both these coins are very fine, and weigh, one 17 grs., the other 16 grs.

No. 94.—A specimen of the Black Money of Edward the Black Prince. At the end of the legend occurs the letter N very distinct, and impossible to be mistaken for any other letter. This would indicate a new mint. Most of the Black Money of Edward the Black Prince was struck at Lectoure, now in the department of Gers. For this N I would suggest Niort, in the ancient county of Poitou.

I shall conclude this paper with a notice of the royal farthing tokens issued by James I. and Charles I. Snelling gives a list of mint-marks to be found on them. I add to those of James I. the following ten, viz., 𝔗𝔜, ball, book, castle, crescent, dagger, three lis, lion passant, star, and trefoil. To those of Charles I., I add eight, viz., 𝔗𝔜, bell, blackamoor's head, cross of Calvary, fret, hook, pellet enclosed in annulet, shield. Of James I. there is a very small token, which Snelling thinks was intended for a half farthing; it has only one MM., the fret, and is sometimes, indeed generally, found silvered.

This coin has a peculiarity which has never been noticed in print: under the crown, and between the sceptres there is always a letter; those in my collection, and in that of Captain Murchison, give A. B. C. D. and F.

I remain, my dear sir,
Yours very faithfully,
HENRY CHRISTMAS.

III.

JETTON OF PERKIN WARBECK.[1]

In the "Revue Numismatique" for the months of September and October of last year, there appears an interesting notice by M. A. de Longpérier, in which he publishes, among other jettons, or counters, of Tournay, one bearing the name of Perkin Warbeck—that interesting and mysterious historical personage. As far as it relates to this pretender, we propose to give a brief transcript of this article for the benefit of our English readers, to many of whom the "Revue" may be inaccessible, inasmuch as anything relating to Perkin cannot fail to be interesting on this side the Channel.

This jetton is as follows:—

> *Obv.*— + VIVE PERKIN IETOIS DE TOURNAI, round a cross ending in fleurs de lis, with four branches of rose-trees—one round each arm, ending in roses in each of its quarters.
>
> *Rev.*— O MATER DEI MEMENTO MEI. MM. A tower. (The Arms of Tournai)—Three circles, each containing a rose with four petals; between the three circles, three fleurs de lis; above each, an arched compartment.

---

[1] Perkin Werbecque, par Adrien de Longpérier.—"Revue Numismatique," Nouvelle Série, tome vi. p. 384.

M. de Longpérier publishes another jetton, very similar in detail to this one, but reading VIVE LE ROI instead of VIVE PERKIN. This, he suggests, was struck on the occasion of the entrance of Louis XI. into Tournay, A.D. 1478.[2] And he points out the curious fact resulting from a comparison of the two pieces, that the name of Perkin is treated with the same honour on the one, as that of the king of France on the other.

He then enters, with considerable research, on Perkin in his historical aspect. The name Warbeck, it appears, is spelt "Warbeck," Werbeck, Werbeque, Werbecque, Waerbeck, and Waarbeck, by different authorities. In his own confession, according to Hall, Perkin's father is called John Osbeck, and, lastly, in the Register of the Irish Commons, 1497, March 28, he is called Parkyn Wosebeck. Perkin is a diminutive of Peter. The general outlines of his story are too well known to require repetition here. I shall merely content myself with abstracting the more novel points brought in prominence in M. de Longpérier's notice.

It appears that Margaret, Duchess Dowager of Burgundy, the widow of Charles the Bold, and the sister of our Edward IV., was continually hatching all the plots in her power against Henry VII. and his peaceful possession of the throne. The attempts of Lambert Simnel had preceded by some five years the first appearance of Perkin at Cork, in 1492; and although it was not till after this that the Duchess of Burgundy affected to recognise him, and to be impressed by an overpowering

---

[2] There is a variety of this reading VIVE LE ROI, but without the rest of the obverse inscription, in the British Museum. It has a remarkable mint-mark of three masks, or heads. Its reverse reads NOMEN SIT NOMEN.

conviction of the truth of his claim, yet we may suspect her of having originated the whole attempt from its beginning, and having chosen for her tool some reputed natural son of Edward IV., or, at all events, some one with an accidental likeness to the ill-fated Richard, Duke of York, who perished in the Tower. The value of the piece described above, as M. de Longpérier observes, consists in its being an historical document and record for ever of the then prevailing belief in the Tournay origin of this semi-mythical personage. Yet although of Tournay, Perkin must, from the fact of his perfect knowledge of our language, which is on record also, have had either one English parent, or at least have resided in this country for some considerable time. The account of his parentage, as given by himself in his public confession, does not seem altogether conclusive, and appears somewhat too circumstantial. Besides, such an utterly worthless and pusillanimous character as he seems to have been, would probably under severe pressure confess anything required of him.

M. de Longpérier goes on to remark, that the absence of his royal name (Richard IV.) on the piece described above has caused great surprise to English antiquaries; but he suggests that Perkin was too well known in Tournay to dare to assume it; that he there received all the more favour, as an expedition against the enemy of the Plantagenets and of the Duchess Margaret was sure to be a popular one; and that we must not be surprised to find the legend VIVE PERKIN on a jetton of Tournay, because the countrymen of the young pretender could sympathise with his enterprises without on that account being taken in on the subject of his identity. Now, well known in Tournay, Perkin must have been, if we are to believe his confession, which describes his father and his maternal grandfather as persons, from their offices, likely to have been very generally known in their town and district. Yet, on this supposition, it seems a wilful and shameless piece of perversity in the Duchess Dowager to have assigned thirty guards of honour to a person whose parentage was so notorious; and a no less singular want of skill on her part in not selecting for her tool one whose birth was a subject of greater mystery. But no doubt it was a mystery at that time to a certain extent, and it is one tenfold more at the present time, and though his countrymen were not shy of calling him by his unregal appellation (which M. de Longpérier disagrees with Hall in thinking implied any idea of contempt, but gives as a diminutive merely), yet the Duchess is apparently more modest than they are on the piece which she is supposed to have struck for him just before his attempt upon Deal; and as she seems to have been in considerable difficulty how to style him, the result was the emission of that well-known but anonymous coin, with its quaint, and, under the circumstances, excessively impudent threat of vengeance, audaciously borrowed from the Book of Daniel and the banqueting hall of Belshazzar. It is perhaps not wholly uninteresting to remark, in conclusion, that in our present Bible version the denunciation reads "MENE TEKEL PERES;" but in Wycliffe's translation from the Vulgate we find "MANE TECHEL PHARES," the exact lettering of the coin, if we change the final E of "MANE" into "MANI." This piece has been so frequently described, that it seems superfluous to do so here; the best account of many is to be found in Mr. Hawkins's Catalogue of the Anglo-Gallic coins in the British Museum.

J. L. W.

IV.

SILVER COIN OF CARAUSIUS.

The Numismatic Society is indebted to the kindness of the Earl of Verulam for the exhibition of a remarkably fine and well-spread silver coin of Carausius, lately discovered upon the site of the ancient city of Verulam. In the woodcut above is given a representation of this coin, which may be thus described:—

> *Obv.*—IMP. CARAVSIVS P. F. AVG. Draped and laureated bust of the emperor, to the right.
>
> *Rev.*—CONSER. AVG. Neptune represented as an old man, seated upon a large shell, his body naked, but his lower extremities draped, with his right hand holding out an anchor, and with his left leaning upon a trident. In the exergue R. S. R.

This type, though not unpublished, is of extreme rarity, so much so as not to be noticed in the catalogue of the coins of Carausius given by Akerman in his Coins of the Romans relating to Britain. It is, however, engraved by Stukeley, pl. xxx. 7, and in the Monumenta Historica Britannica, pl. v. 12, from a coin in the Hunter Collection at Glasgow. A very similar type is also known in copper, and may be seen in Stukeley, pl. xiii. 9, and Mon. Hist. Brit., pl. vi. 31, where it is engraved from a coin in the possession of Mr. C. Roach Smith.

There is something **singularly** appropriate in representing Neptune **as the Conservator Augusti on the coins** of one who **owed first his elevation to** the rank **of High Admiral of the** Roman **fleet, and, next, his** successful usurpation of the imperial power in Britain, entirely to his **naval** skill. The ocean god is certainly as much in **his** place on the coins of Carausius, as he **was on the coins of** Agrippa three hundred years before. **We accordingly** find him on some of his **other coins as COMES AVG., but** on these he is standing, **and not seated.**

The representation of Neptune on **the** coin now under consideration is singular in many respects. The attitude, the drapery, the seat, and the anchor are all unusual. I have described the seat as being formed of a large shell, but I cannot speak with confidence on this point. It certainly has the appearance of a large whelk, with **its point** in the direction of the feet of the figure, and placed within a valve of another shell; and yet it may be a rock, though **there** seems too much method **about it for that;** nor, though not altogether unlike it in **shape,** can **it well** be the prow of a ship, which might not unnaturally be expected in such a position. **The anchor is an** attribute of Neptune's **very** rarely found upon coins; in fact, besides these of Carausius, I am not aware of any other Roman coins on which Neptune appears holding an anchor, except the denarii of Hadrian,[1] on which he reclines leaning **on a** dolphin, and holding an anchor in his right hand, **but** without the trident. The exergual letters **R. S. R.** possibly point out Rutupium as the place of mintage **of this** coin, which is altogether an elegant and pleasing specimen of the medallic art of the period. J. E.

---

[1] Cohen, ii. 394.

V.

MODERN ART AND THE NEW BRONZE COINAGE.

Without entering on the old question of "Britt.," or "Brit.," with regard to which a paroxysm of popular ignorance appears to recur once in every ten years or so; or inquiring too curiously into the chances of extensive and indetectable forgery of coin which can be minted of genuine metal at a large profit, I would venture to say a few words on the new so-called bronze coinage from a purely artistic point of view, believing that as works of art the new coins have not received by any means so much public attention as they deserve.

The first feeling that must strike almost every observer on seeing the three new substitutes for our old-fashioned, dirty, and not inodorous "coppers," will, I am afraid, be one of decided disappointment, which will not be at all relieved by a subsequent and more careful examination. Scrutiny, indeed, only serves to make their artistic defects more palpable; and their whole design is so manifestly inferior to that of the earlier issues, that we can hardly believe it to have been the work of the distinguished engraver whose initials we find, or think we find, on the coins.

Of course the greater hardness of the metal, which necessitates a lower relief in the coin, and almost precludes the possibility of obtaining a perfect impression of the die, is answerable for many of the shortcomings of the new issue. Out of the five new pennies, for instance, now before us, all of them selected as better than average impressions, one only shows any trace of initials under the shield of Britannia, and even in that one, we can only be certain that one of the letters is a W. The entire surface, moreover, on both obverse and reverse, is seamed and flawed in all directions by imperfections and cracks in the dies, while portions of every coin are more or less imperfectly, and even doubly, struck. In nearly all of the coins, also, a raised line following the outline of the head on the obverse is more or less distinctly visible on the reverse, suggesting a remarkable mechanical problem, which may possibly be found easy of solution when all the phenomena of "double-striking" have been satisfactorily explained. Low relief, however, and imperfect impression are in no way responsible for the graver faults in design and drawing, which unfortunately are so many and so palpable,—though the bronze coinage of Napoleon III., of which ours is an attempted copy, prove that low relief and hardness of metal are not entirely incompatible with boldness of design and sharpness in execution. No doubt the bronzing which will arrive with age and use will much improve the appearance of our now too glittering pence and halfpence, by adding greater distinctness of outline, but this will also render the defects of the design and composition more conspicuous. It is to these that I would now call attention.

Let us first take the obverse into consideration. Whether for coins in low relief, a "couped" bust is preferable to one continued to the outer margin of the coin may be an open question when the metal of which the coin is composed is of such malleable nature as to admit of so large a surface being brought into perfect relief without endangering the dies; but in the present instance the widespread bust is, we believe, at the root of most of the defects in the striking of the coins; and were it not so, if the "continuation" is to be covered with such feeble and commonplace allegorical drapery as it is in the present coins, there can be no doubt whatever which is the more artistic. It is really remarkable how much the appearance of the coin is improved when this portion of it is covered. This improvement, however, is not entirely due to the drapery being out of sight. Covering the drapery hides the singularly ungraceful line of the shoulder, and destroys the unpleasant similarity of outline in back and front, which the ribbon breaking the line of the nape of the neck is intended to disguise, but cannot.

It is this similarity and equality of the several portions of the design which is one of its gravest faults. If a line were drawn across the neck, the head and the portion of the bust shown would be as nearly equal in bulk as the halves of an hour-glass, while a line drawn vertically down from the top of the head would also divide the bust into almost as equal halves. There is, in fact, throughout a most inartistic balance of equality, instead of an artistic balance of proportionate diversity of parts.

As a likeness, the head is inferior to that of any former copper issues. The line in front of the eye extends considerably too low, and as one fault always begets another, the upper line of the wing of the nostril is disproportionately depressed.

The shape of the head is also very incorrect, more particularly in the upper portion of the forehead, while the curves of the hair at the back of the head are peculiarly unpleasing in shape, as well as wretchedly executed. The likeness on all the coins is bad; but that on the halfpenny is the best, and that on the penny the worst of the three.

On the reverse we are again met by the same discordantly symmetrical arrangement as on the obverse, in the introduction of a ship and a lighthouse of exactly equal bulk, one on each side of the principal figure, which precisely balance each other, and set all rules of composition at defiance. But what shall we say of the principal figure itself? We are accustomed to ridiculously small heads in our representation of Britannia, but in this case it really appears that the *minimum* has been attained at last. Allowing the largest possible development for the covered portion of the head, the figure cannot be less than ten heads high, and, unless the head be of a very peculiar shape, considerably more. The length of the face is hardly, if at all, greater than the width of the arm near the shoulder, or the length of the back of the hand without the fingers, while the neck is precisely of the same thickness as the upper arm. The attempt to make up in helmet what is wanting in head, merely serves to make the deficiency more signal, and even the shape of the helmet itself is conspicuously ungraceful.

Altogether, on both obverse and reverse, the design is feebler and the work less satisfactory than in any former coin of the reign; nor can it be allowed that the defects and demerits of the new coin are in any way compensated for by the affectation of 18th century capitals in the legend. After such long delays in the execution of the dies, a more satisfactory result was not unreasonably to be anticipated; and we only express the universal feeling of those who have hitherto taken a pride and pleasure in the artistic excellence of the coins issued from the English Mint, when we enter a protest, though now unfortunately too late, against the New Bronze Coinage as a sample of our taste and ability in this important branch of National Art. S. E.

VI.

ON SOME COINS OF CONSTANS II. AND HIS SONS, DISCOVERED IN THE ISLAND OF CYPRUS.

On my return from the East in September, 1858, I made the acquisition at Athens of a mass of 512 coins, then lately discovered in the Island of Cyprus. The *bizarre* character and the rarity of nearly all the types attracted me towards the investment; and I hoped that such a find as this might throw some little light upon a very obscure period of numismatic history, or at least, when catalogued and put on record, afford valuable data in aid of future investigation.

To commence, all these coins, without, I believe, one exception, are countermarked with the monogram of Constans II. thus, (Ⱶ) or (Ⱶ). This is stamped into the coin, with a little round field of its own, indented in every conceivable position on the obverse or reverse. We have every reason to believe that this was done when the piece was struck: it is generally plain and legible enough, and on the smaller types occupies a large portion of the coin, to the utter mutilation of the effigies or legend. Even in those comparatively rare cases where the whole of the countermark does not appear, some traces of it are easily discernible on closer investigation. I have, therefore, omitted to represent it in the plate, but on every coin of this find its presence is to be understood.

One and all these 512 coins are of a rich red copper hue, now and then coated with verdigris, but seldom

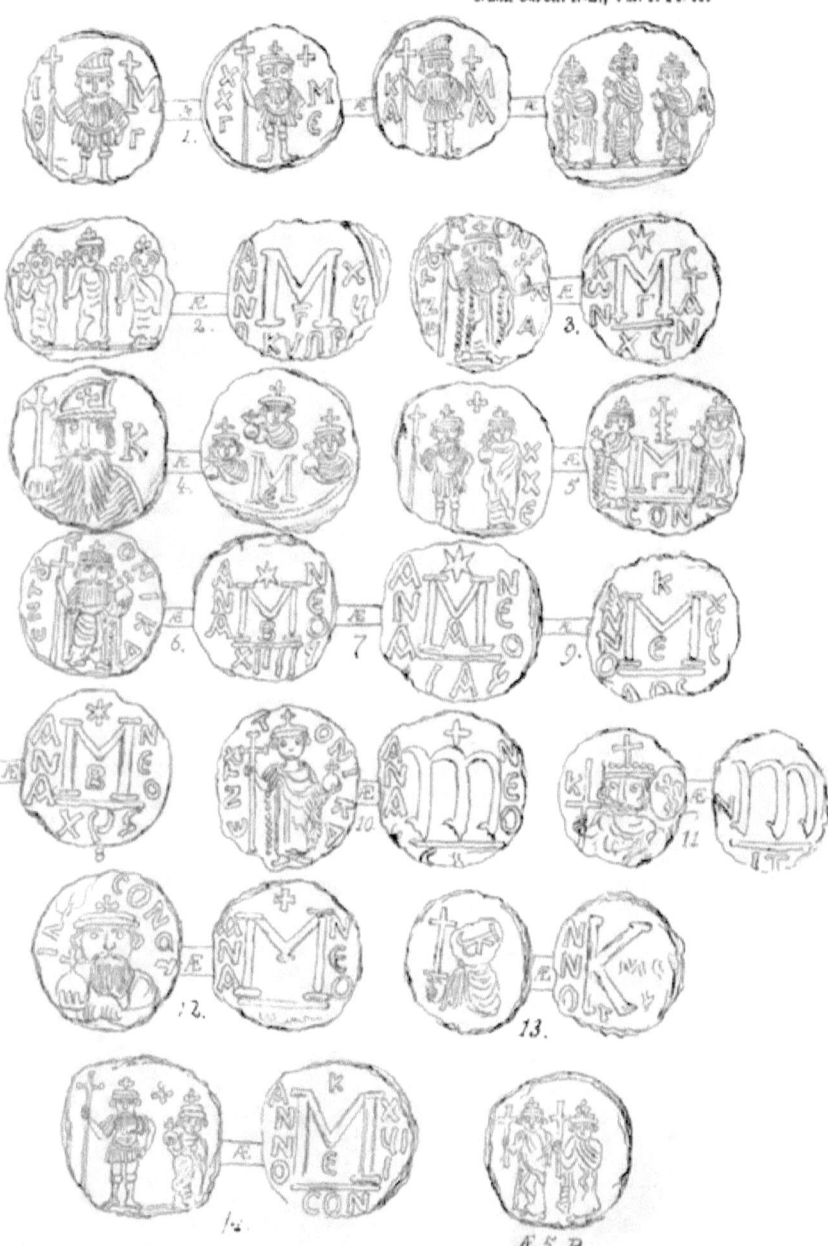

BYZANTINE COINS FOUND AT CYPRUS, 1858.

LEICESTER WARREN.

blackened. Thus they are easily distinguishable when incorporated with others in a collection, and the 137 coins of this find now in the British Museum can be recognised among the trays of the same period, at first sight, even without the aid of the ticket preceding them.

It is also noticeable that many of these coins could never have been in circulation, but were buried fresh from the die. Even in this state they are extremely difficult to decipher from their generally uncouth fabric, and the ignorance or carelessness with which they are struck. Their shape and size also are variable in the extreme. The workmen probably struck a number of these impressions on large plates of metal, and the single coins were then separated by shears into the quaint octagonal or triangular forms which the awkwardness of the clipper allowed them to assume.

Thus can we well understand that in numismatic monuments of this description, it is only by the comparison and collation of numerous specimens of each type that the details can be satisfactorily made out.

We have in this find examples of several types in great numbers, but it is only in one variety of the εν τουτο νικα type that we get anything like a coin of frequent occurrence elsewhere. Some of the other varieties are now probably published for the first time, or at all events have been hitherto very imperfectly described from the want of sufficient materials for the task.

With regard to the place of mintage from which this hoard issued, we have three coins undoubtedly struck at Cyprus (pl. ii. 2). A coin of this island, different in detail, but very analogous in its general appearance, is published by Mons. de Saulcy in his work on the Byzantine Series, pl. viii. 3, and there rightly ascribed to Heraclius I., Heraclius Constantine, and Martina. This is proved by a specimen originally in my possession, now in the British Museum, where the monogram of the elder Heraclius is perfectly clear above the large M on the reverse. This coin has, however, no connection with the hoard now under examination, the three Cyprus pieces of which must be, after due consideration, attributed to Constantine Pogonatus, with his two brothers, Heraclius and Tiberius; for the fifteenth year of Pogonatus (668 A.D.), in which these coins are dated, is the first year of his association with his brothers after his father's death, which had then just taken place; and our last dated coin in the present find of Constans and his three sons is of his twenty-fifth year, or two years before his death. (See pl. ii. 5.) Thus our hoard presents us with an interesting series of dates, among which but few are wanting from the eleventh year of Constans II. to the fifteenth of Pogonatus[1] with his brothers, or the year of their father's death.

Otherwise the attribution of these pieces to Heraclius I., Heraclius Constantine, and Martina would leave a considerable gap unaccounted for, from the date of their association until this eleventh year of Constans II. (Pl. ii. 7.)

It is a remarkable fact that while endeavouring to trace out the types of our present find, or their analogues, in the authorities on the subject, in some cases little can be found resembling these coins, while in others, when a specimen somewhat similar occurs, Sicily is often suggested as their place of mintage. This island was certainly very active in coining during the reign of the elder Hera-

---

[1] Pogonatus, of course, reckons the years of his reign from the time of his association with Constans, his father.

clius, and frequent are the examples inscribed with its name, especially of the ανανεοσις types. The various imperial combinations, from his accession until and throughout the epoch of this find, are also represented on products of this mint. Nor should we be surprised if, of whatever mintage this hoard eventually proves to be, an intimate relation were discovered to exist between it and the monetary establishments of Sicily, somewhat analogous to the transfers of mints from one place to another, such as are found during the lower empire period.

Now on the general question as to where our hoard was issued, we have one bit of firm ground in three of its pieces being inscribed ΚΥΠΡ, and referring themselves undoubtedly to Cyprus, the locality in which they were discovered. The fact, likewise, of their discovery at this place, and the probability of the great mass of these pieces having never been in circulation, are also *prima facie* evidence pointing to a Cyprus mintage.

Once for all I would remark, that I have no wish to dogmatise on this point, and I am merely throwing out the following suggestions in the hopes that some abler numismatist may carry them to their full extent.

We have then here a number of pieces of uncommon type, and semi-barbaric, or, at least, ultra-provincial fabric. In the whole mass the only letters with any apparent reference to a mintage place are the ΚΥΠΡ above quoted, the CON in the exergue of two types (see pl. ii. 5, 14), and the ΚΩΝΣΤΑΝ reading vertically to right and left of an εν τϑτο νικα reverse (see pl. ii. 3),—of which presently. The fabric of the two types with CON would warrant some hesitation in ascribing their emission to Constantine, and we should rather suggest them to be the efforts of provincial mints, which have copied ignorantly, or *de industriâ*, to ensure a wider circulation, the exergual mark of the capital.

The very remarkable type giving us ΚΩΝΣΤΑΝ would seem to evidence an unusual position for Constantine, the emperor's name;[2] but should we incline to attribute our hoard to Cyprus emission, these letters might also present an ingenious expedient for a double allusion to the reigning prince, and Constantia (Κωνσταντεια, as it is written by Epiphanius, in his words πολυανδροτατη πολις), the capital of the island and the ancient Salamis, where no doubt their principal monetary establishment would have been; but in our very scanty supply of contemporaneous Cypriot authorities, I should be unwilling to insist *at present* on this attribution. Any how, Constantinople can hardly be referred to, and the coincidence of the locality whence these coins came, to say the least, is curious.

The absence of every other exergual mark prevalent at this time among our hoard, increases to a certain extent the probability of their Cyprus manufacture; for even should we attribute the doubtful specimens bearing CON to the capital, why should Constantinople and Cyprus alone appear in our 512 pieces? whereas, allow the types reading CON to be provincial copies, and the want of all foreign mints in a hoard, the great portion of which was probably never put into circulation, is precisely what we should be led to expect.

Yet in our endeavoured attribution of the mass of this find to the Island of Cyprus, there is one important historical event by no means to be lost sight of. We know that in 648 A.D. (that is the seventh year of the reign of Constans II.) Moyawiah, the general of Othmán, invaded

---

[2] It is hardly necessary to remind our readers that the emperor is never written "Constans" on his coins.

Cyprus, which capitulated on an agreement that the Saracen general should share the revenues with the Greek emperor. Now it is after this event that our find was struck, and its semi-barbarous fabric accords well with the mixed nature of the island's political institutions during that period. The Greek population of the country was then probably little disturbed; and the **Saracens, always** ready to copy the coinage of their neighbours, would interfere little with the Greek currency of **the island, or** the employment of Greek workmen: thus even supposing a nominal and tributary Saracen supremacy, the years and titles of their "half-masters" at Byzantium might still be recorded as before. Very superior, however, are these coins to the common run of the so called Saracen imitations struck at times far in the interior of their dominions, and by chance workmen of the mint, for these pieces are seldom legible in their dates; yet it **is a** remarkable circumstance that these very types which our catalogue describes were among those most generally copied in the Saracen states.

The presence in our hoard of great numbers, **and several,** I believe, unpublished varieties **of the** εν τѹτο νικα types, would seem likewise to demand **a few words** on this subject, which is not without its difficulties and its interest, and to the materials for the investigation of which I venture to hope that the catalogue of this find may add its quota.

I should preface my observations by suggesting that in most of what **has** been written on this subject, there seems too great a desire to view these **types as all of one epoch,** **or,** at least, as referring to one event.

The word ἀνανέοσις, or as it woul̃d be classically written ἀνανέωσις,[3] must mean "a renewal," *renovatio*, or

---

[3] Ducange would seem to think **this** word ought to be completed thus ἀνανεόωσις, but surely ἀνανέωσις is the commoner

restauratio. When this type was supposed to have originated with Justinian Rhinotmetus on his recall from exile, it was then translated "return," from ἀνανέομαι, "to go back;" but besides the utterly overwhelming numismatic evidence against this supposition, we may remark that such an use of the word would be far too classical for even the Heraclian era; its letters, however, never read satisfactorily farther than ανανεο on any coin I have yet seen. Of the symbol which accompanies it, when joined with a numeral, I shall treat in the catalogue. Examples of the Sicilian type are elsewhere engraved, and described as if the legend went as far as αναντος; but no specimen has been brought under my notice sufficiently well preserved to establish this point beyond question.

The εν τѫτο νικα type as struck at Carthage is, doubtless, the earliest of this series, and came in with the Heraclian dynasty. The Sicilian types must have followed this closely, and the word αναντωσις as it appears on these has, I believe, been rightly referred to the circumstances under which the tyranny of Focas was suppressed. There are many legends quite as strange in Byzantine numismatics, yet the RESTITUTOR ORBIS of Aurelian is perhaps the most analogous expression to be found, to which we may add the FEL. TEMP. REPARATIO of the lower empire. Now, although the elder Heraclius first minted these types, yet, as far as our present hoard is concerned, in which we have about 202 of these coins, I should doubt the existence among them of one single specimen referrible to his reign; I believe rather the sum total of these to have been struck after the eleventh year of Constans II.

---

form; and from the obverse, εν τουτο for ἐν τούτῳ, we learn that the o is evidently equivalent to the ω in many instances, and in modern Greek no distinction exists between the two letters.

Mons. de Saulcy has justly remarked how servilely, and with how careful an imitation of detail, Constans has copied and reproduced alike the legends and the types of his ancestor Heraclius. This is a fact of which whoever tries to separate a mixed heap of the coins of these two sovereigns must soon become painfully aware.

It is remarkable enough that in all our number above stated we only encounter two beardless effigies, with the additional and confirmative difference of the cursive *m* on the reverse in place of the usual square letter. One other specimen occurs beardless, but slightly moustached, to supply a link with the main number of bearded portraits, and prevent any idea of attributing the two above named to the elder Heraclius. On pieces unconnected with this hoard a decided preponderance of these εν τϋτο types have beardless effigies, and a very large proportion of these beardless portraits elsewhere are accordingly to be assigned to the first Heraclius. Some few, like our two, may belong to Constans, struck probably before his eleventh year, at which period he is nearly always represented with a beard. I have never yet seen anywhere a single bearded specimen that from its fabric could be assigned to the elder Heraclius.

So favourite and peculiarly a Heraclian type as this εν τϋτο νικα would be copied naturally among the rest by his imitative descendant Constans; whether the word "renewal" may not have acquired a secondary importance and appropriateness from one of the crises which the empire underwent during the reign of Constans also, seems not unlikely, although no positive opinion can be maintained on this subject till a fuller history of the reappearance of this type has been collected.

The normal and representative specimen of this type

under Constans is the εν τΗτο νικα obverse, conjoined to the ανανεο reverse with a numeral. But each of these legends appear in our find disjoined from the other likewise. For instance, αναινεο takes a fresh obverse of the emperor's bust and the legend INPER (*sic*) CONST, while εν τΗτο νικα substitutes as its obverse KΩNΣTAN and a numeral in one case, and ANNO with a numeral and an illegible exergue in the other. (See the plate *passim*.)

Catalogue of the Cyprus Find.

CONSTANS II. ALONE. FROM A.D. 641.

No. 1.
    Obv.—INPER CONST. Full-faced, bearded bust, with diadem surmounted by a cross. Orb in right hand.

    Rev.—The large M; above it a cross; to the right, ANA; to the left, NEO. The NEO is on other specimens often blundered, and thus sometimes reads like three in Roman numerals (Pl. ii. 12), for which it has been often mistaken. 2

No. 2.
    Obv.—Bust, with head indistinct from the countermark; holding a long cross in the right hand. No legend decipherable.

    Rev.—The large K; to right ANNO, to left various illegible figures. (Pl. ii. 13.) . . 2

No. 3.
    Obv.—The bust of the emperor to the waist, holding long cross; to his right, K; to his left, a countermark of a small winged Victory. The emperor unbearded, but with a moustache.

    Rev.—The cursive M; traces of ANA to the right; in the exergue, IT? (Pl. ii. 11) possibly IΓ, that is 13. 1

        (M. Sabatier, in his new work on the Roman series, has published a silver coin of Heraclius and Heraclius Constantine, in which a small

COINS OF CONSTANS II. AND HIS SONS. 51

Victory is represented as crowning the emperor. See his Pl. Sup. xvii. 44.)

No. 4.

Obv.—The beardless effigy of the emperor, standing, full-faced and diademed. The long cross in his right; the orb in his left. EN TЫTO NIKA.

Rev.—The cursive M in two specimens; **as usual, on** the third, to the right, ANA ; left, **NEO**. The exergue doubtful. (See Pl. ii. 10.) . . 3

No. 5.

Obv.—The emperor as before, but always bearded, and the diadem more ornamented. The details of this type more elaborate than the last.

Rev.—The large M, lettered from A to E between the limbs to the right, ANA ; left, NEO; in the exergue the numerals IA. XII. XIII. XIIII. and XV. (11th, 12th, 13th, 14th, and 15th years.)

In the left corner of the field, between the last symbol of the numeral and the O of ANANEO, there appears the sign ↳ or ϛ.[4] (See Pl. ii. 6, 7, and 8.) . . . 52

Coins of the same type as above, **but** with **illegible** exergues 76

───
128

[4] Of this, in many specimens perfectly distinct and legible symbol, I am at present quite unable to offer any adequate explanation. It closely resembles the Upsilon in form, if it be not actually one and the same letter. We may conclude it is to be read as an integral part of ANANEO rather than the numeral preceding it, as it disappears on the KΩNΣTAN type after the very numeral XV which it followed on the ANANEO type. (See Pl. ii. 3 and 8.) The most convenient theory would be to suppose this equivalent to Σ, ΣI, or ΣIΣ, the remaining portions of the word ANANEOΣIΣ ; but unless some of the "litteræ nexæ" of the period come to our assistance, I fear there is little to bear out this reading. I think also there is small chance of its being the Omega required to follow ANANEO were the word to be continued in an uncontracted form, thus, ANANEOΩΣIΣ, as this is a very unlikely way for a Byzantine to write the word at this period.

No. 6.

   Obv.—EN TSTO NIKA. The emperor as before, bearded and full length. This type of rather better workmanship, and elaborate in its details. The letters rather broader.

   Rev.—The large M; above it a star; lettered beneath, from A to E; to the right, KΩN; left, CTAN; in the exergue xϞ; sometimes written xϘ. (See Pl. ii. 3.) 62

No. 7.

   Obv.—EN TSTO NIKA. The emperor as in No. 5.

   Rev.—The large M; lettered as usual below; above it, a K; to the right, ANNO; to the left, XVI. The exergue doubtful. (See Pl. ii. 9.) 7

CONSTANS II. AND CONSTANTINE POGONATUS.
FROM A.D. 654.

No. 8.

   Obv.—The emperor, bearded and diademed, standing, full-faced, in military costume, holding a long cross in his right hand. To his left, Pogonatus, diademed, in a long robe, with the orb in his right hand.

   Rev.—The large M; above it a K; and numeral letters between the limbs from A to E; to the right, ANNO; to the left, XV. XVI. or XVII. In the exergue, CON. (Soleirol, No. 638, describes a coin somewhat similar, giving the exergual mark SCL.) (See Pl. ii. 14.) 59

CONSTANS II., CONSTANTINE POGONATUS, HERACLIUS, AND TIBERIUS. FROM 659 A.D.

No. 9.

   Obv.—Full-faced bust of Constans, with a very long beard, wearing an open kind of diadem, leaning to one side; sometimes a small cross on it. In his right hand a globe, surmounted by a long cross. On his left, in the field, a large K for Constantine.

Rev.—The large **M**; the bust of Pogonatus above it; to the right, that of Heraclius; to the left, that of Tiberius; in the exergue sometimes ᴏ; but generally with no exergual mark, but lettered under the M from **A** to **E**, which variety seems unknown. Soleirol apparently had three specimens reading ᴏ. There are endless minor varieties in the treatment of the diadem and the drapery of **the mantle** on the obverse. **One** specimen bears in **the** field ҂, instead of **the** large **K**, **to the** left of the bust of Constans. This **is not a** countermark, as the usual **one appears** elsewhere **on** the coin. (See Pl. ii. 4.) **No date or legend.** 80

No. 10.

Obv.—The emperor standing, in military costume, full-faced and bearded; wearing a kind of mitre, leaning **to** the left. A long cross in his right hand; his left rests on his hip; to the right, Iᴏ. XX. KA. XXΓ. (19, 20, 21, 23); **to** the left a large M, lettered below from **A** to **E**. These letters generally large **also**. **On the** coins of the latest date the **tiara has given** place to the diadem **on** the obverse.

Rev.—Pogonatus, Heraclius, **and** Tiberius, full-faced, standing in robes of peace; all diademed, and holding orbs. Sometimes Δ to the right, or A to the left; **in a** few instances the M to the left of **the** obverse has no letter under it. This type **varies** much in size and fabric. Soleirol, No. **647, is** an imperfect description **of it.** He suggests Sicily as the mintage **place,** and describes his three specimens **there** given as badly preserved. (Pl. ii. 1.) 160

No. 11.

Obv.—The emperor in military dress, full-length and full-faced, standing to the right, holding a long cross; he is diademed and bearded. To his left Pogonatus in a robe of peace with an orb in his right hand; in the field **to** the left XXE (25); above, between the **figures,** a small cross.

Rev.—The large M, surmounted by an elaborate cross on steps, Heraclius full-length and full-face to the right, holding the orb; Tiberius to the left as before. In the exergue CON, under the M, a Γ. (Pl. ii. 5.) Another variety differs in having no large M between the figures on the reverse, who both hold crosses instead of orbs. (Pl. ii. 5 B. The last coin on the page.)   5

CONSTANTINE POGONATUS, HERACLIUS, AND TIBERIUS. FROM A.D. 668.

No. 12.

Obv.—Pogonatus, Heraclius, and Tiberius standing full-faced, all holding in their right hands short crosses or sceptres, also diademed and in robes of peace.

Rev.—The large M, below it Γ; to the right, ANNO; to the left, XV. In the exergue, KYΠP. Countermarked as usual with the rest.

(Pl. ii. 2.)   3

Names.	Number of Coins.	Dates of Years.
Constans II. alone	205	11, 12, 13, 14, 15, 16.
Constans II. and Constantine Pogonatus	59	15, 16, 17.
Constans II., Constantine Pogonatus, Heraclius, and Tiberius	245	19, 20, 21, 23, 25.
Constantine Pogonatus, Heraclius, and Tiberius	3	15.

Total 512

We learn from this table that in his fifteenth and sixteenth years Constans was being struck on anonymous coins by himself, simultaneously with the issue of pieces of himself and his son Pogonatus.

The system of numeration adopted in the coins of this

find is quaint in the extreme from its confusion of Greek and Roman numerals.

IA 11
XII 12   IB } Occur elsewhere about this period.
XIII . . . 13   IΓ }
XIIII . . 14
XV 15
XVI . . . 16
XVII . . 17   18 is wanting.
IΘ 19
XX 20
KA 21   22 and 24 wanting.
XXΓ 23
XXE . . . 25

"Surfrappes," or counterstruck coins are common in this find. I shall conclude by the mention of those which are decipherable.

Upon the EN TSTO and ANANEO type (pl. ii. 6, 7, 8) are struck the KΩNΣTAN type (pl. ii. 3), the Constans and Pogonatus type (pl. ii. 14), the four bust type (pl. ii. 4), and the four figure type (pl. ii. 1).

The last-mentioned type is again struck upon the KΩNΣTAN type (pl. ii. 3), and on the four bust type (pl. ii. 4).

J. L. W.

VII.

ENGLISH AND FOREIGN STERLINGS FOUND IN SCOTLAND.

For the following catalogue of a hoard of coins lately discovered in Dumfriesshire, we are indebted to Mr. George Sim, of Edinburgh. The whole of them were made over to the Scottish Exchequer Chamber, in accordance with the recent regulations as to treasure-trove in Scotland.

Though not presenting any remarkable features, either in the number of the coins discovered, or in the rarity of any of the types, this find is still of interest, as showing the proportionate quantities of the coins issued from the various English mints of the period in circulation together, and the amount of intermixture of the foreign imitations of the sterling with them.

As there are only four Scotch coins among them, it would appear that though found in Scotland, this hoard of coins was originally collected together in England, and was probably either buried by an Englishman on one of the numerous expeditions into Scotland at the beginning of the 14th century, or may have been the hidden produce of some Scottish raid over the Border.

Mr. Sim remarks that the sterling of Valenciennes is exactly similar to one found at Kirkcudbright, and described in the Numismatic Chronicle, vol xiii. p. 88, and that of Mons to the one described on the same page. There is some doubt whether the sterling attributed to

Robert III. of Flanders is really his. It belongs, however, to a Count of Flanders, and was struck at Alost.

In the find of coins at Kirkcudbright, the relative proportions of the English and foreign coins was just the reverse of that of the present find. In that instance there were only five coins of Edward I., one of Henry III., and one of Alexander III., to upwards of eighty of foreign mintage, while here there are one hundred and ninety-one English and Scotch coins to four of the foreign imitations.

Description of Coins found on the 30th March, 1860, on the farm of Netherfield, parish of Cummertrees, in the county of Dumfries, by Edward Dalrymple and William Burnie.

ALL PENNIES.

Foreign sterlings:—John of Hainault (of Mons, and Valenciennes), and Robert III. of Flanders, &c.	4
Alexander III. of Scotland	3
John Baliol. Rev. "Rex Scotorum"	1
Edwards I. and II. of England:—	
London	91
Canterbury	49
Durham	23
Newcastle	3
Lincoln	1
York	4
Bury St. Edmunds	4
Berwick	3
Bristol	5
Dublin	1
Illegible	3
	Total 195

Dalrymple 77
Burnie . 118

Total 195

VIII.

ON SOME LOOPED COINS FOUND WITH ANGLO-SAXON ORNAMENTS IN KENT.

THE four gold *solidi* here described, and engraved, though without the loops, in Pl. iii., were found last year at Sarre, near Reculver, in Kent, and formed pendants to a necklace of beads, which—with a splendid gold *fibula* inlaid with garnets, found at the same time—is now in the British Museum. They belong to the end of the sixth and beginning of the seventh century, and are highly interesting, as they mark the period at which the name and effigy of a Byzantine emperor appeared for the last time, under Heraclius, on the coinage of the south of Gaul.

No. 1.
  Obv.—DN. MAVRIC RPPAVG. Diademed bust of Mauricius Tiberius, to the right.
  Rev.—VICTORIA AVGGVI. C . . . . . A cross resting on a globe, and encircled in a wreath. On the left of the cross, M; on the right, A. On the left of the globe, X; on the right, XI. Of good workmanship.

No. 2.
  Obv.—ON MAVIIAPPAHC. Diademed bust of Mauricius Tiberius, to the right.
  Rev.—VIC. OR. AVGGVI. CONOB. Cross and globe as in No. 1, but with AR. instead of MA. Of barbarous workmanship.

No. 3.
  Obv.—ERAC. . VS INP. Diademed bust of Heraclius, to the right.
  Rev.—Barbarous legend. Cross and globe as in No. 1.

No. 4.
  Obv.—CHLOTARIVS RX. Diademed bust of Clotaire II., to the right.
  Rev.—Barbarous legend. Cross and globe as in No. 1.

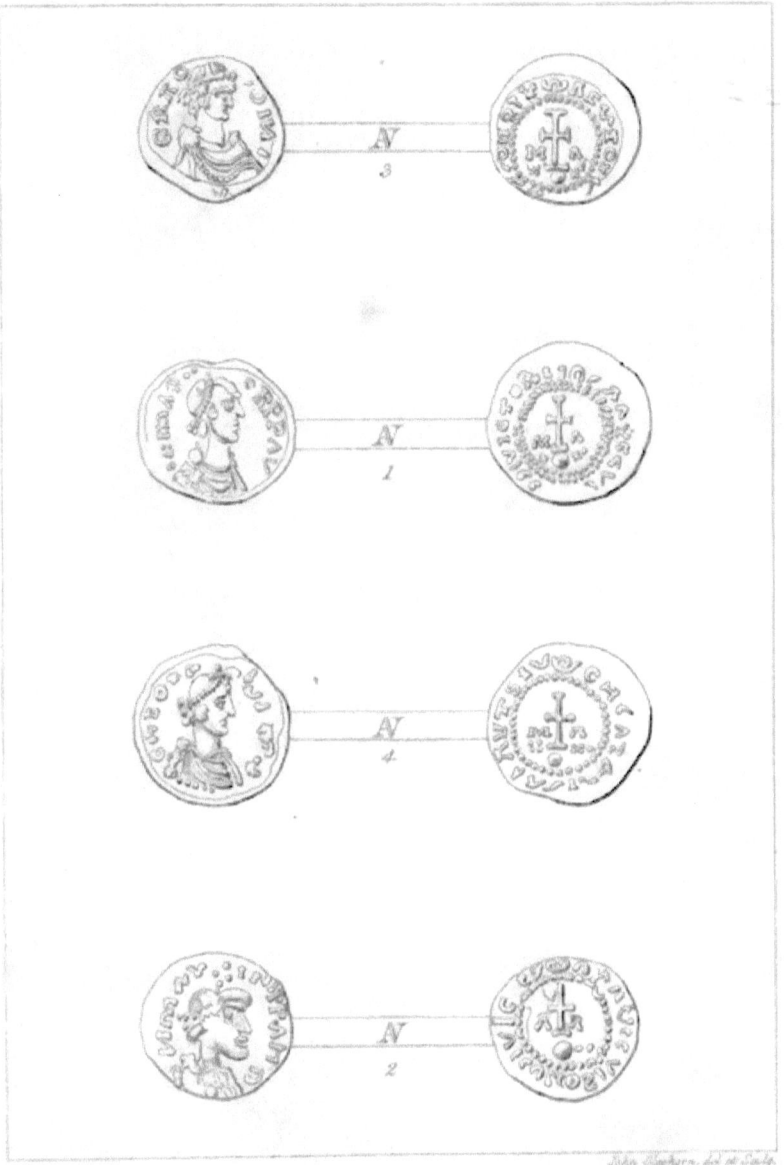

COINS FOUND WITH ANGLO SAXON ORNAMENTS IN KENT.

M. Lenormant describes two varieties of gold coins struck at Marseilles, and in other towns of the south of France, with the name of Mauricius Tiberius, but he does not mention any of similar fabric bearing the names of subsequent emperors. The first variety, like the early Merovingian coinage, is full faced in the *solidus*, but side faced in the *triens*. In the second variety, to which our coins belong, both the *solidus* and *triens* are side faced, and the cross on the reverse is encircled in a wreath, instead of being separated by a straight line from the exergual legend, as in the first variety. He ascribes the former to Gondovald, natural son of Clotaire I, who, with the assistance of Mauricius Tiberius, held possession of the south of Gaul from A.D. 583 to 585; and the second to Syagrius, who in 587 succeeded for a short time in re-establishing the imperial authority in the same quarter.

M. Lenormant further observes that we have no effigies of Merovingian kings on coins imitated from those of the second variety till Clotaire II., who obtained possession of the southern provinces in 613, and he is of opinion that till this date money was coined there in the name of the Byzantine emperor.

This supposition is confirmed by the coin of Heraclius, No. 3, and by two others, both in the British Museum. The first is a barbarous *solidus* of Focas, the reverse of which is similar to that of Nos. 1, 3, and 4; and the second, a *triens* of Heraclius, struck at Viviers, and similar in fabric to one of Clotaire II., bearing the mint-mark of Marseilles, which is also in the national collection. This mintage continues, with a few exceptions, from Clotaire II. to the end of the Merovingian dynasty.

J. F. W. DE SALIS.

NOTICE OF RECENT NUMISMATIC PUBLICATIONS.

The sixth number (November and December) of the *Revue Numismatique* for 1860 has the following papers:—

1. Letter XI. of M. De Saulcy, addressed to M. A. de Longpérier, on the "Numismatique Gauloise," attributing the Gaulish quinarii with the horseman on the reverse, and the legends EBVRO, DONNVS, AVSCRO . COMA, &c., to the Gaulish league against Ariovistus and the Helvetii.

2. Remarks on the names Voluntillius and Ambillius, by M. A. de Longpérier.

3. "Etudes de Numismatique Asiatique," by W. H. Waddington, Esq.

Mr. Waddington here publishes the commencement of an essay on the coins bearing Phœnician, Aramæan, or similar inscriptions. The first portion treats of the coins of the Satraps, and of Tyre. The most important discovery announced, is that the Satraps did not issue coin as governors, but when in command of large forces by a special authority. The paper is of great value in establishing a safe basis for further inquiry.

4. Paper on the coins of Mâcon, by M. Ch. Robert.

In the *Nécrologie* is a well-deserved tribute of respect to the late Colonel Martin Leake.

The principal articles contained in the 3ième and 4ième *Livraisons*, of the *Revue Numismatique Belge*, for 1860, are as follows:—

1. A letter from M. Fénélon Farez, "On a Gaulish coin with the legend L . ARTVE . C . COMIN Ⅱ VIR," in which he repudiates the opinion of De Saulcy, who interprets COMI . N as COMMII. *Nepos*, and suggests that ARTVE is without doubt a proper name, and that VIR may be *Vericus*, the son of Commius. M. Farez suggests that it is a coin of *Pæstum*, and that it was struck in the *duumvirate* of *Lucius Artuenus* and *Caius Cominius*, the latter of the plebeian family *Cominia*. He gives his reasons for this attribution, and appeals to Messrs. Birch and Evans to give their opinion on the subject. There is no doubt that the view of M. Farez is correct, and it had already been accepted by M. de Saulcy in a *Rectification* which appeared in the August number of the *Revue Numismatique*.

2. "On a *solidus* of Aelia Galla Placidia," by M. Julius Friedlaender.

The attribution to *Galla Placidia*, the wife of Constantius (Patricius), of the coins formerly attributed to *Aelia Placidia*, wife of Olybrius, has been often suggested. The coin of *Galla Placidia*, with the name *Aelia* was struck at Constantinople by her nephew, Theodosius II., during the **time** that Johannes I. had usurped the purple at Ravenna, **and on** being restored to her power there by her nephew, she **again struck coins in** the name of her son, Placidius Valentinianus, **with the name** *Galla. Aelia* was the common name for the princesses at Constantinople, viz., *Aelia Eudoxia, Aelia Pulcheria*. M. Friedlaender is probably mistaken in saying that the type of these *solidi* with the legend VOT. XX. MVLT. XXX. has **reference** to the *solidi* of her **son**; it has reference to the **same** type and legend **of the *solidi*** of her nephew, Theodosius II., struck at Constantinople.

3. "**On an Arab** coin with **a** Visigothic type," by M. H. Lavoix.

4. "On some unedited mediæval coins," by M. Chalon.

5. "Plombs des fêtes des Innocents, having reference to the town of Aire-sur-la-Lys," by M. Jules Rouyer.

6. "On some interesting documents relating to the history of coins," by M. de la Fons-Melicocq.— *Two Essays.*

7. "The destruction of Eptiacum about the year 202 of the Christian era proved by coins," by Dr. A. Namur.

8. "On the most ancient coin known of Abdul Malek," **by** M. H. Sauvaire.

9. "On some curious Jettons," by M. Preux.

10. "On a medal of honour presented by the **United Provinces** to Captain Logier," by M. de Coster.

11. "Notice of J. Boskam, the engraver," by **M. A.** Pinchart.

In the *Numismatische Zeitung*, December, 1860, No. 25 (twenty-seventh year), are notices of the work by J. Neumann.

Beschreibung der bekanntesten Kupfer Münzen. Prag., 1860.

The twelfth Part of this valuable publication **contains** the papal and Neapolitan coins. Great care has been shown **in the** description of the papal money, and in those of the Rulers of Camerino, Ferrara, Pesaro, and Urbino.

A notice of the later money of the Bishopric of Passau.

Of a medal of M. Römer, the President of **the** Ober-Apellations-Gerichts.

Of an extensive find of coins in Ober-Schwaben, which are to be described at length by Dr. J. Müller. And

Of a medal to the celebrated naturalist Leopold Von Buch, under whom Humboldt studied.

MISCELLANEA.

THE NEW COINAGE.—From the *Gazette* of Tuesday, Dec. 18.
By the QUEEN.—A PROCLAMATION.
VICTORIA, R.

Whereas we have thought fit to order that certain pieces of money of bronze or mixed metal should be coined, which should be called " Penny Pieces," " Halfpenny Pieces," and " Farthing Pieces :" every such penny having for the obverse impression our effigy laureated, with the inscription " Victoria. D. G. Britt : Reg : F. D.," and for the reverse impression the figure of Britannia seated upon a rock in the sea, her right hand resting upon a shield, and holding in her left the trident, with a ship and pharos in the distance, and the inscription " One Penny," with the date of the year; and every such halfpenny piece having for the obverse impression the aforesaid effigy and inscription, and for the reverse the figure of Britannia, with the same emblems as described for the penny, and the inscription " Halfpenny," with the date of the year; and every such farthing piece having for the obverse impression the aforesaid effigy and inscription, and for the reverse the figure of Britannia, with the same emblems as described for the penny, and the inscription " Farthing," with the date of the year: all which said moneys of bronze or mixed metal have been and shall be coined in a mixed metal or bronze, composed of copper, tin, and zinc ; and whereas pieces of money of the description aforesaid have been coined at our Mint, and will be coined there, we have, therefore, with the advice of our Privy Council, thought fit to issue this Proclamation ; and we do hereby ordain, declare, and command that all such pieces of money of bronze or mixed metal so coined, and to be coined as aforesaid, shall be current and lawful money of the Kingdom of Great Britain and Ireland, and shall pass and be received as current and lawful money of the said kingdom, every such penny piece as of the value of one penny of present lawful money, every such halfpenny piece as of the value of one halfpenny of present lawful money, and every such farthing piece as of the value of one farthing of present lawful money; provided that no person shall be obliged to take more of such penny pieces in any one payment than shall be of the value of 1s. after the rate aforesaid, or take more of such halfpenny or farthing pieces in any one payment than shall be of the value of sixpence after the rate aforesaid.

Given at our Court at Windsor, this 17th day of December, 1860, and in the 24th year of our reign.

God save the Queen.

THE COINAGE.—A return relating to the operations of the Mint was issued April 17, 1860. The number of sovereigns coined in 1859 were 1,547,603; of half-sovereigns, 2,203,813, a greater number than those for the former year, when 803,234 sovereigns and 855,578 half-sovereigns were coined. The total value of all the gold coinage manufactured at the Mint during the last ten years was £54,490,265. The number of florins coined in 1859 was 2,568,060; of shillings, 4,561,920; of sixpences, 4,688,640; of fourpences, 4158; of threepences, 3,584,328; of silver twopences, 4752; and of silver pence, 7920. In copper the coinage was as follows:— 1,075,200 pence, 1,290,240 halfpence, and 1,290,240 farthings. Half-farthings have not been coined since 1856.

SALE OF COINS.—The choice collection of coins, &c., formed by the late Rev. J. Lewin-Sheppard, of Frome, to which were added some other coins, have been lately dispersed under the hammer of Messrs. Sotheby and Wilkinson. The following were the more interesting specimens of the Rev. Mr. Sheppard's collection:—Roman Silver.—Lot 18. Marciana; rev., CONSECRATIO, eagle—£3 14s. Lot 33. Carausius, an unpublished denarius; obv., bust laureated, to the right; rev., FEDES (sic) MILITVM, female standing, holding two military ensigns; R.S.R. in exergue—£7 12s. 6d. British Gold.—Lot 61. Eppillus; obv., EPPI. (Eppillus), horse to right; rev., COM.F (Comi filius) in circlet; well preserved; size, 1¾, wt. 20 grs.—£8. Lot 62. Tasciovanus; obv., ornated tablet, inscribed TASC. (iovanus); rev., horseman to left, a pellet beneath; size, 2, wt. 20½ grs.—£5 10s. British, Saxon, and English Silver.—Lot 64. Cunobelinus; obv., CVNOBELINVS., bare bust to right; rev., TASCIO., horse to right, crescent above. Fine; size, 2, wt. 26 7-10 grs.; varied from Mr. Huxtable's specimen, lot 507, which sold for £15, the present realized £30 10s. Lot 69. Ecgberht, King of Kent, or rather Eadbhert of Northumberland; sceatta, with obv., an animal resembling a dragon; rev., EOTBEREDTVI., and cross; vide Hawkins, No. 103. Wt. 14½ grs.—£4 3s. Lot 71. Offa; obv., King's head to right;

rev., ornamental cruciform type, including the moneyer's name, PEHTVALF. Fine; wt. 17¾ grs.—£5. Lot 72. Offa; obv., O.F.M.R. and O. in centre of an ornament, extending to the edge of the coin; rev., ALH. MVN. in the field; cross, crook, &c. Fine; wt. 19 grs.—£14 10s. Lot 73. Coenwlf; obv., bust; rev., LVL+. in ovals between the angles of a cross, terminating in large triangular compartments, in imitation of coins of Offa. Fine; wt. 18 grs.—£3 15s. Lot 83. Anlaf; obv., trefoil ornament; rev., the so-called Danish sacred ensign, but without the badge of the raven. Similar to that in Hawkins, No. 128. Wt. 26 grs.—£3 4s. Lot 85. Saint Peter, penny; rev., EBRAICIT., and in centre the Carlovingian monogram. Fine; wt. 19 1-5 grs.—£5 10s. Lot 88. Ceolnoth, Archbishop of Canterbury; obv., rude full-faced bust; rev., BIARNRED. MONETA. Fine; wt. 23¼ grs.—£13 10s. Lot 93. Ecgbeorht, sole monarch; obv., bust to right; rev., TIDBEARHT., and in centre a monogram somewhat like that of Charlemagne; *vide* Hawkins, No. 157. Wt. 22 grs.—£4 12s. Lot 102. Aelfred, obv., + ELFRED. M.—X +., portrait rudely executed; rev., DVDD. MONETA. in three lines, as the pennies of Burgred. Mr. Hawkins, at p. 58 of his *Silver Coins of England*, mentions this identical rare coin, and states, " It is difficult to suppose that Maximus was intended, and as difficult to form any other reasonable conjecture." Probably unique. Wt. 18 grs.—£9. Lot 104. Aelfred, halfpenny; obv., CIV.REI.; head to right; rev., large monogram (retrograde) of London, occupying the whole field; wt. 10 grs.—£6 10s. Lot 126. Harthacnute; obv., + HARDE-CNVToo., diademed head to left; rev., + BRACIT. ON. VIBEIS., cross, as in Hawkins, No. 216—£3 5s. Lot 135. Eustace; obv. and rev., as in Hawkins, No. 282, lion, &c. Fine —£3 1s. Lot 164. Mary Queen of Scots, testoon; date 1562. Fine, though double struck; from the Bindley collection—£4. Lot 170. Oliver Cromwell, silver pattern for a two-shilling piece; obv., bust of the Protector without the &c. before PRO.; rev., PAX, &c.; 1658, probably the work of Simon. Plain edge. Fine; wt. 6 dwts. 11 grs. Mr. Cuff's specimen, lot 1,288 (1854) produced £18 5s.—14 guineas. Lot 228. Maryland, Lord Baltimore's shilling, sixpence, and groat, by Nicholas Briot; a fine set—£10. Lot 235. Edward V., angel, M.M., rose and sun combined; scarce—£10. Lot 247. Simon's petition crown of Charles II.; obv., splendidly executed bust, laureated, &c., SIMON beneath; rev., four shields, &c., 1663; on the edge or rim is inscribed the well-known curious petition, *vide Num. Chron.*, vol. xvi. p. 133. Fairly preserved; enclosed in a silver box, within a modern red morocco case—£40.

IX.

AN ACCOUNT OF A FIND OF COINS IN THE PARISH OF GOLDBOROUGH, YORKSHIRE.

[Read before the Numismatic Society, April 28, 1859.]

I HAVE great pleasure in giving an account to the Numismatic Society of a very curious find of coins that has taken place in the parish of Goldborough, in Yorkshire, and for the preservation of which we are indebted to the Hon. and Rev. Mr. Lascelles, the vicar of the place.

It appears that, in the autumn of 1858, some workmen were digging the foundations for the rebuilding the wall of the churchyard at Goldborough, when they came upon an earthenware pot, which was immediately broken into fragments, and was found to contain a number of pieces of silver, such as ingots, several portions of silver bracelets, one very large and perfect silver buckle, and a considerable number of coins. The character of the find bears remarkable analogy to the much larger one at Cuerdale, in Lancashire, in 1840; but there is this difference, that whereas in the Cuerdale find the great bulk of the coins were Saxon, and there were only two or three Oriental coins interspersed among them, in this find nearly the whole of the coins are Oriental, only two Saxon coins having been met with—one of Alfred, and the other of Eadweard the Elder.

The coin of Alfred is a great curiosity; it is, indeed, only half a coin; but its size is double that of the usual

Saxon pennies, and, with one exception, no similar coin has been met with. Those who are interested in the Saxon coinage will probably remember a specimen engraved by Mr. Hawkins, Pl. xiii. No. 178, in his work on the "Silver Coins of England," of which he gives the following account:—"A very peculiar piece will be found (see No. 178), $1\frac{5}{10}$ inch in diameter, and weighing 162 grains. It is right to make the reader acquainted with the existence of so curious a piece, though it must be considered more in the light of a medal than of a coin. It is in the possession of Mr. Garland," or rather it was, in 1828; for whether Mr. Garland is still alive, and whether he still retains it, or what may have become of it if he is now dead, this, no one, I believe, knows. Mr. Garland's coin, or medal, reads:—

Obv.— +AEL
FRED RE
X SÅXO   (*In four lines.*)
NVM

Rev.— EL̊I
M̊ · O̊ —   (*In two lines.*)

The fragment discovered at Goldborough, weighs 53 grains, and is here engraved.

It is not too much to say that but for the previous occurrence of the perfect specimen of which I have spoken, no one, however imaginative, could have determined to what king it was to be assigned.

The other coin has no especial merit, and belongs to a class which, as all collectors know, is sufficiently abundant. It reads :—

Obv.— + EADVVEARD REX; in the centre a small cross.

Rev.—
EDELLF
✠ ✠ ✠
A   ×ꟼO
∴ (M)

The remaining coins are all Oriental, and may be arranged as follows. They are, in number, thirty-five, of which seven have become hopelessly illegible ; the rest may be thus described :—

OF THE ABBASSIDE DYNASTY.

1. Al Motámed ala Allah.   A.H. 276
                                A.D. 889

2. Ditto, bearing the name of Taher.

3. —   A.H. 290—299
                                A.D. 903—912
   and struck during the khaláfat of Al Moktafi or Al Moktader.

4. One struck at *Al Shash.*

5. Another, which belongs to this dynasty, but is so much worn as to be nearly illegible.

6. One bearing the name of Al Moktafi, and the date A.H. 292
                                A.D. 905

7. Al Motadhed.   A.H. 280
                                 A.D. 893
                                 and struck at *Al Shash.*

8. Of this dynasty; but with no date or place of striking.

9. Al Moktader billah.   A.H. 297
                                 A.D. 910

OF THE SAMANIAN DYNASTY.

10. Ismail ben Ahmed.
    (Al Motadhed.)   A.H. 282
                                 A.D. 895
                                       Al Shash.

11. Ismail ben Ahmed.
    Al Motadhed billah.   A.H. 286
                                 A.D. 899
                                       Al Shash.

12. Ismail ben Ahmed.
    Al Motadhed billah.   A.H. 286
                                 A.D. 899
                                       Samarcand.

13. Ismail ben Ahmed.
    Al Motadhed billah.   A.H. 288
                                 A.D. 901
                                       Samarcand.

13. Ismail ben Ahmed.
    Al Motadhed billah.   A.H. 289
                                 A.D. 902

14. Ismail ben Ahmed.
    Al Motadhed billah.   A.H. 291
                                 A.D. 904
                                       Al Shash.

15. Ismail ben Ahmed.
                                 A.H. 291
                                 A.D. 904
                                       Al Shash.

16. Ismail ben Ahmed.
    Al Motadhed billah.   A.H. 279—289
                                 A.D. 892—902
                                       Al Shash.

A FIND OF COINS AT GOLDBOROUGH.

16. Ismail ben Ahmed.
    Al Moktafi billah.   A.H. 289—294
                                  A.D. 902—907
                                        Al Shash.

17. Ismail ben Ahmed.
    Al Moktafi billah.   A.H. 292
                                  A.D. 905
                                        Al Shash.

18. Ismail ben Ahmed.
    Al Moktafi billah.   A.H. 292
                                  A.D. 905
                                        Samarcand.

19. Ismail ben Ahmed.
                                  A.H. 293
                                  A.D. 906
                                        Maaden.

20. Ismail ben Ahmed.
    Al Moktafi billah.   A.H. 294
                                  A.D. 907
                                        Samarcand.

21. Ismail ben Ahmed.
    Al Moktader.   A.H. 29—
                                  A.D. 90—

22. Ismail ben **Ahmed**.
                                  A.H. —8
                                  [A.H. 279—295]
                                  [A.D. 892—907]
                                        Al Shash.

23. Ismail ben Ahmed.
                                  [A.H. 279—295]
                                  [A.D. 892—907]
    sine anno aut loco.

24. Ahmed ben Ismail.
    Al Moktader billah.   A.H. 298
                                  A.D. 911

25. Ahmed ben Ismail.
    Al Moktader.   A.H. 298
                                  A.D. 911

26. Nasr ben Ahmed.
    Al Moktader billah.   A.H. 301—320
                                  A.D. 913—932

(*Seven illegible.*)

From the comparison of the dates we are able to obtain from these coins, it is easy to ascertain the limits of the period within which they must have been struck, and thence to deduce some conclusions as to the date when this hoard must have been deposited.

Thus, from the coins of Alfred and Eadweard the Elder, we know that none of these can be earlier than the first year of Alfred, A.D. 872, nor later than the last year of the reign of Eadweard, or A.D. 925; that is, that so far as we can ascertain from the Saxon coins, they range over a period of fifty-three years.

This period is, however, more limited when we come to examine the dates of the Oriental coins. Thus, the earliest is a piece of the Abbasside dynasty and of the Khalif Al Motámed ala Allah; on this the date is clearly A.H. 276 (A.D. 889), corresponding with the eleventh year of Alfred the Great; and we have, subsequently, the well-defined dates, A.H. 280 (893), 282 (895), 286 (899), 288 (901), 289 (902), 291 (904), 292 (905), 293 (906), 294 (907), 297 (910), 298 (911), while from one of the coins bearing clearly the name of Nasr ben Ahmed, the fourth prince of the Samanian house, who reigned between A.H. 301—331, or A.D. 913—943, we might conclude that one at least of these coins was as late as that date, or eighteen years after the death of Eadweard the Elder. Here, however, we have another limitation in the name of the khalif who appears also on this coin, Al Moktader billah. As this prince did not reign longer than A.H. 320 (A.D. 932), we may be sure that the coin cannot be later than this period. Now the year A.D. 932 is seven years after the death of Eadweard, during the reign of his son, Athelstan; and it is possible, therefore, by taking the extreme limits as mentioned above, that these coins do range over a period extending from A.H. 276 — 320 (A.D. 889—932), or forty-three years. As, however, the last coin mentioned does not give its actual date, but only an inferential one, derived from comparing the dates of the prince's reign with that of his spiritual sovereign the khalif, it is quite possible that this coin may have been struck before the death of Eadweard, in A.D. 925, and, therefore, that the actual limit of these coins is between A.D. 889—925, or thirty-six years.

With regard to the discovery of Oriental coins intermixed with Saxon or other money of the North of Europe, I have already given the fullest information I could, in a paper I read before this Society in January, 1850,[1] in which I gave an account of the vast number of such coins which have been found all along the shores of the Baltic. I then stated that, curiously enough, almost all these coins belong to one or two Oriental dynasties, and that their date lies within very narrow limits. All this is confirmed by the circumstances of the present find, no less than by that of Cuerdale, to which I have already alluded.

W. S. W. VAUX.

---

[1] Num. Chron. vol. xiii. p. 14.

X.

OBSERVATIONS ON SOME DOUBLE-STRUCK COINS OF THE BACTRIAN KING, AZES OR AZAS.

OF the abundant series of coins which bear the name of the Bactrian king, Azas, two types, figured as Nos. 10 and 12, in the seventh plate of Wilson's "Ariana Antiqua," are perhaps those most common.

The first bears on the obverse an elephant, and on the reverse an Indian bull; the other has on its obverse a seated figure of the Greek goddess, Demeter, and on the reverse a standing figure of Hermes with his caduceus.

The legends on both types are precisely the same, being on the obverse, in Greek letters,

ΒΑΣΙΛΕΩΣ ΒΑΣΙΛΕΩΝ ΜΕΓΑΛ Ο Υ ΑΖ Ο Υ,

and on the reverse, in Arian Pali letters,

MAHARAJADHIRAJASA . MAHATASA AYASA.

In the year 1849, while examining a very well preserved specimen of the latter type, which I procured from Jhelum, in the Punjab, I discovered beneath the Pali legend of the obverse the faint outlines of the Greek letters "ΩΝ."

I examined, in consequence, every individual of the same type which fell into my hands with peculiar care; and at last, in 1851, I was rewarded by finding among a parcel of coins purchased for me at Rawul Pindi, an entire series of these curious palimpsests.

They were bought by Mr. Carnac, who states the Affghan who sold them assured him they were all taken out of a tope near Jellalabad, in Affghanistan—a story which their appearance did not belie, as when I first received them they were mostly adhering to each other, and covered with a thick coat of verdigris.

On cleaning, I found them to be all coins of Azas, and, with one exception, of the two types described above. Most of those, however, which bore the second type exhibited traces of having been re-struck upon older defaced coins; and in every case the original type appeared to have been that of the bull and elephant.

Altogether, the number of specimens which I have secured (mostly of this find), on which similar marks are to be found, amounts to nearly a dozen, exhibiting the defacement of the original device in almost every stage of completeness; in some a few faint traces of the original legends alone survived; in others, again, it is difficult to say which of the two types predominates; indeed, one of my coins presents to the eye the figure of Hermes or the elephant, according to the position in which it may be held, while on the other side the knees and lower extremities of the seated goddess vanish into the hind quarters of the Indian bull!

Beyond my own collection, I have also met with similar re-struck coins of Azas (there is one in the cabinet of the British Museum); there can therefore be little doubt that the re-coinage was one of large extent.

Moreover, as the only type obliterated is that of the elephant and bull, while that substituted is also always that of Demeter and Hermes, it seems probable that the re-coinage was in pursuance of a general design to recall one from circulation in favour of the other. It may be inferred, however, from the comparative abundance in which the condemned type still occurs, that the object was not completely attained.

Knowing, as we do, the various motives which have actuated monarchs in recorded instances to call in and re-coin their own or their predecessor's currencies, it may seem rash to attempt any explanation of the particular caprice which influenced Azas to this measure.

Still, meagre as our materials are, and premature as it would be to dogmatize on the matter with the information we have hitherto possessed, there are, I think, to be found in the general study of the coinage of Azas, some facts which may warrant a conjecture, and on so interesting a subject it is scarcely possible to refrain from one.

In the first place, there is a good deal to show that Azas was not only a potent monarch, but that he was likewise a conquering one. His coins, occurring as they do in large numbers, of many different types, and with an unusual variety of mint-marks, prove that he must have ruled at once for a long period, and over a wide extent of country; and certainly none but a successful conqueror could have reigned long and widely in a country so politically situated as Upper India must have been at the time he flourished. When, however, we find beyond this, that his coins are especially abundant and various, as compared with those of monarchs who must have been of the same dynasty with himself, we cannot help believing that he either founded or extended the dominion of that dynasty—in either case, necessarily by conquest.

I might strengthen this position by further evidence and arguments; but the simple fact that Azas was a conqueror is all that is necessary for my present purpose, and this fact is not likely to be controverted.

Of his adversaries there may be wider room for conjecture. It can, however, scarcely be doubted that among them were numbered some one or other of the representatives of the Greek sovereigns of India. Indeed, it is scarcely needful in the present state of our numismatic knowledge to adduce formal proof of the fact; it may therefore suffice to say the execution of the coins of Azas prove them to be of a date when Greek art and Greek intelligence still asserted their supremacy, while there is sufficient proof that a Greek dynasty still existed at a yet later date, and that among the mint-marks found on the coins of princes of this dynasty, are some which are found also on the coins of Azas.

Keeping these facts in view, there is something of significance in the character of the types of both the coins which, it has been seen, were called in to be re-struck, and of the types which were substituted in their place.

The first, we have seen, were an elephant and an Indian bull—types which figure conspicuously among the emblems of Buddhism. Nor are they the only traces of that faith to be found on the coins of Azas—the lion is another ordinary type. Perhaps, too, the well-known singular cross-legged figure, which is found on the obverse of more than one variety of Azas' coins, may indicate a leaning to the same faith. I may even cite, in addition, a very curious standing figure, from a rare type in my own cabinet, which closely resembles some curious sculptures of the great Sakya Muni in the act of teaching.

But whether it be probable or not that the emblems on the defaced coinage were selected on account of their significance in Buddhism, there can at least be no doubt that those of the coinage which replaced it were selected from the storehouse of Grecian mythology; as, for instance, Demeter with her cornucopiæ, and Hermes with his caduceus.

Guided, therefore, by these indications—the career of

Azas as a conqueror; his consequent antagonism to the remaining Greek rulers of India; the probable Buddhist character of the bulk of his coinage, and especially of the earlier type under consideration; the ascertained defacement of the latter, and its re-coinage with types of an undoubtedly Greek character; I would venture to offer as a conjecture (and purely as a conjecture) the following explanation.

I suppose that the religion which Azas himself professed, at least in the outset of his career, was probably Buddhism; that the bull and elephant were adopted, among his other earlier types, from the influence of that religion; and that their calling in and re-coinage with types borrowed from Grecian mythology took place after his acquisition of some portion of the territories which had, since the early conquests of the Bactrian monarchs, exclusively owned a Greek sway; and I would further conjecture, that the adoption of the new types indicates not so much the abandonment on the part of Azas of his own religion, as a concession, probably only for a time, to the prejudices of his newly acquired subjects.

I would, in conclusion, make a few observations on the monograms which these coins bear. On the re-struck coins I have never found but one[1]—that figured as Nos. 113 and 132 of the table in "Ariana Antiqua," and No. 23 of Major Cunningham's paper in the Numismatic Chronicle.[2] This the latter gentleman reads from the Arian version of it as "Salapi," and proposes to assign it to ΣΑΛΑΠΕΙΣΑ, which he supposes to be the same with

---

[1] It occurs also on the coins of Azas bearing the types of the Indian bull and the lion. See "Ariana Antiqua," Pl. vii Fig. 8.
[2] Num. Chron. vol. viii. p. 175.

the ΣΑΛΑΓΕΙΣΑ of Ptolemy, and identifies it as the modern Sealcote.[1]

To this reading I see no objection from my own specimens and the plate of the coin in the "Ariana Antiqua." I think the letter "sh" exists also in the Arian monogram, which I would read, therefore, "Salapisha," or "Shalapisa." The Greek letters certainly admit of being rendered as ΣΑΛΑΠΕΙΣΑ.

Major Cunningham does not give at length his reasons for identifying this place with Sealcote. If, however, he be correct in his supposition, it would well accord with the conjectures I have formed, for Sealcote must have been a city of importance from a period of remote antiquity, as it is situated in what was unquestionably the stronghold of Greek sovereignty in India, viz.: the upper part of the Punjab.

On the coins of the earlier type I find at least three monograms; for one of which, No. 114 of Wilson, Major Cunningham proposes to read ΤΑΞΙΛ, for Taxila. On the coins of Azas, however, it is most frequently accompanied by the letter "a" of the Arian alphabet, and this is probably the initial letter of the name. I must admit, however, I am not prepared to offer any more satisfactory solution for this or the other two monograms which occur on this class of coins.

They possess, however, one peculiarity to which I would draw attention—the occurrence, in conjunction with them, of certain minute varying Arian letters. These are found, in conjunction too with other monograms, not unfrequently

---

[1] The modern "Sealcote" derives its name, I think, from the tribe of "Syál" Jats, who inhabit much of the country between the Jhelum and Ravi. Jhung is also surnamed from them "Jhung-Syál."

on the coins of several monarchs besides Azas—as Azilisas, Gondophares, Hippostratus, and Hermæus.

Major Cunningham, in his paper on monograms, already cited, notices the occurrence of Greek letters of low numerical value on the coins of some of the earlier Bactrian kings, and suggests they may indicate the date according to the year of the king's reign. The results of my own examination of the coins of Apollodotus and Menander are confirmatory of this view, and I am inclined to suggest these Arian letters may have been employed in a manner more or less analogous.

I do not pretend, however, at present to offer any complete scheme explanatory of their use. I would only observe, if my previous remarks are accepted as probable, that the two letters "a" and "s," which alone I have found on the recalled coinage, occupy in all probability a low position in the arithmetical series. I would further merely add, that the vowel mark for "1," occurring as it does in conjunction with nearly all the letters, may perhaps designate, as in the Greek numerical series, the first place in the decimal series; and as in one instance "k" also seems to occur in composition, it may, too, similarly represent "20" in either series.

These remarks, however, are merely thrown out as hints to other inquirers, and I am not myself disposed to place any undue reliance on their value.

E. Clive Bayley.

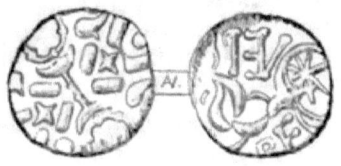

XI.

AN ACCOUNT OF BRITISH GOLD AND ROMAN SILVER COINS FOUND AT LIGHTCLIFFE, NEAR HALIFAX, IN THE YEAR 1827.

[Read before the Numismatic Society, Jan. 24, 1861.]

For the following particulars of this most interesting discovery we are indebted to the kindness of Thomas Bateman, Esq., of Youlgrave, Derbyshire.

In the year 1827 a workman, digging for gravel in the immediate vicinity of the old Roman road, at Lightcliffe, near Halifax, came upon a fictile vase, apparently of Roman fabric, within about twelve inches of the surface of the ground. Its contents proved to be a number of coins, principally Roman denarii, but among them were four ancient British coins in gold. Three of these were of the now well-known Yorkshire type, with the inscription VOLISIOS in two lines across a wreath on the obverse, and the rudely formed horse and DVMNO-CO-VEROS on the reverse. (See Ruding, pl. A, 83, and Hawkins, pl. i. No. 8.) The fourth coin was a variety, hitherto unpublished, of the type engraved in the Numismatic Chronicle, vol. i. pl. ii. No. 11, and vol. xiv. p. 71, No. 7. A representation of it is given above, which may be thus described :—

> *Obv.*—A wreath formed of rectangular leaves running in opposite directions on either side of a band connecting two crescents placed back to back. In front of each crescent a large beaded ring-ornament between two pear-shaped figures. There are small pointed crosses in two of the spaces among the leaves of the wreath.
>
> *Rev.*—VEP (VE in monogram) *retrograde;* [CO]RF; an extremely disjointed horse to the left, his tail forming the rim of a wheel.

It will be seen that this coin differs from those that have already been published in having the VEP of the legend retrograde, and in the very peculiar formation of the tail of the horse. Nothing is known as to what the legend VEP CORF was intended to designate, and it is difficult to assign even a conjectural meaning to it. As to the type of the coin, there can, however, be no doubt. It is evidently a direct descendant of that of the Macedonian Philippus, though only the wreath and the horse survive to prove the relationship; and the wheel-like form of the tail of the horse is all that is left to remind us of the chariot that was drawn by its better-formed ancestors.

The cruciform objects on the obverse of the coin are remarkable, as similar, though smaller crosses are frequently found on the reverse of the gold coins of ANTE-DRIGVS and others of the west of England, which it will shortly be seen belong to nearly the same period as this.

As was the case with the discovery of ancient British coins of the same class at Almondbury in 1829—a locality not many miles distant from Lightcliffe—these gold coins were accompanied by a number of Roman denarii. At

Almondbury these were all family or consular coins; but at Lightcliffe there were found in addition several imperial coins, including one of Caligula, with the reverse of Agrippina, probably struck about A.D. 40. The testimony of this coin is valuable, as affording an approximate date for the gold coins supposed to have been struck by the Brigantes, some of which belong in all probability to even a later period. The recent discovery of British coins at Nunney, near Frome, proves that the native coinage survived in the western parts of England till after the accession of Claudius, and there are good grounds for believing that that of the northern district may have continued some years longer than it did in the west.

In the following list of the Roman coins, it has been thought best to preserve the descriptions as given to Mr. Bateman, merely annexing references to Cohen's "Médailles Consulaires" for the types. Of some of them there were duplicates. It is stated that some of the silver coins were, when found, coated with bitumen.

ACILIA.

Obv.—Head. SALVTIS.

Rev.—Valetudo holding a serpent; letters not easy to be read. (Cohen, No. 3.)

ANNIA.

Obv.—Female head, with the caduceus and the bilanx on each side, with letters.

Rev.—Victory in a four-horse chariot, commemorative of a victory in Spain. (Cohen, No. 1.)

CARISIA.

Obv.—Head of Victory.

Rev.—Two-horse chariot; beneath, T . CARISI. (Cohen, No. 1.)

Considia.

Obv.—Female head; behind, PAETI.
Rev.—Four-horse chariot, with Victory; under, C . CONSIDI. (Cohen, No. 4.)

Obv.—Helmeted head; no letters.
Rev.—Four-horse chariot; under, C . CONSIDI. (Cohen, No. 2.)

Cornelia.

Obv.—Head of the Sibyl; one consulting her, and holding a palm-branch; under, L . SVLLA.
Rev.—Trophies; over, IMPER.; under, ITERVM. (Cohen, No. 17.)

Obv.—Head, without letters.
Rev.—Four-horse chariot; beneath L . SCIP . ASIAG. (Cohen, No. 3.)

Obv.—Head. C . P . R.
Rev.—EX . S.C . CN . LEN . Q. A garland, shield, and circle. (Cohen, No. 10.)

Claudia.

Obv.—Head of Diana; her quiver behind.
Rev.—Goddess holding two torches; around, M . F . P. CLODIVS. (Cohen, No. 6.)

Crepereia.

Obv.—Female head.
Rev.—Neptune driving two sea-horses, holding his trident. Q. CREPER . M . F . ROCVS. (Cohen, No. 2.)

Eppia.

Obv.—Head covered with an elephant's skin and proboscis; in front, an ear of corn; by the sides, SCIPIO IMP.—Q METELL.
Rev.—Hercules leaning on his club. LEG . F.C . EPPIVS. (Cohen, No. 1.)

FLAMINIA.

Obv.—Female head; by the side, PRI . FL.
Rev.—Two-horse chariot.   L . FLA.   (Cohen, No. 2.)

JULIA.

Obv.—Elephant; under CAESAR.
Rev.—Augurs' instruments and the axe.   (Cohen, No. 10.)

Obv.—Head of Venus.
Rev.—Æneas carrying his father, Anchises, on his back, and holding the image of Pallas. CAESAR. (Cohen, No. 9.)

Obv.—Head of Victory; no letters.
Rev.—Neptune, with one foot on the globe, holding his trident in his left hand, and the aplustre in his right; by the side, CAESAR IMP. (Cohen, No. 44.)

Obv.—Head of Augustus; no letters.
Rev.—The emperor standing in the rostrum of the forum, by the side, IMP CAESAR. (Cohen, No. 58.)

JUNIA.

Obv.—Female head; around it LIBERTAS.
Rev.—The lictors with Brutus; under, BRVTVS. (Cohen, No. 12.)

LUTATIA.

Obv.—Helmeted head.
Rev.—An oak garland; inside, a galley; above, Q. LVTATI; under, Q—.   (Cohen, No. 3.)

NÆVIA.

Obv.—Female head; by the side, S . C.
Rev.—Three-horse chariot; under, C . NAE . BALB. (Cohen, No. 1.)

SCRIBONIA.

Obv.—Covered head of Concord: around it, PAVLLVS LEPIDVS CONCORDIA.

Rev.—The puteal in the forum; around it PVTEAL SCRIBON. (Cohen, Aemilia, No. 10.)

SERVILIA.

Obv.—Helmeted head.

Rev.—Victory in a two-horse chariot; under, P.SERVILI. M.F. (Cohen, No. 6.)

IMPERIAL.

AUGUSTUS.

Obv.—Head.
Rev.—Two shields. (Much broken.)

Obv.—Head of Augustus; no letters.
Rev.—A capricorn; under, AVGVSTVS. (Cohen, No. 52 or 54.)

CALIGULA.

Obv.—His head and titles, C CAESAR, &c.
Rev.—Agrippina's head, with letters. (Cohen, No. 2 or 3.)

J. E.

XII.

ON AN UNPUBLISHED VARIETY OF THE COINS OF ETHELSTAN, KING OF EAST ANGLIA.
(A.D. 825—852.)

[Read before the Numismatic Society, Feb. 21, 1861.]

Obv.— + EÐELSTAN . REX.   Bust to the right.
Rev.— + MON . MONETA.   In three lines.

This variety is mentioned in Hawkins' "Silver Coins,"[1] from a MS. list of Combe's, which does not state in what cabinet it exists, and Mr. Hawkins says that it is not now known. Besides, it is there attributed, as many others, *without the head*, to Guthrun, a Dane, who succeeded St. Eadmund in 870, and who, on being converted to Christianity, was baptized in 878 by the name of Ethelstan, and reigned down to 890. No mention is made of a coin *with the head*.

According to Mr. Haigh's classification,[2] this coin

---

[1] Hawkins' "Silver Coins of England," pp. 36, 37. 1841.
[2] "An Essay on the Numismatic History of the ancient kingdom of the East Angles," by D. H. Haigh. 1845.

belongs to Ethelstan, who was either the brother or son of Ethelwulf, it is not certain which, and who is mentioned in the Saxon chronicles as having been appointed, on the death of Ecgbeorht, deputy sovereign of the kingdoms which the latter had subdued, viz., Kent, Essex, Surrey, and Sussex. His coins date from 825 to 852. Those with the bust seem to be very rare. There are three engraved in Haigh,—one from the cabinet of the late Rev. T. F. Dymock, and the other two from that of the late J. D. Cuff, Esq., but all different in the reverse from this one. The obverse is similar to Nos. 4, 5, and 6, on pl. i.; and the reverse is something like No. 7 on the same plate, though this latter is a coin *without the head*, and reads MOM + MOMETA, in three lines. As to Ethelstan or Guthrun above mentioned, Mr. Haigh attributes to him the coins which were first made known to Numismatists by the Cuerdale find, with the legend ED EL . TA . RE, ED . EL SAN RE, &c., &c., not one coin of the twenty-four that were found, reading correctly ED EL STAN RE.

The above coin may then be safely attributed to Ethelstan I., King of the East Angles, from A.D. 825 to 852.

Nothing more can be said, save that this variety is in excellent preservation, and is the only coin of Ethelstan I. *with the head*, that the Museum possesses.

FRED. W. MADDEN

XIII.

ON A COIN OF MALLUS IN CILICIA.

Among the coins added to the National Collection by purchase at the sale of the collection of Mr. James Whittall, of Smyrna, one of the most remarkable is a silver piece of the town of Mallus in Cilicia. The silver money of this place is of extreme rarity; and I believe that the present is the only example in any collection in England. It is also of a different type from any other of which the description is known to me; and I have little doubt that it is unique.

It is not necessary to say anything as to the position and history of Mallus, excepting that it is uncertain by what people it was founded. Of the probable character of the religion we must, however, speak briefly. At so great a distance from Greece Proper, and where the influence of the earlier (I will not say the earliest) population was evidently unextinguished by the Greek settlers, we must not look for a purely Hellenic mythology. This, indeed, we scarcely find in Asia Minor, excepting in those tracts on the western coast where the Greek settlers had firmly established themselves in such large numbers as to give new territorial names to portions of the ancient countries. In Ionia and in Æolis alone can we expect to find Hellenic religion generally free from the influence of an earlier local belief. It is the more important to bear this in mind, as our information is usually conveyed, whether in the forms of art or in the words of literature, in a Greek shape, and we are therefore apt to trace it to a Greek original. But if we do so, we must make the Baal of Tarsus a Greek Jupiter, and the Baal of Tyre a Greek Hercules.

From the few coins of Mallus known to us, the divinities worshipped at that place and represented on its money appear to have been Minerva, Mercury, Venus, Hercules, and Bacchus—the first three, probably, having been the chief objects of worship. Minerva has a perfectly Greek character; the same is the case with Mercury and Hercules; Venus appears to have an Asiatic character, and probably this may also be said of Bacchus. It may be conjectured that the worship of Minerva and Mercury was introduced by Greek colonists, the other divinities being already reverenced by the older inhabitants.

The coin of Mallus forming the subject of this paper may be thus described:—

> *Obv.*—Minerva, seated to the left, holding a spear with her right hand, and resting her left arm upon a shield; behind her, the trunk of a tree.
>
> *Rev.*—ΜΑΛ. Mercury standing, facing, wearing a chlamys, and bearing in his right hand the caduceus. To his right, Venus, standing, turned to the left, with her right arm on his shoulder, and her left arm resting upon a column. ℞. Size, 5½. Weight, 159·8 grs.

It may be remarked that it is difficult to distinguish with certainty which is the obverse: according to the general rule it would be as described, what I have called the obverse being slightly convex. The supposed reverse is, however, the more important side.

The weight is 159·8 grains troy, which is rather below

that of most specimens of the usual denomination of the silver coins of Pamphylia and Cilicia. It would involve a long inquiry to discuss fully the evidences of the origin of this denomination; but the chief facts may be briefly stated. It may be supposed, on account of the fondness of the Asiatics for divisions by three, to be two-thirds of a tetradrachm which weighed not more than about 240 grains; for we may at once dismiss the idea that it is a debased Æginetan didrachm from our not finding any pieces certainly of that talent in Asiatic Greece. The standard of the supposed tetradrachm is too low to be Attic, and we are therefore led to suppose it was what we may term the later Phœnician, with which it well corresponds. In this case, each one of these Asiatic pieces would be equal to two of the common Persian silver coins with Daric types, of which three went to the tetradrachm, which was of the later Phœnician weight.

The art of the coin is fair in character, and delicately, but rather slightly, though stiffly executed. Were it of Greece, or the west coast of Asia Minor, it would be referred to the latest part of the fifth century, B.C.; but we have not a sufficient knowledge of the art of the Cilician and Pamphylian cities to speak with so great certainty as to the age of their coins. Probably, however, it is not later in date than the first half of the following century. In many respects the style recalls the very beautiful coins, of the same weight, struck at Celenderis in Cilicia, perhaps, as a series, the finest of any issued by the cities of the east of Asia Minor.

The obverse type requires no detailed explanation. It simply represents Minerva seated, probably as the protector of the city. The reverse type is far more remarkable. It would, at first sight, seem to represent Venus detaining

Mercury, as she is represented by ancient artists detaining Mars. It might appear, therefore, to relate to the amour of Mercury and Venus, from which sprang Hermaphroditus. The circumstance, however, that Mercury, as already shown, seems to have been here a Greek divinity, and Venus an Asiatic one, appears to be fatal to this conjecture. Even if we suppose the representation to be that of this Greek myth, we cannot see any motive in Venus's resting upon a column. In late, and especially in Græco-Roman, designs, it is not unlikely that such an incongruity might occur; but the fitness of every part of an early Greek type does not allow any such latitude. The column must imply rest, or stability, and is probably connected with the foundation of the town, or, at least, in some manner distinctly refers to the place. A copper Greek imperial coin of Mallus, struck under Herennia Etruscilla, destroys the first explanation, and seems to support this. On its reverse, Mercury and Minerva are represented standing facing one another, while, on the ground beneath them, is a pig. This would seem to intend an oath taken by these divinities in favour of Mallus, probably for its protection. The composition is so similar to that of the silver coin that a similar explanation must be adopted for the latter. We should therefore suppose that Mercury and Venus are represented upon it as protectors or founders of the city, and that the same is the case with Minerva on the other side, without hazarding any more precise explanation. The only reason that we can assign for the substitution of Minerva for Venus on the Greek imperial coin, is that, the bust of the Empress having usurped the place of the former, she took that of Venus as the more important divinity.

R. S. POOLE.

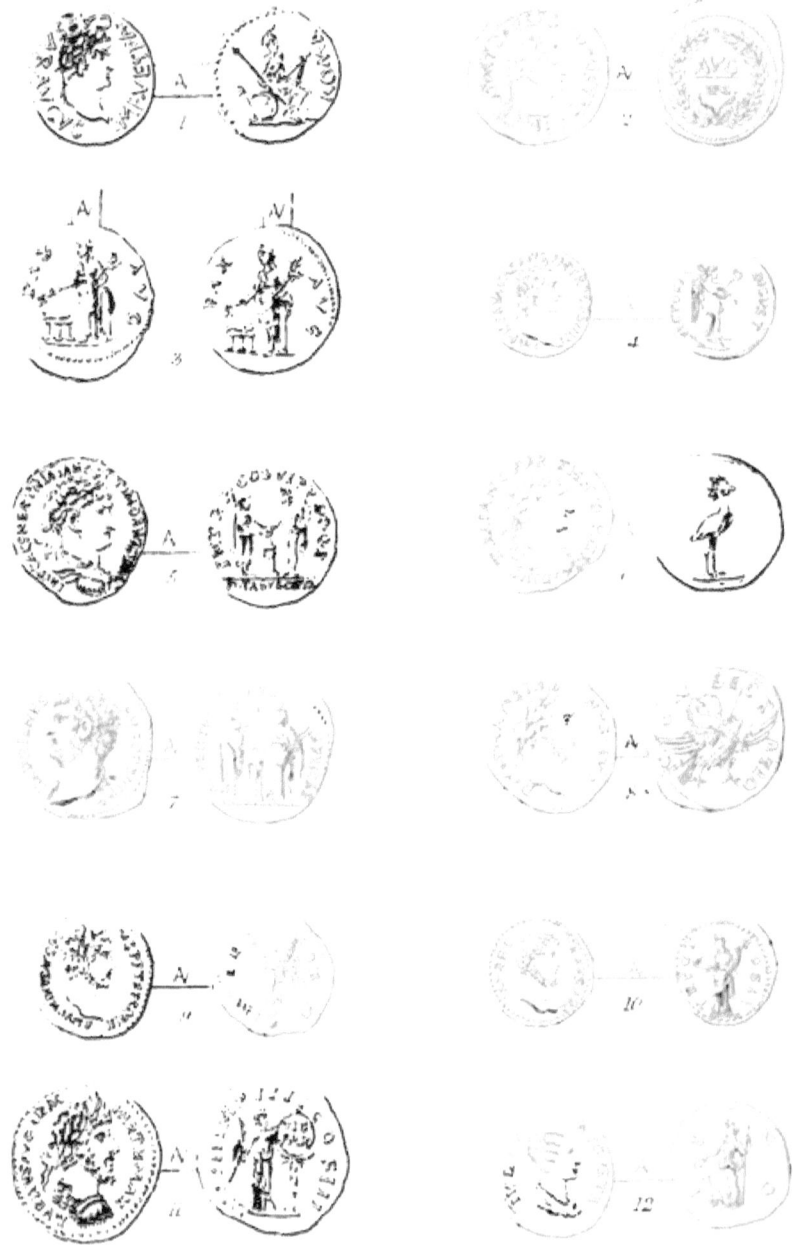

XIV.

ON SOME UNPUBLISHED ROMAN COINS.

[Read before the Numismatic Society, November 22, and December 13, 1860.]

I HAVE much pleasure in laying before the Numismatic Society this evening, casts of some Roman gold coins, almost all unpublished, or else of types described as only existing in silver in M. Cohen's "Médailles Impériales;" and also an impression of a rare and unpublished medallion in bronze of the Emperor Hadrian. In a large and comprehensive work like that of M. Cohen's, some errors and omissions must necessarily occur. I have already furnished him with a list of some of the omissions I have noticed; but as they have not yet appeared in print, and when they do, can only appear in a "supplement," or in the "errata," I think it desirable that a more special notice of them should be given.

Without further preface, I pass to the description of the coins :—

AUGUSTUS.

Obv.—CAESAR . AVGVSTVS. Head, to right, bare.
Rev.—MAR . VLT. (in field). Mars, helmeted, naked, standing to the left, in a tetrastyle temple, holding the legionary eagle and a standard.

Described in silver in Cohen. No. 168.

Claudius.

(1) *Obv.*—TI . CLAVD . CAESAR . AVG . P . M . TR . P . VIIII . IMP . XVI.   Head, to right, laureate.

Rev.—DE . BRITANN., written on a triumphal arch, surmounted by an equestrian statue, to the left, between two trophies.

There is here a slight difference from the coin reading DE . BRITANNI., as the statue on that is to the right, while here it is to the left.

(2) *Obv.*—TI . CLAVD . CAESAR . AVG . P . M . TR . P . VI . IMP . XI.   Head, to right, laureate.

Rev.—DE . GERMANIS.   Same type.

Both these coins are described in silver in Cohen. Nos. 16 and 25.

(3) *Obv.*—TI . CLAVD . CAESAR . AVG . P . M . TR . P .   Head, to right, laureate.

Rev.—IMPER . RECEPT., written on the prætorian camp, at the door of which stands a soldier near a military standard.

This coin is described in Cohen (No. 33) from Morell. It is in the Museum.

Nero.

Obv.—IMP . NERO . CAESAR . AVG . P . P.   Head, to right, laureate.

Rev.—IVPPITER . CVSTOS.   Jupiter, seated, to the left, holding a thunderbolt and sceptre.

Described in silver in Cohen.   No. 16.

Vespasian.

(1) *Obv.*—IMP . CAESAR . VESPASIANVS . AVG.   Head, to right, laureate.

Rev.—COS . VII.   Cow, walking, to the right.

Described in silver in Cohen.   No. 57.

(2) *Obv.*—IMP . VESPA . CAESAR . AVGVS. Head, to right, laureate.

Rev.—ROMA. Rome, helmeted, seated to the right, on a shield, holding a spear and parazonium. Near the shield is a sword. (?) (Pl. iv. No. 1.)

This coin is unpublished. It is of colonial fabric, and is one of the magnificent collection of Roman coins presented to the Museum by Mr. de Salis.

Titus.

(1) *Obv.*—T . CAESAR . IMP . VESPASIAN. Head, to right, laureate.

Rev.—IMP . VIII. Bull, butting, to the right.

Described in silver in Cohen. No. 41.

(2) *Obv.*—T . CAESAR . IMP . VESPASIANVS. Head, to right, laureate.

Rev.—COS . VI. Rome, seated, to the right, on two shields, holding a spear; beneath the shields a helmet. On either side, in the field, a bird flying; at her feet, Romulus and Remus, suckled by a wolf.

Unpublished.

(3) *Obv.*—IMP . TITVS . CAES . VESPASIAN . AVG . P. M. Head, to right, laureate.

Rev.—TR . P . VIIII . IMP . XIIII . COS . VII . P. P. Quadriga, to the left; on it a flower.

Described in Cohen (No. 77) from Wiczay. It is in the Museum.

(4) *Obv.*—IMPERATOR . T . CAESAR . AVGVSTI . F. Head, to right, laureate.

Rev.—AVG . EPHE . (PHE in monogram) in crown of laurel. (Pl. iv. No. 2.)

Described in silver in Cohen, (No. 7.) This coin was struck at Ephesus, and was presented to the Museum by Mr. de Salis.

(5) *Obv.*—IMP . T . CAESAR . VESPASIANVS. Head, to right, laureate, with the *ægis*.

Rev.—CONCORDIA . AVG. Concord, seated, to the left, holding a patera and cornucopiæ.

Of colonial fabric. Unpublished.

(6, 7) *Obv*—T . CAES . IMP . VESP . CEN . and CENS Head, to right, laureate.

Rev.—PAX . AVG. Peace, standing, to the left, near a tripod, on which is the purse of Mercury, (?) or a wine-bag (ἄσκος), holding a caduceus and olive-branch, her left arm resting on a pillar. (Pl. iv. No. 3.)

These two coins are unpublished, and differ from the coin of Titus in Cohen (No. 53). The object represented on the tripod seems never to have been satisfactorily explained. Eckhel, in his "Cat. Mus. Vindob.," describes it as "Tripus, super quo, cornu-copiæ;" but certainly nothing resembling a cornu-copiæ can be seen on the coins in the Museum. Morell is at a loss too, and says, "Tripus, in quo quoddam obscurius expressum reperitur repositum;" he also suggests "hostiæ femur." M. Cohen, in his description of two similar types of Vespasian, calls it "la bourse de Mercure." Now, judging from the four specimens in the British Museum,—two of Vespasian, and two of Titus,—I am rather inclined to think that it much resembles a wine-bag (ἄσκυς); and as the tripod was often used as an altar, it seems not at all improbable for wine to have been sacrificed at the time of peace. The question is not one of much moment; but if these minutiæ can be accurately ascertained, the coin is better described.

Domitian.

Obv.—CAES . AVG . F . DOMIT . COS . III. Head, to right, laureate.

Rev.—PRINCIPS . (sic) IVVENTVT. Female figure (Hope), walking, to the right, holding a flower in her right hand, and raising her robe with her left.

Differs from Cohen (No. 203) in the legend.

NERVA.

Obv.—IMP . NERVA . CAES . AVG . P . M , TR . P . COS . III . P . P. Head, to right, laureate.

Rev.—VICTORIA . AVGVST. Victory, walking, to the right, holding a wreath and palm. (Pl. iv. No. 4.) A quinarius.

This coin is unpublished. Mr. Wigan's coin, given in Cohen (No. 61), is of the second consulate.

TRAJAN.

(1) *Obv.*—IMP . CAES . NER . TRAIANO . OPTIMO . AVG . GER . DAC. Bust, to right, laureate, with *paludamentum* and cuirass.

Rev.—VOTA . SVSCEPTA (in exergue) P . M . TR . P . COS . VI . P . P . S . P . Q . R. The emperor, standing, to the right, before an altar, holding a sceptre. On the opposite side, Genius, standing, to the left, holding a patera and cornu-copiæ. (Pl. iv. No. 5.)

Unpublished.

(2) *Obv.*—DIVO . TRAIANO . PARTH . AVG . PATRI. Bust, to right, laureate, with *paludamentum* and cuirass.

Rev.—No legend. Phœnix, to the right, *without the branch of laurel.* (Struck after his death.) (Pl. iv. No. 6.)

The usual type of this coin is the Phœnix standing on a laurel-branch. This variety is unpublished, and was purchased for the Museum at the late Lord Northwick's sale.

Trajan and Trajan Sen.

Obv.—IMP . TRAIANVS . AVG . GER . DAC . P . M . TR . P . COS . VI . P . P. Bust, to right, laureate, with *paludamentum* and cuirass.

Rev.—DIVVS . PATER . TRAIAN. Bust to right, bare, with *paludamentum*.

Unpublished.

Hadrian.

(1) *Obv.*—HADRIANVS . AVG . COS . III . P . P. Head, to the left, bare.

Rev.—ADVENTVI . AVG . AFRICAE. The emperor, and the personification of Africa standing facing; between them a tripod. The Emperor, to the right, raises his hand, and Africa, to the left (with trunk of an elephant on her head), holds a patera and branch; at her feet a calf. (?) (Pl. iv. No. 7.)

This coin is described in Cohen (No. 56) from Caylus. The object at the feet of Africa is there called a *lion*, but it far more resembles a *calf*.

(2) *Obv.*—HADRIANVS . AVG . COS . III . P . P. Bare bust, to right, with *paludamentum*.

Rev.—ROMA . AETERNA. Rome, helmeted, seated, to the left, on a cuirass, holding the heads of sun and moon in her right hand, and spear in her left; behind her a shield.

Cohen (No. 463) gives this same type, with the legend ROMAE . AETERNAE. This may be an error of the printer, and the coin I describe may be the same. There is also a variety in the Museum—Head, to right, bare, *without* the *paludamentum*.

(3) *Obv.*—DIVVS . HADRIANVS . AVG. Head, to right, laureate.

Rev.—CONSECRATIO. Eagle, conveying Hadrian to heaven. (Pl. iv. No. 8.)

M. Cohen was not aware that the British Museum possessed this coin, as, after his description of it, he has put " Catalogue du Cabinet des Médailles de 1700." It was purchased at Lord Northwick's sale.

(4) *Obv.*—HADRIANVS . AVGVSTVS . P . P. Head, to right, radiate.

Rev.—COS . III. Salus, half-naked, standing, to the right, holding an uncertain object in her right, and placing her left on the shoulder of young figure (Antinoüs?), naked, but with a mantle flowing from his left shoulder over the arm, standing, facing, and holding a "scipio," round which is entwined a serpent; behind him, the statue of Apollo, on a pedestal, holding in his outstretched hand a bow. (?) Æ. MEDALLION. Size 8. (Pl. v. No. 3.)

This rare and curious medallion was purchased for the British Museum at the late Lord Northwick's sale, and the type is described in the catalogue as " Æsculapius and Hygieia; and behind, the statue of Priapus on a base." M. Cohen has described a large brass coin of Hadrian,[1] from Vaillant, the legend of the obverse wanting, and the reverse, COS . III . S . C. " Salus presenting a stick, round which is entwined a serpent, to young Hercules, naked, standing, and carrying a 'strophium' on the left arm: behind him, the column of Trajan." Evidently, from this vague description of Vaillant's, the coin he had seen must have been in indifferent preservation. M. Cohen did not know of the existence of this medallion until I showed it to him when he was last in England. He then referred me to the above-quoted large brass of Hadrian, and there can be no doubt that these are one and the same coin.

---

[1] "Médailles Impériales," vol. ii. p. 192, No. 732.

There are three opinions concerning the male figure, whether it is Æsculapius, young Hercules, or Antinous? and there are three concerning the statue, whether it is that of Priapus, or the column of Trajan, or that of Apollo? For my part, I do not think it is Æsculapius, for it is a *young* figure, and though Mionnet describes a young Æsculapius on coins of Parium, in Mysia, with which description Mr. Poole does not agree, I am far more inclined to think it young Hercules or Antinous, but especially Antinous. The object in the background is not the statue of Priapus, nor do I think it the column of Trajan, the statue of Apollo being far more in accordance with the type.

I can make another suggestion. Is it Antinous as Apollo? for often he is represented on coins in the form of a young god—Bacchus, Mercury, and *especially* Apollo; and we find in Ovid that Apollo and Bacchus were considered the handsomest of the gods, Sappho thus addressing her lover, Phaon,

> "Sume fidem et pharetram, fies manifestus Apollo,
> Accedant capiti cornua, Bacchus eris."

In conclusion; should not the three figures be (as I have here described them) those of Salus, Antinous, and Apollo, the god of health? The extravagant affection of Hadrian for Antinous, shown in his deep lamentations for his death, might easily have caused a medallion to have been struck in commemoration of his recovery from some slight illness.

The work of this medallion is unusual; it more resembles that of a gem. Notwithstanding that it is not in first-rate preservation, it is still a very fine coin.

Antoninus.

(1) *Obv.*—ANTONINVS . AVG . PIVS . P . P . TR . P . COS . III. Head, to right, laureate.

    Rev.—IMPERATOR . II. Victory, on a globe, to the left, holding a wreath and palm. Quinarius. (Pl. iv. No. 9.)

Described in Cohen (No. 162) with "*Musée Tiepolo*" after it. The British Museum possesses it.

(2) *Obv.*—ANTONINVS . AVG . PIVS . P . P. Head, to right, laureate.

    Rev.—LIB . V. (in field) COS . IIII. Liberality, standing, to the left, holding a tessera and cornucopiæ.

Unpublished.

Faustina, Sen.

Obv.—DIVA . AVGVSTA . FAVSTINA. Bust, to right.

Rev.—EX . S . C. Carpentum, to the right, drawn by two mules.

Unpublished.

L. Verus.

(1) *Obv.*—L . AVREL . VERVS . AVG. Bust, to right, bare.

    Rev.—TR . POT . COS . II. Providence, standing, to the left, holding globe and cornucopiæ. Quinarius. (Pl. iv. No. 10.)

The inscription on the reverse differs from Cohen (No. 44).

(2) *Obv.*—L . VERVS . AVG . PARTH . ARM . MAX. Bust, to right, laureate, with *paludamentum* and cuirass.

    Rev.—TR . P . VI . IMP . III . COS . II. Verus, galloping, to the right, holding a spear, which he is levelling at a prostrate foe.

This same type occurs with the fifth year of the Tribunitian power. Cohen, (No. 66.)

(3) *Obv.*—L . VERVS . AVG . ARM . PARTH . MAX. Bust, to right, laureate, with *paludamentum* and cuirass.

Rev.—TR . P . VII . IMP . IIII . COS . III. Victory, half-naked, standing, looking to the right, holding a palm, and attaching to a palm-tree a shield, on which is inscribed VIC . PAR. (Pl. iv. No. 11.)

This coin is unpublished.

Julia Domna.

Obv.—IVLIA . AVGVSTA. Bust, to right.

Rev.—IVNO. Juno, veiled, standing to the left, holding a patera and sceptre; at her feet a peacock. Quinarius. (Pl. iv. No. 12.)

Unpublished.

Caracalla.

Obv.—ANTONINVS . PIVS . AVG . GERM. Bust, to right, laureate, with *paludamentum* and cuirass.

Rev.—P . M . TR . P . XVII . IMP . III . COS . IIII . P . P. Victory, seated, to the right, on a cuirass, holding a shield with her left hand on her left knee: on the ground behind her a shield. (Pl. v. No. 1.)

Geta.

Obv.—P . SEPT . GETA . PIVS . AVG . BRIT. Head, to right, laureate.

Rev.—TR . P . III . COS . II . P . P. Emperor, in military dress, standing, to the left, holding the parazonium and a spear, and placing his right foot on a captive. (Pl. v. No. 2.)

These two coins are described in Cohen (Nos. 167 and 100) from Caylus; but both are in the British Museum. That of Geta was found under the walls of a mud fort in the Sholapoor collectorate, to the east of Poonah, in the Mahratta country.

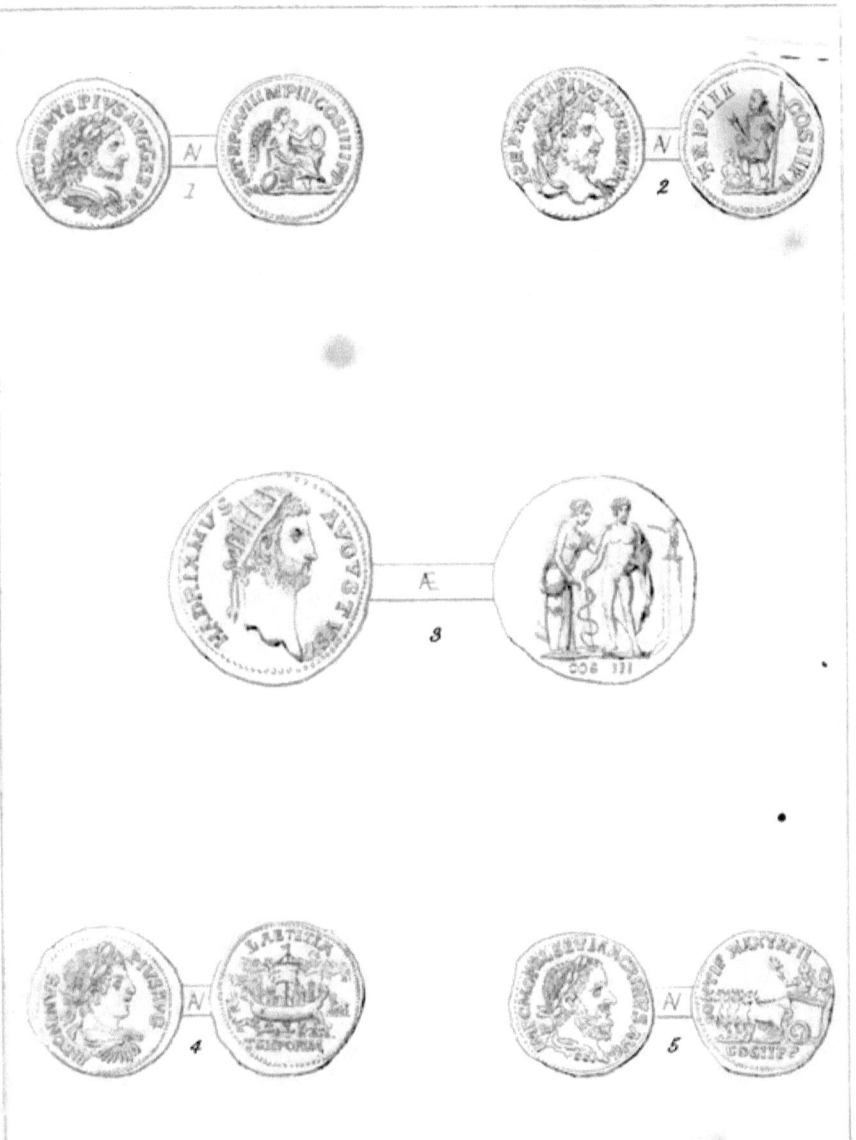

UNPUBLISHED ROMAN COINS.

I must return to mention a rare type of Caracalla: it may be described as follows:—

> *Obv.*—ANTONINVS . PIVS . AVG. Young bust, to right, laureate, with *paludamentum* and cuirass.
>
> *Rev.*—LAETITIA . TEMPORUM. The vessel of the circus in full sail; above are four quadrigæ, to the left, two on each side of the sail; beneath, are a lion and two deer, or antelopes (?), to the right, and a bull and a panther to the left; on the right side of the vessel is a bear, and on the left an ostrich. (Pl. v. No. 4.)

M. Cohen has published this coin, but has not described it fully. There is an engraving in his work of a coin of Severus, in *silver*, of nearly the same type—the type in *gold* of that emperor being mentioned by Vaillant, but not known to exist. Now this gold coin of Caracalla gives so many more details than have been described, that I feel myself quite justified in specially making mention of it, and at the same time it may not be uninteresting if a few remarks are made on the occasion of this coin being struck. After the overthrow of Albinus, which took place in 950 (A.D. 197), Caracalla was styled "Destinatus Imperator." In 951 (A.D. 198), when only ten years of age, he was invested with the tribunitian power, and created *Augustus*. His father, Severus, entered upon his third consulship in Syria, in 955 (A.D. 202), taking him as a colleague. This same year they returned to Rome, to celebrate the "decennalia" and the nuptials of Caracalla with Plautilla, and great *fêtes* and shows are given in honour of the event. In Dion Cassius mention is made of a structure in the form of a ship, which was placed in the amphitheatre, capable of holding four hundred wild beasts; and it is stated that, on the ship suddenly falling to pieces, there bounded out bears, lionesses, panthers, lions, ostriches, wild asses, bisons, so that seven hundred wild and grazing beasts were to be seen running about together, which afterwards were slain: he adds, that during the seven days the festivities lasted, the whole of these animals were killed.[2]

It was on this occasion, evidently, that the coins of both Severus[3] and Caracalla were struck—the " Lætitia Temporum" was the celebration of the "decennalia," the marriage of Caracalla, and the largesses given to the public. M. Cohen has put the date of the silver coin of Severus as 954 (A.D. 201), but as he did not return to Rome till the following year, this must be an error. He likewise gives the above gold coin of Caracalla to the years 957-962 (A.D. 204-209), but I am of opinion that it was struck at the same time as that of his father's, in 955 (A.D. 202). It could not be as late as 962 (A.D. 209), for Severus started for Britain in 960 (A.D. 207). There are two other coins, which are certainly struck the same year —one with the legend CONCORDIA . FELIX. "Cara-

---

[2] Dion Cassius, lib. lxxvi. 1. I quote the passage as it stands, for the benefit of my readers:—

"Τῆς δὲ ἐξαμένης ἁπάσης τῆς ἐν τῷ θεάτρῳ εἰς πλοίον σχῆμα κατασκευασθείσης, ὡς τετρακόσια θηρία καὶ δέξασθαι καὶ ἀφεῖναι ἀθρόως, ἔπειτα ἐξαίφνης διαλυθείσης, ἀνέθορον ἄρκτοι λέαιναι, πάνθηρες, λέοντες, στρουθοί, ὄναγροι, βίσσωνες. (βοῶν τι τοῦτο εἶδος, βαρβαρικὸν τὸ γένος καὶ τὴν ὄψιν), ὥστε ἑπτακόσια τὰ πάντα καὶ θηρία καὶ βοτὰ ὁμοῦ, καὶ διαθέοντα ὀρθῆναι, καὶ σφαγῆναι, πρὸς γὰρ τὸν τῆς ἑορτῆς ἀριθμὸν ἑπταημέρου γεγονυίας, καὶ ἐκεῖνα ἑπτάκις ἑκατὸν ἐγένετο."

[3] There is another coin of Sept. Severus, bearing on the reverse the legend P . P . COS . III. The circus, in which is the emperor, seated, to the left, presiding at the games, in which eight figures take part (three spectators, two groups of wrestlers, and at the left extremity of the circus a figure, standing, holding a spear?) This coin is evidently struck the same year as the Lætitia Temporum, viz. A.D. 202.—*N. Brit. Mus.*

calla and Plautilla, standing, joining hands; between them, Concord, standing;"[4] the other, with the legend PROPAGO . IMPERI. "Plautilla and Caracalla, joining hands;"[5] besides there are several others that were struck during the years 955-960 (A.D. 202-207), in which year, as I have before stated, Severus left Rome for Britain.

This coin is in so perfect a condition, that I have thought it worthy of engraving, that in Cohen, of the silver coin of Severus, not at all giving a good idea of the type. Whether my description is recognisable with the objects represented, I leave others to judge.

Macrinus.

Obv.—IMP . C . M . OPEL . SEV . MACRINVS . AVG.
    Bust, to right, with *paludamentum* and cuirass.

Rev.—PONTIF . MAX . TR . P . II . COS . II . P . P.
    Emperor in quadriga, to the left, holding a branch and the reins, and crowned by Victory, standing behind him. (Pl. v. No. 5.)

Unpublished.

Fred. W. Madden.

---

[4] This coin, in *gold*, is in the British Museum and in the cabinet of Mr. E. Wigan.

[5] Only in gold. Musée de Vienne.

XV.

ON SOME REMARKABLE GREEK COINS LATELY ACQUIRED BY THE BRITISH MUSEUM.

[Read before the Numismatic Society, December 15, 1859.]

I HAVE much pleasure in laying before the Society a short account of some remarkable Greek coins which have been lately acquired by the British Museum.

The first to which I call attention is a very remarkable dodecadrachm, belonging unquestionably to Macedonia or Thrace, and of very early date. It is engraved in Pl. vi. No. 1, and may be described as follows:—

> *Obv.*—A figure seated in a chariot, to the right, drawn by oxen, holding in his right hand a whip; above the oxen is a helmet, and underneath a flower—perhaps a lotus. The chariot wheel has four spokes.
>
> *Rev.*—A large triquetra within a square, in each angle of which is the same flower as under the oxen on the obverse. Æ. Size 11¾. Weight 624·3 grs.

It is impossible to determine to what king, people, or city of Macedon or Thrace this remarkable coin belongs; but there can be no doubt that it must have been struck at a very early period, the whole of the workmanship being most Archaic in character. In proof of this, let any one look at the form of the helmet on the coin, and then compare it with some of the Greek helmets still in existence (as for instance, Colonel Leake's from Olympia, or Sir W. Temple's, both now in the Museum), the dates of which can be given, at least approximately. The coin

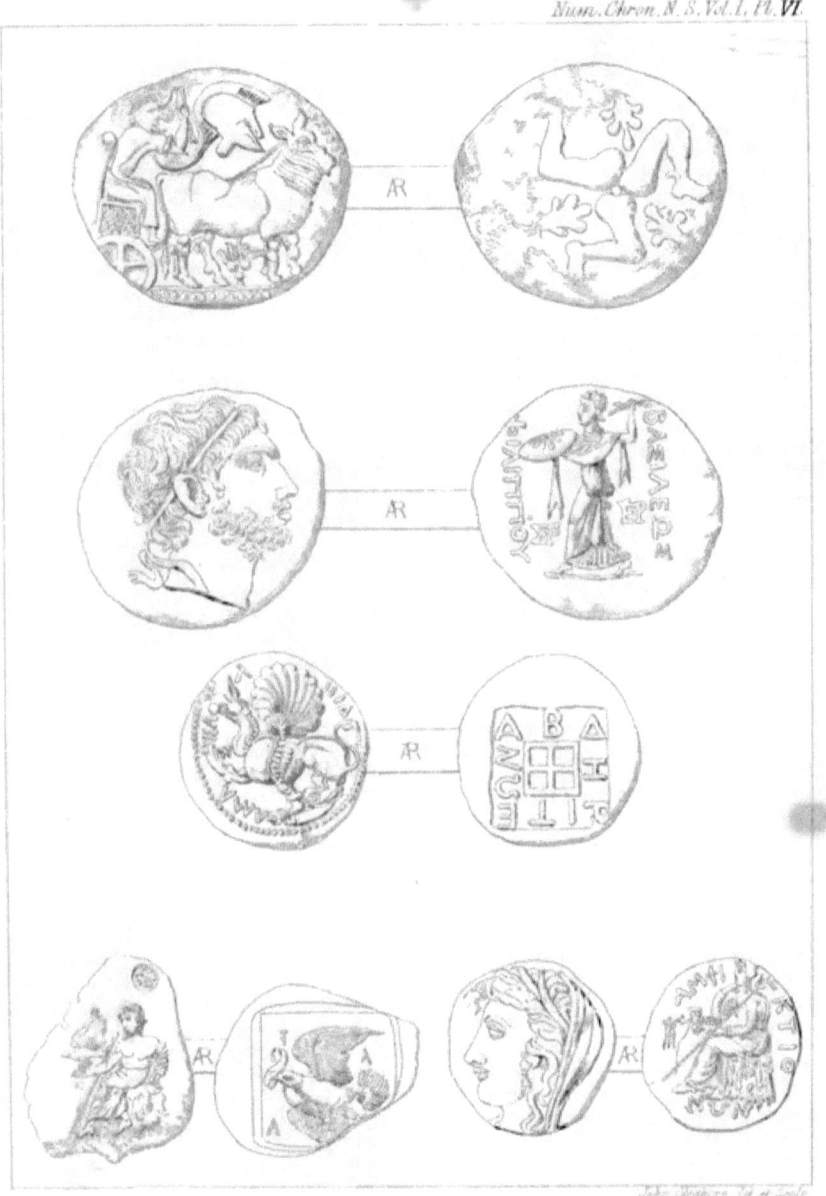

REMARKABLE GREEK COINS.

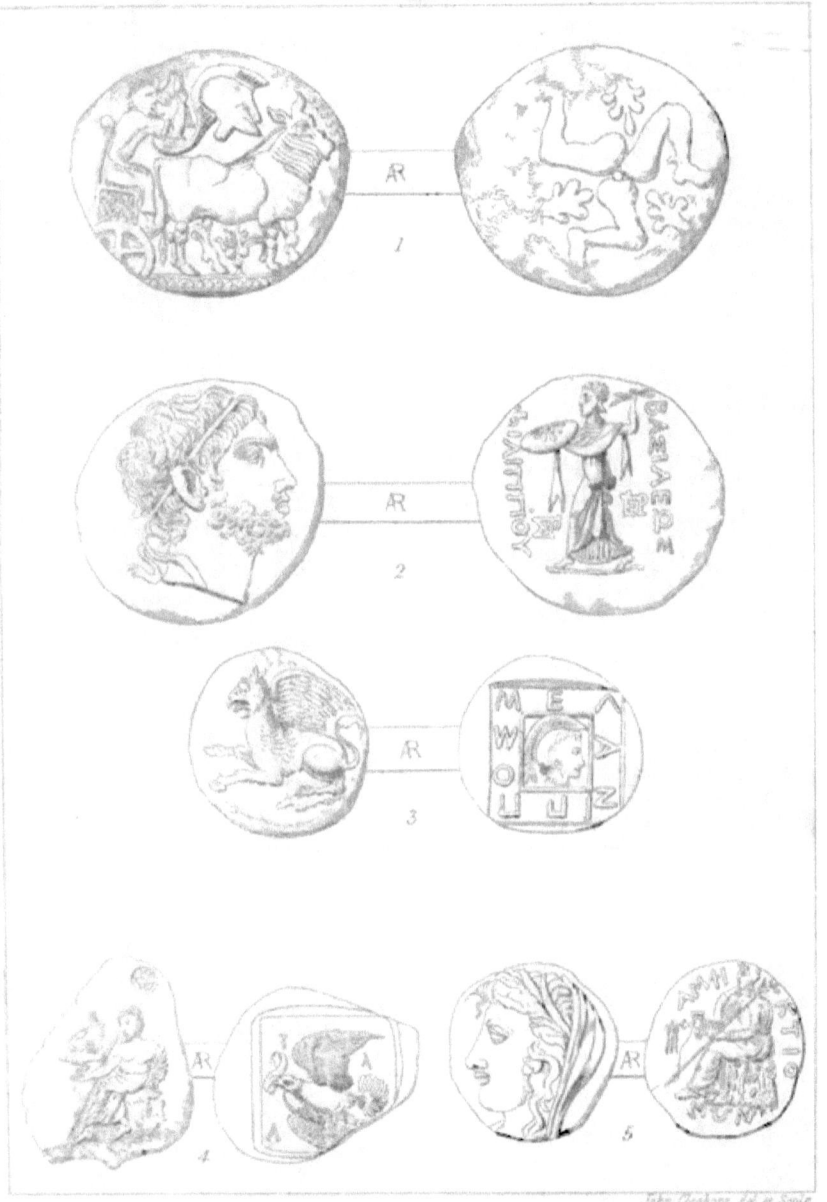

REMARKABLE GREEK COINS.

is almost unique, as only two or three other specimens are known to exist. One of them is in the collection of the Bodleian Library, but is far inferior to the one engraved here, and, at the same time, slightly different from it. The coin before me was obtained by Professor Verkovich, Professor of Latin at Belgrade, while travelling in northern Macedonia, at a place called *Istib;* and the fact of its discovery in this locality goes far to establish the correctness of the attribution. The type of the reverse bears much resemblance to that on some of the coins of Sicily; at the same time, the workmanship is much more rude than that of any of the Sicilian coins. It should be remembered, in studying this peculiar type, that the bulls on the obverse of the coins of Geta, King of the Edonians, exhibit a striking analogy with the ox on the present coin—a circumstance which is the more important in determining its date, as this peculiar representation of the animal is not found elsewhere, while the date I assign to this coin of about 500 to 550 B.C. is not much earlier than that of Geta. It weighs 624·3 grs.

The next coin to which I call the attention of the Society is a very fine specimen of the coinage of Philip V. of Macedonia, procured also from Professor Verkovich. It forms No. 2 in Pl. vi., and may be described as follows:—

> *Obv.*—Head of Philippus V., to the right, bearded and diademate.
>
> *Rev.*—ΒΑΣΙΛΕΩΣ ΦΙΛΙΠΠΟΥ. Pallas, striding, to the left, with her right hurling her thunderbolt; over left arm, the ægis; before her the monogram ΣP; behind her the monogram EP. Æ. Size, 9½. Weight, 209 grs.

This coin, which is in splendid condition, is, for this size, the tetradrachm, nearly unique. There is one in General Fox's collection, but it is not nearly so fine, and has also received some injury on one side. In the didrachm and drachm sizes, it is less rare, but the type of the reverse appears invariably to be that of a club, with the letters of the name within a wreath of oak leaves. As is well known, the almost universal type on the obverse of the tetradrachms of this king is the head of the mythical hero, Perseus, with the *harpa* behind the neck, in the centre of a Macedonian shield. The reason of this type is probably as suggested by Colonel Leake, because Philip pretended a lineal descent from this hero when he was unable to prove his connection with the royal house of Macedon, which had been wholly destroyed by Cassander. His true ancestor was Antigonus, Rex Asiæ, who was himself descended from an ancient Argive family, which colonized Macedonia at a very early period.

3. The next coin, which is engraved as No. 3 in the plate, was also procured from Professor Verkovich, and is a magnificent specimen of the coinage of Abdera, in Thrace. It represents:—

    Obv.—Griffin, seated, to left, with the wings extended.
    Rev.—ΜΕΛΑΝΙΠΠΟΣ, placed round a square, in the centre of which is a helmeted head, perhaps that of Minerva. Æ. Size, 5½. Weight, 193·5 grs.

The name Melanippus is, I believe, new, and has not been met with before on the not otherwise rare didrachms of this town. It may be remarked that, as the place was colonized by the people of Teos under the leadership of Anacreon, the Ionic dialect prevailed in this Thracian town, and also that the griffin, the usual type of the money of Teos, was adopted at Abdera; hence, where there is no legend, there is always some doubt whether the coin belongs to Teos or Abdera. In the present instance we need have no doubt, as apart from the evidence of the weight, this specimen, like the others to which I have already alluded, was procured by Professor Verkovich himself, during his wanderings in Upper Macedonia. As a general rule, the most Archaic in style belong to Teos, the later and finer to Abdera.

The fourth coin to which I call attention is one that belonged to the late Lord Northwick, and was procured for the British Museum at the sale of his coins. It is engraved as No. 4 in the plate, and is a coin of Elis.

> *Obv.*—Zeus Olympius, seated, to the left, with a bird flying from his extended right hand.
>
> *Rev.*—An eagle, flying, with a serpent in his mouth, and in the field, ϜΑΛ, retrograde. The whole within a sunk square. Æ. Size, 5. Weight, $185\frac{1}{2}$ grs.

This a very remarkable and uncommon specimen of the coinage of Elis. It belongs to an Archaic period, probably at least as early as the commencement of the Peloponnesian war. The head of Zeus was, as is well known, a frequent type of Elis, and the eagle is of course used with a reference to him. Connected with the worship of Zeus, we find also that of Hera, and some of the finest specimens preserved of Greek coinage, as those of Elis, give the head of the Greek Juno, surmounted with the high diadem, as the symbol of her supremacy among the goddesses.

The last coin to which I shall on the present occasion invite your attention, is a magnificent and extremely rare coin of Delphi, which I may describe as follows. It forms No. 5 in the plate.

Obv.—Veiled head of Ceres, to the right.

Rev.—ΑΜΦΙΚΤΙΟΝΩΝ. Apollo of Delphi, seated, to the left, on a richly ornamented seat, his head supported on his right arm, which again rests upon a lyre, and with the left holding a small branch of laurel, which passes over the left shoulder. In the field, a small tripod. Æ. Size, 5¼. Weight, 188 grs.

This is one of the most rare coins of Delphi; indeed there are but three or four of this type known. They are quite unlike the usual types of this celebrated place; but at the same time there is no reason to doubt the correctness of the attribution. It is well known that the Amphictyonic Council met at Delphi; and it has been supposed with much probability that the coins bearing this type refer to this event. If so, they are rightly judged to be among the most interesting of the Greek coins, as well as among the most beautiful in point of execution. The ordinary coins of Delphi, like the common coins of Athens, have nothing in consonance with the celebrity of the place to which they belong; they are insignificant, and even poor, in execution. Delphi is supposed to have derived both of its other and more usual types—the heads of the ram and the goat—from Crete; but this is, I think, difficult of satisfactory proof.

W. S. W. Vaux.

XVI.

ON AN ENGLISH JETTON, OR PATTERN-PIECE.

For the opportunity of making our readers acquainted with the remarkable silver jetton, or pattern-piece, of which a representation is given above, we are indebted to the courtesy of Mr. Webster, of Russell Street, Covent Garden, into whose hands the original has lately fallen. The woodcut gives so faithful a picture of the piece, that it is needless to enter into any detailed description of it. It is difficult to say which is the obverse and which is the reverse of a medal of this kind, on which there is neither head nor title for our guidance, and where both types seem of equal importance. The engraver has, however, selected the side on which appear the three crowns, in pale, for the obverse, and has done so, possibly, from finding on the other side five terminations of a cross fleury, alternating with the lions passant, which are placed around the rose; inasmuch as they are similar to those on the reverse of our English nobles. There cannot be the least doubt that the types of both obverse and reverse, whichever way we may take this curious piece, are such as to prove it to belong to this country. The difficulty is to determine at what period and on what occasion it was struck, and what are the allusions contained in the two mottoes which appear upon it; and on these points we must confess ourselves unable to give any very decided opinion. The type of the three crowns, in pale, is frequently found upon the Irish coins of Edward IV., Richard III. and Henry VII.; and good reason has been shown for considering them to have been the ancient arms of the kingdom of Ireland.[1] Mr. J. Gough Nichols, who has been kind enough to favour us with some remarks upon this singular piece, is inclined to connect it with the Irish coinage; and, under any circumstances, it seems probable that the three crowns on the one side bear reference to Ireland, in the same manner that the expanded rose on the other side is emblematic of England. The three crowns, however, ceased to appear on the coins of Ireland in the days of Henry VII.; whereas, from the fabric and style of the piece under consideration, it belongs to a period decidedly more recent, and many years after the harp had supplanted the three crowns on the Irish coinage.

If the three crowns are to be taken, as has been suggested in another quarter, as those of the three kingdoms of England, Scotland, and Ireland, we must regard the piece as a jetton, or pattern, struck, under James I., in honour of the union of the three kingdoms; but the mottoes seem hardly appropriate in this case, especially when we consider the pointed allusion to the union that are to be found on many of the coins of James, such as " Quæ Deus conjunxit nemo separet," " Henricus rosas regna Jacobus,"

---

[1] See Sainthill's "Olla Podrida," vol. i. p. 166; vol. ii. p. 60; *Gent.'s Mag.*, June, 1845, p. 603; and *Arch. Journ.* vol. ix. p. 23.

"Tueatur unita Deus," &c. It seems probable, therefore, that some other attribution must be sought, and Mr. Webster is inclined to regard the coin as having been struck by the adherents of Lady Jane Grey, in the year 1553, immediately after the death of her cousin, Edward VI. It is certainly very remarkable, as confirmatory of this suggestion, that, on the reverse of a forged shilling of Lady Jane Grey, probably fabricated about the close of the last century, the same motto—" Si Deus nobiscum quis contra nos"—is to be found, as appears on this undoubtedly genuine piece. This would give a presumption that the motto in question had been assumed by " Jane the Quene," or her party, and was, therefore, adopted by the fabricator of her spurious coin, as appropriate for his purpose; still, we have not, at present, been able to find any documentary evidence of the motto having been used by Lady Jane Grey, or the Northumberland party. It is, however, a curious fact, in connection with the present inquiry, that this motto—" Si Deus nobiscum quis contra nos"—is prefixed to that violent attack on the Northumberland party—*the Pistel, or Letter, of poor Pratte, sent to Gilbert Potter, in the tyme when he was in prison, for speakinge on our most true Quene's part, the Lady Mary, before he had his ears cut of.*[2]

Without committing ourselves to any of the suggestions which are here put forth, we invite attention to this curious jetton, or pattern-piece, in the hope that some correspondent may be able to penetrate the mystery with which it is now enveloped, and point out its connection with some event of English history, which, in all probability, it was intended to commemorate.   J. E.

[2] See the "Chronicle of Queen Jane." Camd. Soc. 1850, p. 115, Edited by J. Gough Nichols, Esq., F.S.A.

XVII.

"THE THREE VALENTINIANS."

In Eckhel, Mionnet, and Akerman, we read that the coins of Valentinianus II., excepting when they are specially marked by the epithet of IVNior, are not able to be distinguished from those of Valentinianus I., nor from those of Valentinianus III. when this latter is not called PLAcidius. Yet, from a careful comparison, the coins speak for themselves. Valentinianus I. is represented on his coins as a strong, stout, full-faced man; Ammianus Marcellinus[1] says, "Corpus ejus *lacertosum* et *validum*," while Valentinianus II. is represented as a young man. It is well known that when the younger Valentinianus ascended the throne with Gratianus after his father's death, he was then only four or five years of age, and that when he died he was only a few months above twenty. Possessing this knowledge, the difficulty of comparison between the coins of the *man* and those of a *boy* is considerably lessened, and in order to help in preventing any mistakes that might arise, I here give a complete list of all the coins in the British Museum without the word IVNior, and which it is utterly impossible—chiefly from the style of face, and partly on account of some of the mint-marks, which do not appear in the time of Valentinianus I.—to give to any but Valentinianus the son. As to Valentinianus III., the types of the obverses and reverses, which resemble those

---

[1] Amm. Marcell. xxx. 9.

of the other emperors of the period, are sufficient warrant for their attribution. His coins in the Museum without the name PLAcidius, being only two, I give them at the end of the paper.

1. *Obv.*—D.N VALENTINIANVS.P.F.AVG. Bust, to right, diademed.
   Rev.—VOTA.PVBLICA. River-god (the Nile), seated on ground, to the left, holding in right hand a boat, and in left a sceptre, and leaning left arm on an overturned vase, from which water is flowing. Æ. III.

Treviri (Treves.)

2. *Obv.*—D.N.VALENTINIANVS.P.F.AVG. Bust, to right, diademed, with *paludamentum* and cuirass.
   Rev.—VICTORIA.AVGG. The Emperors of the West and East, both with a *nimbus*, seated, facing, holding between them a globe; above, behind them, Victory, standing; on the ground, between their knees a palm. In field, left and right, T-R. (Treviris.) In exergue, COM. (Constantinæ [Arles] moneta.) *N*.

3. *Obv.*—The legend and bust being the same, I shall only mention reverses till there is any difference.
   Rev.—VIRTVS.EXERCITVS. Emperor, standing, to left, holding the *labarum*, and resting left hand on shield. In exergue, TR.P.S. (Treviris pecunia signata.) Æ. (large).

4. VIRTVS.ROMANORVM. Rome, helmeted, seated on cuirass, to left, holding Victory on a globe, and reversed spear. In exergue, TR.P.S. Æ.

Lugdunum (Lyons.)

5. VICTORIA.AVGG. The two Emperors of the West and East, seated, &c. In field, left and right, L.-D. (Lugduno.) In exergue, COM. (Constantinæ moneta.) *N*.

6. VRBS . ROMA. Rome, helmeted, seated to left, holding Victory on globe, and sceptre. In exergue, LVG . P.S (Lugduno pecunia signata.) Æ.

7. VICTORIA . AVGGG. Victory, walking, to left, holding wreath and palm. In exergue LVG . P. (prima). Æ. III.

Constantina (Arles.)

8. VICTORIA . AVGG. The two Emperors of the West and East, &c. In exergue, COM. (Constantinæ moneta.) N.

9. VICTORIA . AVGGG. Same type as No. 7. In exergue, P . CON. (Prima Constantinâ.) Æ. III.

Roma (Rome).

10. CONCORDIA . AVGGG. Female figure (Rome?) helmeted, seated on a chair with lions' heads, and placing right foot on prow, holding sceptre and globe, which is starred. In exergue, COMOB. (Constantinæ moneta 72.) N.

11. VICTORIA . AVGVSTORVM. Victory, walking, to right, dragging captive in right hand, and holding trophy over left shoulder. In exergue, R.P. (Româ prima.) Æ. (large.)

12. VRBS . ROMA. Same type as No. 4. In exergue, R.B. (Româ 2.) Æ.

13. *Obv.*—Same legend. Bust, to right, helmeted, with *paludamentum* and cuirass, showing both hands, the right holding a sceptre, on the top of which is a globe, with the monogram of Christ, and the left holding a shield.

   Rev.—GLORIA . ROMANORVM. Rome, helmeted, seated on shield, holding Victory on globe, and reversed spear. In exergue, S.M.R.Q. (Signata moneta Româ quarta.) Æ. II.

14. *Obv.*—Same legend. Bust, to right, diademed, with *paludamentum* and cuirass.

THE THREE VALENTINIANS. 115

Rev.—REPARATIO . REIPVB. Emperor, standing, to left, holding in left hand a Victory on globe, and lifting with right a female, turreted, kneeling on right knee before him. In exergue, S . M . R . B. (Signata moneta Româ secunda.) Æ. II.

15. CONCORDIA . AVGGG. Rome, helmeted, seated, facing, looking to left, holding globe, and reversed spear. In exergue, S . M . R . T. (Signata moneta Româ tertia.) Æ. III.

16. VICTORIA . AVGGG. (?) Two Victories, standing opposite each other. In exergue, R . T. (Româ tertia.) Æ. III.

Mediolanum (Milan.)

17. CONCORDIA . AVGGG . Θ (9.) Female figure (Roma?), helmeted, seated, holding sceptre, which rests on prow, and a shield resting on a stick, on which is inscribed VOT . X . MVLT . XX. In exergue, MDOB. (Mediolano 72.) *N*.

18. VIRTVS . ROMANORVM. Same type as No. 15. In exergue, MD. P.S. (Mediolano pecunia signata.) Æ.

19. VICTORIA . AVGGG. Same type as No. 16. In exergue, MD. P.S. Æ. III.

Aquileia.

20. VICTORIA . AVGG. The two Emperors of the West and East, &c. In field, left and right, A - Q. (Aquileiâ.) In exergue, COM. (Constantinæ moneta.) *N*.

21. VIRTVS ROMANORVM. Same type as No. 15. In exergue, AQ. P.S. (Aquileiâ pecunia signata.) Æ.

22. SECVRITAS . REIPVBLICAE. Victory, walking, to left, holding wreath and palm. In exergue, S.M . AQ . P. (Signata moneta Aquileiâ prima.) Æ. III.

23. GLORIA . ROMANORVM. Emperor, to right, dragging a captive in right hand, and holding *labarum*, on

which is the monogram of Christ, in left. In exergue, S.M. AQ. Æ. III.

24. VICTORIA . AVGGG. Same type as No. 16. In exergue, S.M. AQ. P. Æ. III.

Siscia (Sissek.)

25. VOT . V . MVLT . X within oak wreath. In exergue, SISC . P . Σ. (Sisciâ pecunia or percussa 7.) Æ.

26. CONCORDIA . AVGGG. Same type as No. 15. In exergue, A and B SISC. (1 and 2 Sisciâ.) Æ. III.

27. VICTORIA . AVGGG. Same type as No. 7. In exergue, A and B SIS. Æ. III.

Thessalonica (Saloniki.)

28. VICTORIA . AVGG. The two Emperors of the East and West, &c. In exergue, THCOB. (Tessalonicâ 72.) N.

We find coins of Gratian and Theodosius with the mintmark TESOB. This coin, from its peculiar style, is evidently a copy from the true coin of Valentinianus II.

29. *Obv.*—Same legend. Helmeted bust, with spear and shield.
    Rev.—GLORIA . ROMANORVM. A figure standing on a galley. In exergue, TES . A. (Tessalonicâ 1.) Æ. II.

The coins with the helmeted busts, and a figure standing on a galley, are those which have been generally supposed to belong to Valentinianus II., but have never been attributed with positive certainty.

30. *Obv.*—Same legend. Bust, to right, diademed, with *paludamentum* and cuirass.
    Rev.—REPARATIO . REIPVB. Same type as No. 14. In field, to right, Δ. In exergue, S.M.TES. (Signata moneta Tessalonicâ 4.) Æ. II.

31. VICTORIA . AVGGG. Same type as No. 7. In exergue, TES. (Tessalonicâ.) Æ. III.

32. GLORIA . REIPVBLICE (*sic*.) The Prætorian camp, from the top of each tower a man looking out.(?) In field, to left, A. In exergue, TES. (Tessalonicâ 1.) Æ. III.

33. SALVS . REIPVBLICAE. Victory, walking, to left, dragging captive with right hand. In field, to left, the monogram of Christ. In exergue, TES. (Tessalonicâ.) Æ. III.

Constantinopolis (Constantinople.)

34. CONCORDIA . AVGGG . C. or S.(3 or 6). Female figure (Rome?) seated, sometimes on chair with lions' heads, sometimes on chair without, &c. In exergue, CONOB. (Constantinopoli 72.) *N*.

35. VICTORIA . AVGVSTORVM. Victory, walking, to right, holding wreath and globe, on which is a cross. In exergue, CONOB. Quin. *N*.

36. VOT . X . MVLT . XX. within wreath. In exergue, CONS. (Constantinopoli.) Æ.

37. *Obv.*—Same legend. Helmeted bust, with spear and shield.

   Rev.—GLORIA . ROMANORVM. Same type as No. 29. In exergue, CON. Δ. (Constantinopoli 4.) Æ. II.

38. *Obv.*—Same legend. Bust, to right, diademed, with *paludamentum* and cuirass.

   Rev.—SALVS . REPVBLICAE. Same type as No. 33. In exergue, CONS. B. Æ. III.

Heracleia (Eski Eregli), Perinthus Thraciæ.

39. *Obv.*—Same legend. Helmeted bust, with spear and shield.

   Rev.—GLORIA . ROMANORVM. Same type as No. 29. In exergue, S.M.H. (Signata moneta Heracleiâ.) Æ. III.

40. *Obv.*—Same legend. Bust, to right, diademed, with *paludamentum* and cuirass.
    Rev.—VOT . X . MVLT . XX. within wreath. In exergue, S.M.H.B. (Signata moneta Heracleiâ 2.) Æ. III.

Nicomedeia (Ismid.)

41. *Obv.*—Same legend. Helmeted bust, with spear and shield.
    Rev.—GLORIA . ROMANORVM. Same type as No. 29. In exergue, S . M . N. (Signata moneta Nicomedeiâ.) Æ. II.

42. *Obv.*—Same legend. Bust, to right, diademed, with *paludamentum* and cuirass.
    Rev.—VIRTVS . EXERCITVS. Emperor placing left foot on captive, and holding *labarum* in right hand and globe in left. In field, to the left, a palm. In exergue, S . M . N . B. (Signata moneta Nicomedeiâ 2.) Æ. II.

43. CONCORDIA . AVGGG. Same type as No. 15. In exergue, S.M.N. Æ. III.

44. VRBS . ROMA. Same type as No. 4. In exergue, S.M.N. Æ. III.

45. SALVS . REIPVBLICAE. Same type as No. 33. In exergue, S . M . N . B. Æ. III.

Cyzicus (Chizico.)

46. *Obv.*—Same legend. Helmeted bust, with spear and sceptre.
    Rev.—GLORIA . ROMANORVM. Same type as No. 29. In exergue, S . M . K . D. (Signata moneta Kyzico 4.) Æ. II.

47. *Obv.*—Same legend. Bust, to right, diademed, with *paludamentum* and cuirass.
    Rev.—CONCORDIA . AVGG. Same type as No. 15. In field, to right, +. In exergue, S.M.K . Δ. Æ. III.

48. SALVS . REIPVBLICAE. Same type as No. 33. In exergue, S . M . K . Δ. Æ. III.

49. VOT . X . MVLT . XX. within wreath. In exergue, S . M . K . B. Æ. III.

Antiocheia (Antakiah.)

50. VIRTVS . EXERCITVS. Same type as No. 42. In exergue, ANT . T. (and Δ) (Antiochiâ 3 (and 4.) Æ. II.

51. REPARATIO . REIPVB. Same type as No. 14. In exergue, ANT . B. (Antiochiâ 2.) Æ. II.

52. *Obv.*—Same legend. Helmeted bust, with spear and shield.
    Rev.—GLORIA . ROMANORVM. Same type as No. 29. In field, to left, a wreath; to right, a cross. In exergue, ANT . E. (Antiochiâ 5.) Æ. II.

53. *Obv.*—Same legend, bust, to right, diademed, with *paludamentum* and cuirass.
    Rev.—CONCORDIA . AVGG. Same type as No. 15. In exergue, ANT . A. (B . Γ . Δ and S.) (Antiochiâ (2, 3, 4, and 7.) Æ. III.

54. GLORIA . ROMANORVM. Same type as No. 23. In exergue, ANT. Æ. III.

55. SALVS . REIPVBLICAE. Same type as No. 33. In exergue, ANT . Δ. Æ. III.

56. VOT . XX . MVLT . XXX. within wreath. In exergue, ANT . Δ. Æ III.

Alexandreia.

57. VIRTVS . EXERCITVS. Same type as No. 42. In exergue, ALE . A. (Alexandriâ 1.) Æ. II.

58. SECVRITAS . REIPVBLICAE. Same type as No. 22. In exergue, ALE . A. Æ. III.

59. SALVS . REIPVBLICAE. Same type as No. 33. In exergue, ALE . A. Æ. III.

60. VOT . X . MVLT . XX within wreath. In exergue, ALE . A. Æ. III.

The above is the complete list of the coins in the British Museum, without the word IVNior, that may safely be assigned to Valentinianus II., from their distinctness of portrait; and among them there are one or two which, on account of their exergual letters, could not possibly be of Valentinianus I. It was not till the year A.D. 375 that Valentinianus II. was proclaimed Augustus, that being the year of his father's death, consequently the elder and younger Valentinianus never reigned together.

It may not be inappropriate now to make a few remarks on the mint-marks occurring on the coins of Valentinianus II., and to do so it will be necessary to take a view of part of the coinage from Constantius II. to Theodosius I., inclusive. Owing to a greater number of coins having been found, and the Museum having been enriched by the splendid collection of Mr. de Salis, who has spared neither money or pains in obtaining every interesting coin that has come to his sight, the knowledge of mint-marks has much advanced, though still there are many more connecting links required, and, in consequence, the remarks which follow must be considered only as hypothetical, though I confess they are probable.[2]

I will commence, then, with the coins that may be assigned to Constantina or Arles. "Constantina" was the name given to "Arelate" (Arles) by Constantine

---

[2] The articles of M. de Pétigny and M. Senckler in the *Revue Numismatique* for 1847 and 1851 made great advances in the explanation of the mint-marks of this period, but the absence of sufficient material and too much dependence on the text of Mionnet have caused several unmistakeable errors in their excellent articles. We cannot but hope that Mr. de Salis will soon publish the results of his researches on the Gothic and Ostrogothic coinage—indeed, a history of the coinage of the fourth century and downwards.

the Great, when he improved the town and built a new one on the opposite side of the Rhone. Ausonius (" Urbes Claræ" No. 8) calls Arelate *duplex,* and says that there was a bridge of boats on the river. CON. or CONS. (Constantinople) is always accompanied by a *Greek* letter, while CON. or CONST. (Constantina) is preceded by a *Latin.* The attribution to Arles of the coins formerly given to Constantinople, is due to the late Mr. Borrell, of Smyrna. It was suggested to him by a coin of Fausta with the mintmark CONST., which could not be of Constantinople, because Fausta died before Byzantium was dedicated. The Museum does not possess a specimen of this coin.[3]

The first gold coin that may be attributed to Constantina or Arles is one of Constantius II., with the mint-mark KONSÆ (Constantina Augusti). This form of mint-mark is found also on a gold coin of Julian the Apostate, and on the coins of Valentinianus I. and Valens. It is very probable that the KONSÆ mint-mark of Gratianus, who reigned with Valentinianus I. and Valens from A.D. 375 to A.D. 379, is in existence, though at present the Museum does not possess it. On some large silver coins of Valentinianus I. and Valens we find the mint-mark KA, the exergual letters being S.M.KAP. At first sight, one would be inclined to attribute these coins to Carthage, but they cannot well be of that mint for the three following reasons: —1. If we give these coins to Carthage, we must suppose that that mint was restored for a very short time *only* under Valentinianus I. and Gratianus, as no other coins attributable to it are found from the time of Maxentius and

---

[3] The *exergual* letters are printed CONS. in Borrell's Sale Catalogue, but this I believe to be a mistake, and the coin must have been in bad preservation, so as to conceal the T. (See Borrell Catalogue, p. 81, No. 834.)

Alexander Tyrannus down to the Vandal period. 2. We must suppose that *silver only* was struck there; and 3. We must take no notice whatever of the fabric, which is decidedly Gallic. This is the only instance where the final letter is used in a mint-mark (if we may except SM., Sirmium), the object being in this case to show its difference from Constantinople and Cyzicus. K is never used as the initial of Constantinople, and not invariably of Cyzicus. The P at the end of the *exergual* legend cannot be a *Greek* P., being too low in the alphabet to be used as a differential letter.

The next change that occurs on the gold coins is to COM. (Constantinæ Moneta). This seems to have been introduced late in the reign of Gratianus, and is found *alone* also on the coins of his cotemporaries, Valentinianus II. (See No. 8) and Theodosius I., and when thus *alone*, it signifies "Arles." It is the mint-mark of Gaul and the greater part of the West, and is sometimes accompanied by the letters TR., LD., AQ., MD. in the *field*, and the mint-marks may then be interpreted, "struck at Treves, Lyons, &c., on the same standard as that of Arles."[4] It is curious that on a gold coin of Magnus Maximus,[5] who killed Gratianus in 383,

---

[4] COM. may have been accompanied by letters in the *field* under Gratianus, but as we have no examples of it, is probable that this form of mintage, which supersedes TROB., AQOB., &c., was not introduced till after the reign of Gratianus in A.D. 383.

[5] Since the list of mint-marks appended to my work was printed, Mr. de Salis has made further investigations in the Roman coinage of Gaul and Britain, which have led to the attribution to London of the uncertain coin of Magnus Maximus with the *exergual* mark AVGOB. As it appears from Ammianus Marcellinus and the Cosmography of Ravenna (p. 429, Ed. Pinder and Parthey, Berlin, 1860) that "London" was also called "Augusta" during the Roman domination, there is little doubt that Magnus Maximus, on assuming the imperial power in Britain, issued his first coinage in London, where no mintage had

thereby obtaining the latter's share of the empire (Britain, Gaul, Spain, and Mauretania Tingitana), and the greater part of Italy, instead of the usual mint-mark COM. we should find KONOB (Constantina 72). This form in the *exergue*, accompanied by AR. (Arelate) in the *field*, occurs on a gold coin of Constantinus III., the usurper under Honorius, and on another of this latter's coins we find AR. in the *field*, and COMOB in the *exergue*. AR. (Arelate) was the only mint omitted in the *field*, while COM. was the great Western *exergual* mint-mark.

The mint-mark COMOB.[6] appears in the *exergue* for the first time under Valentinianus II. (No. 10) and Theodosius I. To what place shall it be assigned? To Constantinople? No. It is a *Western*, and *only a Western*,

---

taken place since the latter years of Constantine. On his becoming master of Gaul and Italy the temporary mint of London was given up, and the coins of the later part of his reign, as well as those of his son Flavius Victor, were struck in the then existing mints of Treves, Lyons, Arles, Milan, and Aquileia. We have thus a most satisfactory explanation of this short reappearance of London as a place of mintage. The passages of Ammianus Marcellinus are, " Egressus tendensque ad *Lundinium*, vetus oppidum, quod *Augustam* posteritas appellavit" (xxvii. 8.), and "Theodosius, vero, dux nominis inclyti, animo vigore collecto ab *Augustá* profectus, quam veteres appellavere *Lundinium*" (xxviii. 3.). We Englishmen ought to have thought of this earlier, had we recalled to our memories the line from the " Rejected Addresses"—

"On fair Aŭgusta's towers and trees;"

or those of Swift—

"For poets you can never want'em
Spread through *Augusta Trinobantum*."

Thomson and other poets have, I believe, also used the old name " Augusta" in speaking of London.

[6] The forms CORNOB, IONOB., CONOS., &c., do not exist as mint-marks, and if any coins bear them, they must be barbarous. CORMOB. is found on a gold coin of Anthemius, and RM. signifies " Roma," and the CO. is affixed, and the OB. prefixed, to resemble as near as possible COMOB., and at the same time to designate a mint.

mint-mark, and may be explained by "Constantinæ Moneta 72—money of the standard of Constantina or Arles." It is well known that Theodosius I. and Valentinianus II.[7] reigned as colleagues at Rome, and being the only place of which we have not their coins with letters in the *field*, and COM. in the *exergue*, a suggestion may be ventured that there (?) these coins were struck, the types being intended to imitate those of Constantinople, and the *exergual* letters to resemble, with a slight distinction, the CONOB. of Constantinople. When COMOB. became common to every Western mint, RM. (Roma), as well as the other mints, appeared in the *field*. Theodosius I. also struck coins at Sirmium with SM. in the *field* and COMOB. in the *exergue*.

The form CONOB. occurs *only* on the coins of Constantinople, and for the first time under Gratianus, Valentinianus II. (No. 34), and Theodosius I., and the OB., as in all the other cases, is an indication of value, and signifies that "72 solidi" were coined from one pound of gold. After the time of Anastasius, COMOB. and CONOB. became the general mint-marks of the West and East, and the latter is used indiscriminately after the time of Justinianus I.

Having now given a sketch of the KONSN, COM., COMOB., and CONOB. mint-marks, it will not be necessary for me to mention any other than Treviri, or Treves. The usual abbreviation is TR.—TROB (Treviris 72)[8] occurs for the first time on the gold coins of

---

[7] The Museum possesses a gold coin of Honorius similar to these of Valentinianus II. and Theodosius I., with COMOB in the *exergue*. It is evidently struck somewhere in Italy.

[8] Accompanying the mint-mark TROB. on the coins of these emperors, we find the letters C, S, and T. In M. Senckler's article on "Les Médailles à l'exergue CONOB, etc.," in the *Revue Numismatique*, 1847, p. 401, TROBS is interpreted " *Treviris* LXXII *signatus*, or *Treviris officinâ* II *signatus*,

Valentinianus I.; it also may be found on the coins of Valens, Gratianus, Magnus Maximus, Victor, Valentinianus II.[9] and Theodosius I., and besides may be found on the coins of Constantinus III., usurper in Britain and Gaul A.D. 407—411. To account for the return to an old form of mintage which had been dropped under Valentinianus II. and Theodosius I. for the new form TR. COM., is not very easy, and it is most probable that the coins are barbarous. During the reign of Honorius we have no Gallic coins, that is to say coins bearing Gallic mint-marks, and it is likely that some of the barbarous coins of the period, some having RA. (Ravenna?) in the *field*, and perhaps some of those that bear Eastern mint-marks, were struck in Gaul.[10] Gaul seems never to have recovered from the effects of the usurpation of Eugenius, and although Theodosius I. reconquered it, he did not live long enough to establish complete power there. Late in A.D. 406 the Vandals invaded Gaul, and commenced the destruction of Treves, and in A.D. 413 the Franks, who

and TROAS, *Treviris officinâ I signatus*. I may remark that the form TROAS also is not found. It is a question if the final S may be interpreted *signatus*, and if it may, what is the meaning of C and T? On some of the small copper coins of Valentinianus I. and Valens we find R *Prima, Tertia, Quarta* in full, besides R.B., R.Q., and on the silver R.P., R.T. Now with this before me, I am rather inclined to think that these letters are numerical representations, and signify the number of the mint; C = 3; S = *Secunda*; T = *Tertia*. Not having seen a gold coin with the letter P. (Prima), this mintage may have been confined to the silver and copper. On a gold coin of Valentinianus II., with the epithet IVNior on the obverse, we find in the exergue AQOBF. Here the F is most likely a numerical letter signifying 6, sixth mint. The Aquileia mint ends with the destruction of that town under Valentinianus III.

[9] The form TROB. occurs only on his coins that have IVNior on the obverse.

[10] The silver coin of Arcadius with *exergue* TR.P.S. was struck during the lifetime of Theodosius I.

had sided with Jovinus, proclaimed emperor at Treves, and of whom we have coins with TR. in the *field*, and COMOB. in the *exergue*, in order to avenge his fate, again sacked the town and reduced it to ashes. Thus ended this great capital which had been established as a mint from the time of Diocletian.

I have deemed it necessary to affix the above remarks to the list of coins of Valentinianus II. in explanation of the various forms of mint-marks occurring upon them, of their attributions, and to show that most of the gold coins could not possibly belong to Valentinianus I. The silver and copper show chiefly from their style of face to whom they should belong. I cannot say more than that in my recent work on " Roman Numismatics" there is an entire alphabetical list of the mint-marks occurring in the *exergue*, with explanatory notes attached to them. I would refer those who require any further information on this interesting subject to the above list and notes. Adjoined to this paper is a table showing the mints at which the emperors between the time of Constantius II. and Theodosius I. issued their coinage, the metals, and the *exergual* letters found on the coins, thereby enabling one to see at a glance how the different forms of mint-marks were introduced.

And now to dispel the doubts about the coins of Valentinianus III., and of him the Museum only possesses two coins without the name PLAcidius:—

1. *Obv.*—Helmeted bust, full faced, with cuirass, showing right hand, which holds spear, and on the left side part of a shield, on which is represented the emperor on horseback, to right, and on the ground a captive.

    Rev.—SALVS . REIPVBLICAE . Z. (7) Theodosius II. and Valentinianus III., both with *nimbus*, seated, full-faced, each holding the *mappa* and a cross. In exergue CONOB. (Constantinoplis 72).

This coin is struck by Theodosius II. at Constantinople, soon after Aelia Galla Placidia and her son, Valentinianus III., were restored to their power, and the usurper Johannes, who had assumed the purple at Ravenna, was defeated by Theodosius II. Placidius may have been omitted on his Eastern coins for the same reason that Galla was omitted on those of Aelia Placidia.

2. *Rev.*—VICTORIA . AVGGG. Victory standing to left, holding a long cross; in the field, to right, a star. In exergue CONOB.

In consequence of the absence of a differential letter after the legend, this coin is probably an imitation of the genuine Constantinople type. It resembles the coins of Marcianus, who was colleague with Valentinianus III. after the death of Theodosius II. from A.D. 450 to A.D. 457.

There can be no doubt of the attribution of these coins.

Since the paper has been in type the Museum has added to its collection the following coins of Valentinianus II. :—

LVGDVNVM (Lyons).

1. VIRTVS . EXERCITVS. Same type as No. 3. In exergue LVG. (Lugduno). Æ. (large).

2. VRBS . ROMA. Same type as No. 6. In exergue LVG. Æ. (sometimes P. or S., Prima and Secunda).

3. VOTIS . V. MVLTIS . X. within wreath. In exergue LVG. Æ.

ROMA.

1. VOT. X. MVLT. XX. within wreath. In exergue R.B. (Romà 2.) Æ.

ANTIOCHEIA.

1. VOT. X. MVLT. XX. within wreath. In exergue ANT. Δ. (Antiochià 4). Æ. III.

FRED. W. MADDEN.

NOTICE OF RECENT NUMISMATIC PUBLICATIONS.

Roman Numismatics, by F. W. Madden. J. Russell Smith, 1861. Small 8vo.

Few questions are more commonly asked by those who have but a slight knowledge of Numismatics than this, whether there be not some complete existing handbook to the science, wherein, briefly, of course, yet judiciously arranged, the student may find all the essential particulars he may desire to know of the coinage of different ages and countries.

It is not easy to answer this and similar questions as we would gladly answer them, for there exists no general work on Numismatics to which any practised Numismatist would dream of referring the supposed inquirer. Whether it be from the vast range of the study itself, embracing, as it does, the history in miniature of nearly the whole world—a "survey" far surpassing the famed one "from China to Peru"—and ascending from the present day to the sixth or seventh century before Christ; or, from the fact that no one mind has as yet grasped the whole of this great story, or acquired the diversities of characters, not to say the actual languages, wherein Art has impressed its style, or Commerce defined its measures—certain it is, that no one book has yet appeared for universal use; more than this, we may add our belief that no such volume will ever appear.

Hence it is, that among Numismatic works, none are so common, nor, except from the number requisite for the complete study of coins, so useful, as detached monographs embracing one or more specific subject, some of which (it would be invidious to instance individual cases where so many are excellent) may justly rank, from the ability and research they exhibit, with the works more especially devoted to other branches of Archæology or science.

It is to fill a want (at least to English students), in the case of Roman coins, that this little work aspires. We have indeed, in other languages, some elaborate works on Roman Numismatics, among which those by MM. Riccio and Cohen are entitled to the first place. We have also, in English, the translation by Mr. Akerman of Mionnet's work on this subject, published now more than twenty-seven years ago, which, so far as it goes, is not without value. But the same objection applies to these, and to not a few other works on this branch of Archæology, that their size is too often inconveniently large, and their price beyond the means of the bulk of coin collectors. For their use, a small, well-arranged, compact volume, of moderate cost, was really wanted: let us see how far the one before us answers these conditions.

Mr. Madden commences his work with a carefully drawn up account of what may be called the history of the Roman coinage, including notices of the As and its subdivisions, the gold and silver denarii, &c., with an interesting detailed memoir on the types to be found on the Consular and Imperial coins, with some reference to the character of the portraits exhibited on many of them, and to the titles and surnames borne by the different personages whose coins are enumerated. Many of these, he remarks, are of considerable importance, either as confirming or as elucidating history. Among others, he speaks especially of the famous coin usually attributed to the Junia family, and bearing the inscription EID. MAR. His words are, "This coin, either in gold or silver, has been often doubted; the gold is decidedly false; but there is a specimen in silver in the British Museum, of undoubted authenticity, presented to the nation by Mr. de Salis." It may be added that authentic specimens exist in other cabinets.

He then proceeds to give some account of the various officers, whose titles are found on the coins themselves, such as the Consules, Ordinarii, Suffecti, or Designati, the Viri Consulares, Proconsuls, Censors, &c., with detached notes on some independent subjects, such as the "Nummi Restituti," and the coins bearing the inscription "Votis." On the latter, we wish our author had been a little more explicit, as we could not at first comprehend the meaning of the passage he has marked as a quotation, "that these were the vicennalian vows of the emperor, and he hoped that he might live to the tricennalian," though if, as we presume, a translation from Eckhel, the Latin of this German writer has the merit of being equally unintelligible.

The rest of his work is taken up with a series of lists, as it would seem, very carefully compiled, of the various species of money current during different periods of Roman history, of the Roman families, and of the members of the Imperial houses who ruled from the time of Julius Cæsar to that of Theodosius I. Among the Families, care has been taken to discriminate between those of patrician and plebeian origin, and, in both series, the metal in which they are struck is duly noted, and the degree of rarity they at present possess. Short notes are appended with reference to any remarkable coins, and in all cases, the dates of births and deaths are given, so far as history has recorded them.

Such lists will, we believe, be found of the greatest use to any one who shall be collecting Roman coins, as they give all that can be really required, short of an elaborate and complete history.

We may add, that the reader will find at the end of the volume some clear and valuable notes on mint-marks, a subject to which it is well known that Mr. de Salis has recently paid great attention. Much confusion has long existed on this subject, especially in the coins of the Later Empire, and we rejoice that Mr. Madden has put in print a carefully revised statement of what has at present been made out on this subject, as this will lead those who are interested in Roman coins to make further, and, it may be, still more complete researches

Six lithographed plates accompany the volume, and add much to its practical value and utility. We may be allowed to express the hope that Mr. Madden will not stop with the Roman coins, but will proceed to the more difficult study of Greek Numismatics: he may rest assured that there is ample room for such a volume, indeed for more than one, and that collectors (not to say scholars and students) would hail with much satisfaction a condensed Handbook of Greek Numismatics, similar to the one to which we have just called attention.

MINNESPENNINGAR ÖFVER ENSKILDA SVENSKA MÄN OCH QUINNOR BESKRIFNA AF BROR EMIL HILDEBRAND. *Stockholm*, 1860. 8vo. pp. 454, with 21 plates. (Medals of Swedish private men and women.)

THE name of Hildebrand is well known to every English Numismatist in connection with his researches into our own Anglo-Saxon coinage, so that any work produced by his pen is deserving of notice in these pages. That now before us is a catalogue, chronologically arranged, of all the medals struck in honour of illustrious Swedes, of both sexes, from the days of Birger Magnusson, Earl of Bialbo, and Regent of Sweden in 1252, to those of the Swedish nightingale, Jenny Lind. Though professedly including only the medals of private individuals, there are many among them of the regents of the kingdom, and of some who, like Gustavus Vasa, afterwards ascended the throne. It must, however, be confessed that the majority of the names of those whose memory has been perpetuated by this series of medals are but little known to English readers. There are, however, beside such historical names as Oxenstierna, others of world-wide fame to be found in this catalogue—Berzelius, Swedenborg, Scheele, Puffendorf, Linnæus, as well as some of numismatic note, such as Brenner, Keder, and Hedlinger. It is also curious that among those in whose honour medals have been struck in Sweden are many whose names testify to their English or Scotch descent, and to the connection that has subsisted between this country and Sweden. A Jennings, Hamilton, Ramsay, Bancks, McLean, Murray, Innes, Stuart, or Sheldon might claim a place in a catalogue of British medals should such be ever attempted, though also rightfully inserted in M. Hildebrand's list. Nothing can exceed the care with which this seems to have been compiled. Not only are the descriptions fully detailed, and the size of the medal and the engraver's name given, but the date, the occasion, and the place of striking are also mentioned in all instances where they could be ascertained. In the case of posthumous medals, such information is in the highest degree necessary, though not unfrequently omitted by medallic writers.

The first (January and February) of the *Revue Numismatique* for 1861 has the following papers:—

1. Conclusion of Mr. Waddington's Étude de Numismatique Asiatique.

In the second portion of this valuable essay Mr. Waddington has shown that there are coins of Datames struck at Sinope, and of Ariarathes I., struck at the same town and at Gaziura. He has also assigned strong reasons for attributing certain coins, hitherto classed to a King of Citium, to a Syrian dynast, bearing the name Aba-Hadad, and probably having Hierapolis for his capital. Perhaps the most interesting of the new results here published, is the attribution to Artaxerxes Mnemon of the famous coin in the British Museum, bearing the inscription ΒΑΣΙΛ, and two others with the same portrait, one in the Hunter collection, and the other in that of Lieut.-Gen. Fox. The first of these coins was conjectured by M. Lenormant to be of Cyrus the Younger, but Mr. Waddington has shown that there can be no doubt that this and the other two are of his brother Artaxerxes. The general conclusions are of great importance, and the whole paper requires to be carefully studied by all interested in this curious branch of ancient numismatics.

2. "On some unpublished Byzantine bullæ in the Louvre," by M. E. Miller.

3. "Description of the Merovingian coins of Limousin," (seventh article), by M. Max. Deloche.

4. "On some rare and unpublished coins of Provence in the Bibliothèque of Marseilles," by M. A. Carpentin.

5. "Attribution to the Emperor Henry VI. of an unedited 'Augustale,'" by M. Huillard-Bréholles.

In the *Nécrologie* is a tribute of respect to M. A. Bigot.

The second number (March and April) of the *Revue Numismatique* for 1861 has as follows:—

1. Letter XII. of M. de Saulcy, addressed to M. A. de Longpérier, on the "Numismatique Gauloise," being a most interesting essay on the attribution of certain coins to the Ædui.

2. "On some unpublished imperial Roman, Greek, and colonial coins," by M. J. Sabatier.

Among the most remarkable of the pieces is a bronze medallion of Antoninus Pius, with Diana on the reverse, holding a stag by the horns. Though bearing Latin inscriptions, it is considered to be of Asiatic, and probably Ephesian, mintage.

The following articles are in the 1ère livraison of the *Revue Numismatique Belge* for 1861:—

1. Letter to M. Chalon, "On some unpublished Roman coins of the collection of the late Octave Fontana, of Trieste," from M. J. Sabatier.

We do not quite agree with M. Sabatier on his attribution of the small piece bearing on the reverse the letter K. (Pl. ii. No. 9), which is very similar in fabric to the coins of the Vandal kings, and seems more likely to belong to Karthage than Constantinople. As to the other pieces bearing the K. (Nos. 4, 5, 6)—which M. Sabatier seems to attribute to Fausta, and to explain by Konstantinopolis (an attribution which is impossible: first, from the fact that Fausta died in 327, and Constantinople was not dedicated till 330; and second, because the letter K is never used as the initial of Constantinople on *coins* at that time nor at any other)—we think that they are evidently copied from coins of the Constantine period, and represent, No. 5, Helena, Nos. 4 and 6, though the latter is rather youthful, Constantine the Great. If we may hazard a supposition on the origin of these "small pieces," which, according to us, also belong to the period of Justinian, we should say that this latter emperor, perhaps on the dedication of St. Sophia, or on some other occasion, thought proper to commemorate the first Christian emperor, the founder of Constantinople, and Helena his mother, both of whom were held in the highest reverence by the Greek Church. Such restorations were not unusual in the Upper Empire; and we find, not only Augustus, but several of his successors commemorated by later emperors. K may be the initial of Konstantine, or Konstantinople (?), and if the latter, is the only example, and these "small pieces" were struck to distribute among the Greek local population. C is always the initial on *coins*. The small piece, No. 7, with reverse P, of which we have a specimen in the British Museum, probably belongs also to the time of Justinian, and if it does, the letter P would signify 100. The British Museum possesses coins of that emperor with CN. (250), PKE. (125), and PK. (120), which last was equal to three of the large copper coins marked M. (40.)

2. Second letter to M. Soret, "On some unedited Cufic coins," from M. le Général de Bartholomæi.

3. "On an imitation of a Belgian coin made by Le Comte Palatin de Simmeren et de Deux-Ponts," by M. Chalon.

4. "Documents pour servir à l'histoire des monnaies," by M. de la Fons-Mélicocq.

5 "Monetary history of Liége," an unedited document, by M. Ferd. Henaux.

6. Letter to M. Chalon, "On a jetton of Liége," from M. Dumont.

MISCELLANEA.

THE FIND OF COINS NEAR FROME.—In addition to the Roman coins described (p. 8) as having been found in company with a number of British coins at Nunney, near Frome, there was discovered at the same time a denarius of Caligula. This coin, which is in a fair state of preservation bears on the obverse the laureate head of Caligula, to the right, with the legend; C. CÆSAR . AVG . GERM . P . M . TR . POT., and on the reverse, the radiate head of Augustus, to the right, with DIVVS . AVG . PATER . PATRIAE. Its date is probably A.D. 37, or some six or seven years before the invasion of Claudius. For our knowledge of the discovery of this coin we are indebted to Mr. Singer, of Frome.

SALE OF COINS, 18TH-20TH MARCH, 1861.—The choice collection of coins formed by the late W. Waring Hay Newton, Esq., of Newton Hall, Haddington, and also the cabinet of Monsieur De Carnéieff, of St. Petersburg, have been dispersed under the hammer of Messrs. Sotheby and Wilkinson. The following lots are selected as the more important. Lot 14. Syracuse, Æ, size 10, decadrachm, or medallion. A fine specimen.—£10 10s. Lot. 41. Seleucus II., Callinicus, Æ, size 8; obv., Diademed head, to right; rev., Apollo, standing, leaning on a tripod, holding an arrow; in the field are two monograms. Very fine and rare—£5 2s. 6d. Lot. 46. Alexander II., Zebina, Æ, size 8; rev., Zeus-Nicephorus, seated, a star and Δ under the throne.

A very fine specimen, formerly in the Thomas and Northwick collections—£5 2s. 6d. Lot 49. Tigranes, Æ, size 7, obv., head of Tigranes; rev., Antioch, seated on the rock Silpius, with her right foot resting on the river-god Orontes—£4. Lot 68. Augustus and Agrippa, 2 Æ: rev. COL(onia) NEM(ausus), crocodile, chained to a palm-tree. A perfect specimen, and finely patinated—£2. Lot 70. Nero, 2 Æ; rev., MAC(ellum) AVG(usti), the macellum, with an armed figure standing under the gateway. A perfect specimen, and finely patinated—£5. Lot 71. Nero, 2 Æ; rev., PONTIF. MAX., &c.; the emperor, personating Apollo. Extremely fine—£2 2s. Lot 79. Galba, 1 Æ; rev., ROMA in the exergue. Rome, seated, to left. Extremely fine, and patinated—£3 3s. Lot 85. Antoninus Pius, 1 Æ.; rev., LIBERALITAS . AVG . IIII . COS . IIII.; the emperor, seated on an estrade, attended by the prefect of the prætorium and Liberality, distributing largess to a person standing on the ground. Extremely fine; from the Northwick collection—£4. Lot 96. Alexander the Great, a contorniate; rev., Circus Maximus, with chariot, obelisk, metæ, &c.—£3 13s. 6d. Lot 124. Vespasian, medallion, Æ, of Antiocheia ad Orontem; rev., ΕΤΟΥC . ΝΕΟΥ . ΙΕΡΟΥ . Δ.. (regnal year 4 = A.D. 72); an eagle on an ornamented altar, holding a caduceus in its beak, and a palm-branch in its claw. Extremely fine, from the Northwick collection—£4 10s. Lot 128. Tiberius and Augustus, N; obv., TI . CAESAR . DIVI . AVG . F . AVGVSTVS; laureate head of Tiberius, to right: rev, DIVOS . AVGVST . DIVI . F. laureate head of Augustus, to right; above, a star. Very fine - £6 6s. Lot 156. Oliver Cromwell broad, 1656, by Simon—£5. Lot 171. Mary Queen of Scots, testoon, 1561, with portrait; rev. SALVVM . FAC., &c. Very fine and rare—£7 12s. 6d. Lot 172. Mary, testoon, 1561, as before, and equally fine—£7 15s. Lot 173. Mary, half testoon, 1562. Extremely rare and fine—£9 5s. Lot 187. Mary, écu; rev. CRUCIS . ARMA, &c.; short broad cross, with foliated ends, a thistle in each angle; lion, 1553; rev. DILIGITE, &c., Maria Regina, in cypher, crowned, between two cinquefoils. Both very fine—£6. Lot 189. Mary, half ryal, 1555, with portrait; rev., JUSTUS . FIDE . VIVIT, arms of Scotland, crowned. Extremely rare and fine—£9 2s. 6d. Lot 190. James VI., hat piece, M.M. cinquefoil; king's bust, with high-crowned hat, to right; behind, a thistlehead; rev., TE . SOLVM . VEREOR, 1593, lion sejant, crowned, pointing a sceptre to the word Jehovah, in Hebrew letters. Very fine and rare—£5. Lot 269. Olbia. Æ, size 11, head of Medusa; rev., OAB, an eagle alighting on a fish. Very fine, and rare—£2 3s. Lot 282. Tarentnm, N, size 3½, laureated head of Jupiter, to left, behind, N.; rev.,

MISCELLANEA.

ΤΑΡΑΝΤΙΝΩΝ, an eagle, with expanded wings, perched on a thunderbolt; in the field are two vases. Extremely rare and fine—£13 5s. Lot 283. Tarentum, N, size $2\frac{1}{2}$; obv., ΤΑΡΑΝ-ΤΙΝΩΝ, a diademed female head, to right; rev. ΤΑΡΑΣ, the river-god, Taras, astride a dolphin. Very fine, and very rare—£5 2s. 6d. Lot 295. Catana, Æ, size $7\frac{1}{2}$; ΚΑΤΑΝΑΙΟΝ, head of Apollo, to left, the hair short, and fastened by a trifoliate wreath; rev., charioteer conducting a biga, to right, and without the Victory over the horses. An unusually well-spread specimen, and very fine—£4 4s. Lot 300 Naxos, Æ, size 8, head of Bacchus, crowned with ivy, with a long flowing beard, to right, and the back hair bound in a knot; rev., ΝΑΧΙΟΝ, old Silenus, seated, holding a cantharus in his right hand—£6 12s. 6d. Lot. 311. Chersonesus Tauricæ, Æ, size 4, turreted head of Diana, to right, with her usual attributes; rev., ΧΕΡ, stag, to right; below, ΜΟΙΡΙΟΣ. Extremely fine; not in Mionnet—£8. Lot 320. Aenus, Æ, size 2; head of Mercury, three-quarter face, with petasus; rev., ΑΙΝΙ, goat, walking, to right. A charming little coin—£5 2s. 6d. Lot 330. Amphipolis, Æ, size 3; laureate head of Apollo, three-quarter face; rev., ΑΜΦΙΠΟΛΙΤΕΩΝ on a raised square, surrounding a burning lamp. Of great rarity, and unusually fine—£7 7s. Lot 331. Orthagoria, Æ, size 5; head of Diana, to right; behind, a quiver; rev. ΟΡΘΑΓΟΡΕΩΝ, a helmet, with cheek pieces, surmounted by a star; beneath, ΗΓ, in monogram. Of great rarity, and a fine specimen—£8. The Northwick specimen sold for £33. Lot. 354. Damastium, Æ, size $6\frac{1}{2}$; head of Apollo, to left; rev., ΗΡΑΚΛΕΙΔ.ΚΗ, a tripod and sacrificial knife on a base; the five first letters of the legend on the front of the base. Extremely rare, and in good condition—£7. Lot 369. Phanagoria, Cimmerian Bosphorus, Æ, size $3\frac{1}{2}$, laureate head of Apollo; rev., ΦΑΝΑΓΟΡΙΤΩΝ, in two lines divided by a thyrsus, ornamented with bandelets. Extremely fine—£11 11s. Lot 373. Rhœmetalces, N, size 4, of the year ΒΑΥ $=$ 432. Very fine and rare—£5 15s. Lot 374. Rhœmetalces, N, size 4, of the year ΑΜΥ $=$ 441. Very fine and rare—£5 2s. 6d. Lot 375. Eupator, N, size 4; rev., heads of Lucius Verus and Commodus, facing, of the year ΘΝΥ $=$ 459. Very rare and fine —£5 2s. 6d. Lot 378. Sauromates IV., N, size 4; rev. laureate head of Severus; of the year ΒϘΥ $=$ 492. Extremely fine and rare—£5. Lot 388. Cyzicus, N, size 4; Ajax on one knee, to left, with a helmet in his right hand and a short sword in his left; below, a tunny-fish; rev., a deep square indentation of four compartments. An extremely rare and fine Distater — £11. Lot 389. Cyzicus, the Distater, N, size 3 by 4; head of Hercules, to right; underneath, a tunny-fish or a grain of corn; rev., QUAD.INCVS. Very rare and fine—£11 5s. Lot 401.

Maussolus, King of Caria, Æ, size 7; head of Apollo, three-quarter face, having the laurel crown fastened under the chin; rev., ΜΑΥΣΣΩΛΛΟ, Jupiter-Labradæus, walking, to right, with a long spear in his left hand, and a bipennis over his right shoulder. A brilliant specimen—£16. Lot 402. Cos, insula, Æ, size 6; ΚΟΣ, a nude dancing Apollo, performing on the timbrel in front of a tripod; rev., a crab in the centre of four triangular indentations. A finer specimen than usually met with— £5 12s. 6d. Lot 404. Perekle, Lycia, Æ, size 2½ by 3½; lion's scalp, front face; rev. ΓIPEKΛi, and a triple grapnel. Extremely rare, and very fine—£12. Lot 416. Artavasdes, King of Armenia, Æ, size 3½; head, with the usual tiara; rev., ΒΑΣΙΛΕΩΣ. ΒΑΣΙΛΕΩΝ. ΑΡΤΑΥΑΣΔ.., a figure conducting a quadriga at full speed, to left—£5 5s. Lot 441. The shekel of Simon Maccabæus, Æ, size 5½, wt. 213 grs., of the usual type, and of the year 2. Extremely rare, and very fine—£8. Lot 453. Varahan II., N, size 4½; heads of the king and his queen, side by side, with that of their son facing them. Of the highest degree of rarity, and very fine; wt. 113 grs.—£13. Lot 467. Ptolemy Soter, N, size 6; the pentadrachm, of the usual type—£6 12s. 6d. Lot 468. Arsinoe Philadelphi, N, size 8; the octodrachm, of the usual type—£6 6s. Lot 469. Ptolemy III., Evergetes, N, size 7½; the octodrachm, ΘΕΩΝ, heads of Ptolemy Soter and Berenice; rev., ΑΔΕΛΦΩΝ, heads of Ptolemy Philadelphus and Arsenoe. Fine—£13. Lot 472. Ptolemy V., Epiphanes, N, size 7; diademed head, to right, with an ear of corn on the diadem; type of Mt. Supp. pl. iv. No. 5, but with Δ. in the field and ΝΙ between the legs of the eagle on the thunderbolt, to the left. Of the utmost degree of rarity, but only in fair preservation—£9 9s. Lot 474. Ptolemy VIII., Epiphanes, N, size 7½; bust, to right, with radiated diadem and chlamys; rev., cornucopia, with tæniæ, the mouth surrounded with a radiate semicircle; in the field ΔΙ. Extremely rare and fine—£12 12s. Lot 476. Cyrene, N, size 4; ΚΥΡΑΝΑΙ, Victory, conducting a quadriga, to right; rev., [Γ]ΟΛΙΑΝΘΕΥΣ, Jupiter, standing, to left, in the pallium, and holding a patera in his right hand over an altar of a peculiar form. Extremely rare—£5 2s. 6d. Lot 477. Cyrene, N, size 4½; female, conducting a quadriga, to right; above, a star; rev., Jupiter Aëtophorus, seated, to left, holding a sceptre in his right hand and resting his left arm on the back of the throne; behind, an eagle, perched on the lituus—£7. Lot 478. Hesperides (later, Berenice) Cyrenaica, Æ, size 3; Ε[Υ]ΕΣ, in the angles of a sunk square, in the centre of the head of Jupiter-Ammon, to right, within a circle; rev., Silphian plant. Of the utmost rarity, and in fine condition—£8.

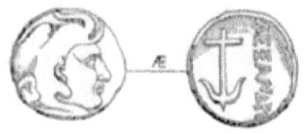

XVIII.

ON A COPPER COIN OF THE CLASS STRUCK AFTER THE DEATH OF ALEXANDER THE GREAT, BY HIS GENERALS, BEFORE THEY ASSUMED REGAL TITLES.

[Read before the Numismatic Society, April 25, 1861.]

THE British Museum has recently acquired a coin which I believe to be entirely new, and of no small importance for the classification of the money struck during the interval between the death of Alexander the Great, B.C. 323, and the assumption of regal titles by the generals, B.C. 306.

It may be thus described :—

> *Obv.*—Young male head to the right, with the horn of Ammon (?) clothed in the skin of an elephant's head.
>
> *Rev.*—[A]ΛΕΞΑΝΔΡΟ[Υ]   Anchor.   Æ, 2½.

This coin was brought from Persia by M. Richard,

interpreter to the Sháh, and purchased of Mr. Webster for the Museum.

The type of the obverse, it is well known, has been assigned with great reason to the younger Alexander, the son of Roxana, by M. Pinder, who supposes the tetradrachms which bear it to have been struck in Egypt by Ptolemy. He mentions a rare copper coin with the same obverse-type, and, on the reverse, ΑΛΕΞΑΝΔΡΟΥ and the type of the staters of Alexander the Great, Victory with the crown and vexillum. Of this coin the Museum possesses four examples, one of which was found at Hamadán, the ancient Ecbatana. In the late Mr. Burgon's opinion, these pieces are always from the far East. Our new coin, from its style, fabric, and size, belongs to the same class. Its remarkable peculiarity is the reverse-type, the anchor, the famous badge of Seleucus. It was, therefore, struck by Seleucus before his assumption of the regal title, and the Alexander, whose name it bears, can only be Alexander the Great, or his son of the same name. M. Pinder's arguments that the tetradrachms with the same head must have been struck by Ptolemy for the younger Alexander, are so weighty, that it seems almost certain that this is the proper type of that sovereign, and if so, Seleucus is shown by this coin to have struck money in the name of Alexander in the same manner as did Ptolemy.

The only difficulty attendant on this explanation is, that it seems strange that the reign of Alexander Ægus should be commemorated by so insignificant a coinage of Seleucus, whereas Ptolemy issued important and well-executed coins. The reply to this is, that the memory of Alexander, the deliverer from the Persians, was greatly cherished in Egypt, and the hieroglyphic inscriptions show that Ptolemy there governed only in the name of his representatives while they lived.[1] Seleucus may have less strongly acknowledged what was but a nominal supremacy, and the large issue of money by Alexander in further Asia, may have rendered any subsequent coinage in the precious metals unnecessary for several years.

REGINALD STUART POOLE.

---

[1] I am of opinion that the copper coins hitherto ascribed to Ptolemy of Epirus, are of Ptolemy I. of Egypt: if so, we have some, with the name Ptolemy alone,—probably issued at Paphos, for they bear what may be the head of the Paphian Venus (comp. the remarkable coin in the Bank, Borrell, *H. P. Rois de Chypre*, p. 68, seqq. fig. xvi.), and Ptolemy afterwards had a mint there,—as well as others, like the tetradrachms which M. Pinder assigns to Alexander Ægus, with the title king, which would be his earliest coinage as king. The former would, if rightly attributed, have been issued by Ptolemy, in his own name, in Cyprus, while he struck in the names of Philip and of the younger Alexander in Egypt, unless, indeed, it was struck between the death of the latter (311), and the assumption of the regal title by Ptolemy (306). (See M. Pinder's paper in the Beiträge zur Älteren Münzkunde, i. p. 194, seqq. pl. viii. Die Aera des Philippus und die ersten Königsmünzen Aegyptens.)

XIX.

ON A HOARD OF COINS DISCOVERED AT HOUNSLOW.

I HAVE been permitted to examine a hoard of coins recently discovered at Hounslow, upon the premises of Mr. Gibson. They consist of two hundred and ninety coins, all groats, with one single exception, and eighty-six pieces of Charles the Bold, Duke of Burgundy, all likewise of the groat size. The English coins are as follows:—

			Specimens.
Henry V. or VI., struck at Calais; an annulet between the pellets in two quarters of the reverse. Ruding, pl. iv. No. 9. (Both very much worn and clipped.)			2
Edward IV., 2nd coinage.	London mint		182
,,	,,	York ,,	32
,,	,,	Bristol ,,	4
,,	,,	Norwich ,,	3
,,	,,	Coventry ,,	1
,,	,,	Dublin ,,	1
,,	,,	London ,, (a half groat)	1
Richard III.	London mint		19
Henry VII. 1st coinage, with open crown. Hawkins, No. 361-2			12
,,	2nd coinage, with arched crown		33
			290
Charles the Bold, Duke of Burgundy. 1466-1477			86
		Total	376

Among the whole mass there is not a single specimen in fine preservation. Many, indeed, are so oxidized and decayed, that the attribution is hardly certain, and the mint-mark not discernible.

The mint-marks on the London groats of Edward IV. are the coronet, annulet, pierced cross (in some instances with a pellet to the right; in others to the left), sun, rose, and heraldic cinquefoil; those with coronet being much more numerous than the others. One of the specimens with the annulet mint-mark has a full-blown rose at each side of the neck; two or three have a rose or cinquefoil on the breast, and one has the letter *C* or *a*; that is, a Coventry or York obverse has been used with a London reverse. The half groat is of the London mint, and has a cross for mint-mark. The whole of these pieces are of the light coinage, subsequent to his third year.

The York groats have the usual mint-marks of lis and sun; those of Bristol, sun and crown; the Coventry specimen, the sun; the Norwich are all so much defaced that the mint-mark is not visible, as is the case with many of York also.

The groats of Richard III. are all of the London mint. The mint-marks are the boar's head, and the united rose and sun. No specimen occurs which combines the two mint-marks on obverse and reverse.

The pieces of Henry VII. offer no peculiarity, and some of the early ones are so decayed as to be barely legible. It is somewhat remarkable that all those with the arched crown (so far as the mint-mark can be made out) have the same mint-mark—the heraldic cinquefoil. The crown has in all the double arch.

The result of this discovery is fully to confirm—if confirmation were required—the attribution which has of late years been made, of certain of the pieces with the open crown, bearing the name of Henry, to the first coinage of Henry VII. Of the twelve specimens of this class, the type is exactly like that of the pieces of Richard III.; they all read HENRIC.; and none of them will turn the scale at 48 grs. If they were of Henry VI., they must all have been struck during the few months of his restoration in 1470-1, which is very improbable; and, moreover, they differ, both in the type of the head and in the legend, from those scarce specimens reading HENRICV., which, from their weight being at the rate of 12 grs. to the penny, like the coins of Edward IV. subsequent to his third year, and from their type resembling that of the coins of Edward IV. rather than those of Richard III., must necessarily be attributed to Henry VI. during his short restoration. The specimens in the hoard under consideration, on the other hand, resemble in type the groats of Richard III., but not those of Henry VI. or Edward IV., and, by parity of reasoning, must be assigned to Henry VII.

Another inference to be drawn from an examination of the hoard, is the remarkable celerity with which the coinage disappeared from circulation. Setting aside the two Calais groats, the earliest coin in the parcel could not have been struck before the year 1464, the fourth year of Edward IV., and none can be later than 1502, the eighteenth year of Henry VII., when he adopted the profile portrait on his coinage. It is, indeed, probable that the latest coins are several years earlier than that date, because all the arched-crown groats have the same mint-mark, and it is therefore fair to presume that they are of the earliest issue of the type. It appears, therefore, that in a hoard containing silver to the value of between £6 and £7 of the period, equal to about £100 at the present day, there were only two coins which could by possibility have been much above thirty years old, and probably were not above twenty. If a hoard of a hundred pounds' worth of silver, concealed at the present day, should hereafter be discovered, it is more than probable that it would contain many pieces of 1816, and would be limited to that date only because everything of a prior coinage was then called in. We therefore see that in those early days, notwithstanding the small facilities for circulation as compared with those of the present time, one coinage replaced another more rapidly than it does now.

The large proportion of Burgundian coins comprised in the find is also a noticeable circumstance, and leads to the conjecture that the parcel may have belonged to some unfortunate adherent of Perkin Warbeck, who was countenanced by the House of Burgundy, and whose conspiracies against Henry VII. caused that monarch so much uneasiness from 1491 to 1499.

J. B. BERGNE.

XX.

ON THE ANGLO-HANOVERIAN COPPER COINAGE.

On the 1st of August, in the year 1714, George Lewis, the Elector of Hanover, ascended the throne of the United Kingdom; and, as nothing in the Act of Succession precluded his retaining his Electoral dominions, Hanover, save during a short period at the commencement of the present century, formed a part of the British empire from the date above given to the accession of the present Queen. In Hanover, the Salic law prevailed; and the death of William IV., therefore, terminated an union which had proved at all times expensive, and frequently disastrous, to England, however advantageous it may have been to Hanover.

The copper coinage of Hanover, during the reigns over England of the princes of the house of Brunswick, comes, therefore, within the province of British Numismatics; though no detailed account of it is at present accessible to the English reader.

The coins present no great variety of types; and, till the year 1814, were struck at two mints only—Clausthal and Zellerfeld. Since the year 1789, the mint at the latter town has been abandoned; and, in 1814, the town of Hanover was enriched with a mint, which has been in full activity ever since.

As most, indeed nearly all, the Hanoverian coins have the initials of the mint-master, it will be necessary to give the names of these functionaries, during the period of the English rule:—

I. CLAUSTHAL.

  I. Christian Philipp Spangenberg, A.D. 1723 to 1751.
  Vacancy from 1751 to 1753.
  II. Johann Wilhelm Schlemm, A.D. 1753 to 1788.
  Vacancy from 1788 to 1792.
  III. Philipp Ludwig Magius, A.D. 1792 to 1800.
  Vacancy from 1800 to 1802.
  IV. Georg. Friedrich Michaelis, A.D. 1802 to 1807.
  V. Johann Wilhelm Lunde, *mint-director*, A.D. 1807 to 1819.
  Vacancy, 1819 to 1821.
  VI. Wilhelm August. Julius Albert, *administrator*, A.D. 1821 to 1838.

II. ZELLERFELD.

  I. Ernst Peter Hecht, *mint-master*, A.D. 1723 to 1731.
  II. Johann Albrecht Brauns, A.D. 1731 to 1739.
  III. Johann Benjamin Hecht, A.D. 1739 to 1763.
  IV. Johann Anton Pfeffer, A.D. 1763 to 1773.
  V. Ludwig Christian Ruperti, A.D. 1773 to 1778.
  Vacancy from 1778 to 1780.
  VI. Christof. Engelhard Seidensticker, A.D. 1780 to 1785.
  Vacancy from 1785 to 1789.

III. HANOVER.

  I. Christian Heinrich Haase, *mint-director*, A.D. 1814 to 1818.
  II. Ludwig August. Brüel, A.D. 1818 to 1838.

The copper struck at Clausthal was brought from that part of the Hartz district which belonged solely to the Electoral house of Hanover. This mint ceased working in the year 1849; and, since that period, Hanover alone has had the privilege of coining money.

The Clausthal coins bear, on the obverse, the crowned cypher of the sovereign, and, on the reverse, the value of the coin and the date; but, when the copper was brought from the mine at Andreasberg, then, in lieu of the crowned cypher, appears the figure of St. Andrew bearing his cross.

The coins of Zellerfeld were struck from copper, the product of that part of the Hartz district which was held in common by the Electoral house of Hanover and the Ducal house of Brunswick Wolfen-büttel. Of this, three-fifths belonged to the former, and two-fifths to the latter.

The coins bear, on the obverse, the wild man; and, on the reverse, the value of the coin, with the date. The wild man holds in his hand a fir-tree, with branches on the right side only. The coins of Brunswick Wolfen-büttel bear the same wild man, but he holds the fir-tree in his left hand, and the branches are on both sides. After 1789, when the business of the Zellerfeld mint was transferred to Clausthal, the Hanoverian wild man bore his fir-tree with branches on both sides.

It is to be noticed that on some of the coins struck at Clausthal and Zellerfeld the letter C. appears. This signifies "*commission;*" and it will be found to occur only during those years in which there was a vacancy in the office of mint-master, or director, and the duties of that office were performed by a commission. After the year 1834, this letter C. is replaced by A.; and the new initial signifies "*administration.*"

We shall now proceed to describe the coins struck in the three mints of Clausthal, Zellerfeld, and Hanover.

GEORGE LEWIS, ELECTOR—GEORGE I., KING OF ENGLAND.

Coins with the Royal Cypher.
Pieces of 1½ Pfennings.

1. *Obv.*—Under the crown of England, G.L.R. in monogram.

Rev.—1½ | Pfenning | Scheide | Muntz | 1718 | In five lines. On each side of the 1½, and under the date, a quatrefoil of clover leaves. Weight, 66 grs.
2. Similar to the foregoing, but stars instead of clover crosses by the 1½; nothing under the date.
3. Similar; but with a star under the date.
4. Similar to No. 1, but two dots after Muntz.   1721.
5. Similar, with date, 1722.

Pfennings.

6. *Obv.*—G. R., crowned.
   Rev.—1 | Pfenning | Scheide | Muntz | 1717 | Two clover crosses, one on each side the numeral; under the date, a rosette of six leaves. Weight, 50 grs.
7. *Obv.*—As before; no dot after Muntz.
8. *Obv.* and *Rev.*—As No. 6; but date, 1719.
9. *Obv.* and *Rev.*—Stars, instead of clover crosses, 1722.
10. *Obv.* and *Rev.*—Like the last; but a rosette under the date.
11. *Obv.*—G. R., crowned; underneath, H. C. B.
    Rev.—1 | Pfenning | Scheide | Muntz | 1723 | A four-leaved rose on each side of the numeral, and a rosette under date.

Coins with the Figure of St. Andrew.

12. *Obv.*—The saint, with a glory round his head, clothed in flowing robes; behind him, a large cross, which he holds with his left arm.
    Rev.—1 | Pfenning | Scheide | Muntz | 1725 | A star of seven rays on each side of the numeral.
13. *Obv.* and *Rev.*—Like the preceding; date 1726.
14. *Obv.* and *Rev.*—Similar; roses, instead of stars.

Coins with the Wild Man.

15. *Obv.*—A wild, bearded man, the head crowned with leaves, holding, in his right hand, a fir-tree, with three branches to the right, his left hand on his side; on the ground, several small trees. In the exergue, E. P. H.

    Rev.—1 | Pfenning | Scheide | Muntz | 1724 | A clover cross on each side the II.

16. *Obv.* and *Rev.*—Same, 1725.

17. *Obv.* and *Rev.*—Same, 1726.

GEORGE AUGUSTUS—GEORGE II., OF ENGLAND.

Pieces of 1½ Pfennings.

1. *Obv.*—G. R. in cypher, crowned; under it, S.
   Rev.—1½ | Pfenning | Scheide | Muntz | 1750.
2. *Obv.* and *Rev.*—Similar; but V instead of U, in Muntz.

Pfennings.

3. *Obv.*—Royal cypher, crowned; underneath, C. P. S.
   Rev.—1 | Pfenning | Scheide | Muntz | 1729 | Clover crosses on each side of numeral.
4. *Obv.*—As usual; no moneyer's initials.
   Rev.— Do. six-leaved roses, instead of clover crosses   1732
5. *Obv.* and *Rev.*—As usual; stars of six rays   1733
6. Do. do. do. C. P. S.   1734
7. Do. do. do. do. clover crosses   1734
8. Do. do. do. stars of six rays   1736
9. Do. do. do. do. do.   1739
10. Do. do. do. a round rose under date   1740
11. Do. do. do. C. P. S., round roses   1741

12.	*Obv.* and *Rev.*—As usual; S., stars of six rays				1742
13.	Do.	do.	do.	round roses	1743
14.	Do.	do.	do.	C.P.S., stars of six rays	1744
15.	Do.	do.	do.	clover crosses	1745
16.	Do.	do.	do.	C.P.S., clover crosses	1745
17.	Do.	do.	do.	stars of six rays	1745
18.	Do.	do.	do.	clover crosses	1746
19.	Do.	do.	do.	stars of six rays	1747
20.	Do.	do.	do.	clover crosses; under date, a rosette	1748
21.	Do.	do.	do.	clover crosses	1749
22.	Do.	do.	do.	I.W.S., clover crosses	1753
23.	Do.	do.	do.	S. star of six rays	1753
24.	Do.	do.	do.	stars of six points	1753
25.	Do.	do.	do.	I. W. S., rosettes of five leaves	1753
26.	Do.	do.	do.	clover crosses	1754
27.	Do.	do.	do.	S.	1754
28.	Do.	do.	do.	I.W. S., clover crosses on each side of moneyer's name, as well as on the reverse	1754
29.	Do.	do.	do.	clover crosses	1755
30.	Do.	do.	do.	clover crosses	1756
31.	Do.	do.	do.	I. W. S., rosettes of five leaves	1757
32.	Do.	do.	do.	do. no stars nor rosettes	1758
33.	Do.	do.	do.	do. do.	1759

COINS BEARING THE IMAGE OF ST. ANDREW.

34.	*Obv.*—Figure of St. Andrew, bearing his cross. *Rev.*—As usual; clover crosses				1729
35.	*Obv.* and *Rev.*—As usual; roses of six leaves				1732
36.	Do.	do.	do.	stars of six points	1734
37.	Do.	do.	do.	do. do. do.	1739

Coins bearing the Wild Man.

38. *Obv.*—The wild man as usual, holding, in his right hand, the fir-tree, with branches on both sides; beneath, C. P. S.

Rev.—As usual; no date; stars of six points.

39.	*Obv.* and *Rev.*—As usual; I. A. B.; clover crosses					1732
40.	Do.	do.	do	do.	do.	do.	1737
41.	Do.	do.	do.	I. B. H.			1741
42.	Do.	do.	do.	do.			1742
43.	Do.	do.	do.	do.			1743
44.	Do.	do.	do.	do.			1745
45.	Do.	do.	do.	do.			1747
46.	Do.	do.	do.	do.			1749
47.	Do.	do.	do.	do.			1752
48.	Do.	do.	do.	do.			1754
49.	Do.	do.	do.	do.			1755
50.	Do.	do.	do.	do.			1756
51.	Do.	do.	do.	do.			1758

52. Do.   do.   do.   do.   under the date, a rose, with five triangular leaves   1759

53. *Obv.* and *Rev.*—As usual; I. B. H.; under the date, a rose, as No. 52   1760

These coins spell the word Muntz, sometimes with V, sometimes with U.

GEORGE WILLIAM—GEORGE III. OF ENGLAND.

The coins struck in Hanover, during this long reign, may be divided into three classes. Those struck by George III., as Elector, those struck by the authority of the King of Westphalia, from 1807 to 1814, and those struck by George III., as king, from 1814 to 1820.

The second class will not come under our notice.

The early Hanoverian coins of George III. resemble those of his grandfather and great-grandfather.

It appears that coins of a larger denomination were required than had hitherto been current, and George III., therefore, struck pieces of four pfennings, and of two pfennings, weighing, respectively, 200 and 100 grains. They are, however, generally deficient from 10 to 15 grains in the four-pfenning piece, and from 5 to 10 in the piece of two-pfennings. One fine example in my own cabinet weighs 190 grains. These coins are found of all the three types.

Coins with the Cypher.

Pieces of four Pfennings.

1. *Obv.*—The royal cypher crowned, as usual; under it, P. L. M.
   Rev.—4 | Pfenning | Scheide | Muntz | 1794

2. *Obv.* and *Rev.*—As usual   1795
3. do.   do.   do.   1796

Pieces of two Pfennings.

4. *Obv.* and *Rev.*—As usual   1794
5. do.   do.   do.   1796
6. do.   do.   do.   1797
7. do.   do.   do.   1798
8. do.   do.   do.   1799
9. do.   do.   do.   1800
10. do. do.   do.   1800
11. do. do.   do.   C.   1801
12. do. do.   do.   G. F. M.   1802
13. do. do.   do.   1803
14. do. do.   do.   1804
15. do. do.   do.   1807

16. *Obv.* and *Rev.*—As usual; under the cypher,
the date, five-leaved roses on each
side the numeral on the reverse   1817
17. do.   do.   As usual   1818

PIECES OF 1½ PFENNINGS.

18. *Obv.* and *Rev.*—As usual; C.   1792
19. do.   do.   do.   P.L.M.   1792

PFENNINGS.

All these coins, save the first, have the word Pfenning abbreviated to Pfenn., and this contraction continued to be adopted till the year 1814.

20. *Obv.* and *Rev.*—As usual; I.W.S.   1761
21. do.   do.   do.   do.   1762
22. do.   do.   do.   do.   1763
23. do.   do.   do.   do.   1764
24. do.   do.   do.   do.   1765
25. do.   do.   do.   do.   1767
26. do.   do.   do.   do.   1768
27. do.   do.   do.   do.   1769
28. do.   do.   do.   do.   1770
29. do.   do.   do.   do.   1771
30. do.   do.   do.   do.   1772
31. do.   do.   do.   do.   1773
32. do.   do.   do.   do.   1774

All these coins have I.W.S. under the cypher.

33. *Obv.* and *Rev.*— As usual; over the crown
I.W.S.   1775
34. *Obv.* and *Rev.*—As usual   1776
35. do.   do.   do.   1777
36. do.   do.   do.   1778

ON THE ANGLO-HANOVERIAN COINAGE. 153

37.	*Obv.* and *Rev.*—As usual			1779
38.	do.	do.	do.	1780
39.	do.	do.	do.	1781
40.	do.	do.	do.	1782
41.	do.	do.	do.	1783
42.	do.	do.	do.	1784
43.	do.	do.	do.	1785
44.	do.	do.	do.	1786
45.	do.	do.	do.	1787
46.	do.	do.	do.	1788
47.	do.	do.	do.	1789
48.	do.	do.	do.	1790

All these coins **have I.W.S.** over the crown. The above have slight variations in the dots after the words Pfenn. and Muntz.

49.	*Obv.* and *Rev.*—As usual			1790
50.	do.	do.	do.	1791
51.	do.	do.	do.	1792

These have **C. under the cypher.**

52.	*Obv.* and *Rev.*—As usual			1793
53.	do.	do.	do.	1794
54.	do.	do.	do.	1795
55.	do.	do.	do.	1796
56.	do.	do.	do.	1797
57.	do.	do.	do.	1798
58.	do.	do.	do.	1799
59.	do.	do.	do.	1800

These have **P.L.M.** under the cypher.

60.	*Obv.* and *Rev.*—As usual			1801
61.	do.	do.	do.	1802

These **have C. under the cypher.**

VOL. I. N.S.   X

62.	*Obv.* and *Rev.*—As usual			1802
63.	do.	do.	do.	1803
64.	do.	do.	do.	1804
65.	do.	do.	do.	1806

These have C. under the cypher.

66.	*Obv.* and *Rev.*—As usual; C.			1814
67.	do.	do.	do. H.	1814
68.	*Obv.* and *Rev.*—As usual; date under the cypher, in place of date on reverse, C.			1817
69.	*Obv.* and *Rev.*—Similar			1818
70.	do.	do.	do.	1819
71.	do.	do.	do.	1820

COINS BEARING THE FIGURE OF ST. ANDREW.
PIECES OF FOUR PFENNINGS.

72. *Obv.*—The saint as usual; underneath C.
    Rev.—4 | PFENNING | SCHEIDE | MUNTZ   1792

PFENNINGS.

73.	*Obv.* and *Rev.*—Similar, but P. L. M.			1794
74.	*Obv.*—The saint as before; in exergue I.W.S. *Rev.*—As usual			1780
75.	*Obv.* and *Rev.*—As usual			1781
76.	do.	do.	do. only S. in exergue	1782
77.	do.	do.	Similar	1783
78.	do.	do.	do.	1784
79.	do.	do.	do.	1785
80.	do.	do.	do.	1786
81.	do.	do.	do.	1787
82.	do.	do.	do.	1788
83.	do.	do.	do.	1789
84.	do.	do.	do. P. L. M.	1793

COINS WITH THE WILD MAN.

85. *Obv.* and *Rev.*—As usual; in exergue of ob-

verse I.B.H.; on reverse rosettes composed of
five triangles on each side of the numeral I. 1762

86.	*Obv.* and *Rev.*—Similar;		I. A. P.		1763
87.	do.	do.	do.		1764
88.	do.	do.	do.		1765
89.	do.	do.	do.		1766
90.	do.	do.	do.		1768
91.	do.	do.	do.		1769
92.	do.	do.	do.		1770
93.	do.	do.	do.	L. C. R.	1774
94.	do.	do.	do.		1775

The following have five-leaved roses on reverse.

95.	*Obv.* and *Rev.*—Similar			1776
96.	do.	do.	do.	1777
97.	do.	do.	do.	1778
98.	*Obv.* and *Rev.*—As usual			1780
99.	do.	do.	do.	1781
100.	do.	do.	do.	1783
101.	do.	do.	do.	1784
102.	do.	do.	do.	1785
103.	do.	do.	do.	1788

The above coins omit the smaller trees on the ground; they have C. E. S. save the last, which bears only S.

104. *Obv.* and *Rev.*—As usual; P. L. M.   1792

The following coins exhibit the fir-tree with branches on both sides.

105.	*Obv.* and *Rev.*—As usual; P. L. M.			1794
106.	do.	do.	do.	1795
107.	do.	do.	do.	1796
108.	*Obv.* and *Rev.*—As usual; G. F. M.			1804

GEORGE AUGUSTUS FREDERICK— GEORGE IV. OF ENGLAND.

The coinage of George IV. proceeded on the same principles as that of his predecessors, nor were any new types adopted. We have of this reign no coins with the wild man, nor any with the figure of St. Andrew. The monotonous royal cypher is all that remains.

Pieces of Four Pfennings.

1. *Obv.* and *Rev.*—As usual; the date under the cypher; on reverse C. 1827

Pieces of Two Pfennings.

2. *Obv.* and *Rev.*—As usual; five-leaved roses on reverse 1821

The following have no roses on the reverse by the sides of the numerals; they exhibit certain slight varieties as to points and stops.

3. *Obv.* and *Rev.*—As usual 1822
4. do. do. do. 1823
5. do. do. do. 1824
6. do. do. do. 1826
7. do. do. do. 1827
8. do. do. do. 1828
9. do. do. do. 1829
10. do. do. do. 1830

Pfennings.

These coins have five-leaved roses on the sides of the numeral on the reverse, and under the royal cypher the initial C.

11. *Obv.* and *Rev.*—As usual 1821

12.	*Obv.* and *Rev.*—As usual			1822
13.	do.	do.	do.	1823
14.	do.	do.	do.	1824
15.	do.	do.	do.	1825
16.	do.	do.	do.	1826
17.	do.	do.	do.	1827
18.	do.	do.	do.	1828
19.	do.	do.	do.	1829
20.	do.	do.	do.	1830

These have B. instead of C. on the reverse.

21.	*Obv.* and *Rev.*—As usual			1826
22.	do.	do.	do.	1828
23.	do.	do.	do.	1829
24.	do.	do.	do.	1830

WILHELM—WILLIAM IV. OF ENGLAND.

The coins of this monarch exhibit a new variety—we have, for the first time, the shield of arms, gules, a horse galloping to the right, argent; crowned by the crown of Hanover.

At the same time, the old device of the crowned cypher was continued. The cypher adopted by William IV. was somewhat more complicated than that used by his predecessors; it consisted of W. interlaced with two R's.

COINS WITH THE CYPHER.
PIECES OF FOUR PFENNINGS.

1.	*Obv.* and *Rev.*—As usual; C.			1831

PIECES OF TWO PFENNINGS.

2.	*Obv.* and *Rev.*—As usual; C.			1831
3.	do.	do.	do.	1833
4.	do.	do.	do.	1834

5. *Obv.* and *Rev.*—As usual; under cypher, IV.;
date on reverse   1834

PFENNINGS.

6. *Obv.* and *Rev.*—As usual; C.   1831
7. do. do. do. C.   1832
8. do. do. do. C.   1833
9. do. do. do. B.   1833
10. do. do. do. A.   1833
11. do. do. do. A.   1834
12. do. do. do. under the cypher, IV.;
on the reverse the date   1834

COINS BEARING THE SHIELD OF ARMS.

13. *Obv.*—A crowned shield as described—
 KÖN. | HANNOVER | SCHEIDE | MUNTZ
 Rev.—2 | PFENNIGE | A.   1835
14. *Obv.* and *Rev.*—Similar; A.   1836
15. do. do. do. A.   1837
16. do. do. do. milled edge   1837

PFENNINGS.

17. *Obv.* and *Rev.*—Similar; A.   1835
18. do. do. do. A.   1836
19. do. do. do. A.   1837
20. do. do. do. B.   1835
21. do. do. do. B.   1836
22. do. do. do. B.   1837

With the accession of Victoria to the crown of England that of Hanover fell to Ernest Augustus, Duke of Cumberland; from thenceforth, Ernest Augustus, King of Hanover. And the coins struck in Hanover cease to be portions of the coinage of the British empire.

There are, however, a few coins which will still deserve

a notice here, because, though not strictly speaking British coins, they were yet struck by the authority and bear the names of British princes. Of these, we shall mention the coins of—

CHARLES, DUKE OF BRUNSWICK AND LUNENBURGH.

This prince was under the guardianship of George IV. from 1816 to 1823, and his coins, or rather some of them, bear his guardian's name and titles as well as his own. Of these we have—

PFENNINGS.

1. *Obv.*—A horse galloping to the right, GEORG. P. R. T. N. CAROLI D. BR. ET L.

   Rev.—1 | PFENNING | SCHEIDE | MUNTZ   1816

The reverse of this coin has clover crosses by the sides of the numeral. In the exergue of the obverse F. R. The legend may be fully expressed thus—

GEORGIUS PRINCEPS REGENS TUTORIS NOMINE CAROLI DUCIS BRUNSWICI ET LUNENBERGENSIS.

2. *Obv.* and	*Rev.*—Similar		1817
3. do.	do.	do.	1818
4. do.	do.	do.	1819
5. do.	do.	do.	1820

The P. R. is sometimes omitted.

6. *Obv.* and	*Rev.*—Similar		1819
7. do.	do.	do.	1820

No moneyer's initials on the above.

PIECES STRUCK DURING THE REIGN OF GEORGE IV. PIECES OF TWO PFENNINGS.

8. *Obv.* and *Rev.*—Similar; GEORG. IV. D. GR. TUT. N. &c., reverse has the initials M. C.   1820

9. *Obv.* and *Rev.*—Similar   1823

PFENNINGS.

The following coins have the initials C. V. C.

10. *Obv.* and *Rev.*—Similar   1820
11. do.   do.   do.   1822
12. do.   do.   do.   1823

EAST FRIESLAND.

This province was under Hanoverian rule from the year 1815, and we have three coins struck in the name and by the authority of George IV. in 1823, 1824, 1825: they bear on the obverse the crowned cypher of the king, and beneath it the numeral IV.; reverse in four lines, $\frac{1}{4}$ | STUBER. | Ost. | FRIESISCH, and the date, the word Stuber being in larger letters than the rest.

HENRY CHRISTMAS.

XXI.

UNPUBLISHED COIN OF CARAUSIUS.

The silver coin of Carausius, of which a woodcut is given above, was discovered, some little time ago, in the neighbourhood of Abingdon, and was communicated to the Numismatic Society in January, 1861, by Henry B. Godwin, Esq., of Newbury, through the intervention of Mr. Akerman. It is, we believe, unpublished; for, though the type of neither obverse nor reverse presents any feature of novelty, yet they have never hitherto been known to occur in association with each other; and the state of preservation of the coin is so admirable that, were it not unpublished, no excuse would be needed for a representation of it being given in our pages. It may be thus described:—

> *Obv.*—IMP. CARAVSIVS P.F. AVG. Laureate bust of the emperor to the left, with his right hand holding a sceptre surmounted by an eagle. His chest and shoulders encased in an ornamental cuirass, over which is thrown an embroidered scarf or *lorum*.
>
> *Rev.*—CONCORDIA MILITVM. Two right hands joined. In the exergue, R.S.R.

As has already been observed, the type of the obverse occurs on other silver coins, and is found associated with the reverses of ADVENTVS AVG., PAX AVG., VBERITAS AVG., and also with CONCORD. MILIT.,[1] where

---

[1] Mon. Hist. Brit., Pl. v., Nos. 5, 27, 36, 37, and 9.

the type is a female figure, holding two military standards. Stukeley[2] also gives it as occurring with the FELICITAS AVG. reverse, with the type of a galley. It is worthy of notice that, on all the coins of Carausius, on which his bust is represented in this manner, it is universally turned to the left, and never to the right. There is considerably more than usual shown of the bust, and the embroidered *lorum*—the badge under the Lower Empire of the consular office, and as such worn by the emperors—is conspicuous upon it.

The type of the reverse is well-known and of not unfrequent occurrence on Imperial coins, from the time of Nerva, downwards; it is also found on the copper coins of Carausius. The "right hand of fellowship" [the *commissa dextera dextræ*] was emblematic of concord in all ages:—

"Id habet concordia signum,
Ut quos jungit amor, jungat et ipsa manus."

The R.S.R. on the exergue of these coins has never been satisfactorily explained. It has, however, been generally considered to refer the coins to Rutupium (Richborough), as their place of mintage. On some few coins the S is replaced by an X, which does not appear to facilitate an interpretation of this mystery. The coin which forms the subject of this notice has since been sold, by Messrs. Sotheby and Wilkinson, for £19!

J. E.

---

[2] Med. Hist. of Carausius, Pl. iii. 1.

XXII.

ON A LEGIONARY COIN OF CARAUSIUS.

[Read before the Numismatic Society, May 23, 1861.]

At the last meeting of the Numismatic Society, I had the pleasure of exhibiting, on behalf of Mr. Joseph Warren, of Ixworth, a cast of a third brass coin of Carausius, having, on the reverse, a ram to the right, with the letters ML on the exergue, but with only the final N of the legend visible; and I observed that, though several specimens of this type were known, yet that the legend had never been satisfactorily completed. I was at that time inclined to accept Stukeley's reading of LEG . VIII . IN . and to regard the latter as an abbreviation of INVICTA, especially as Akerman, No. 90, and the compilers of the Mon. Hist. Brit., pl. viii., No. 31, place the coin with the legend LEG. . . . IN, with a ram for its device, immediately after that of the Eighth Legion with a bull; and Haym, in his "Tesoro Britannico," tab. xxx. 7, gives a coin reading LEG . VIII . . . IN, with the ram for type, and ML in the exergue.

Turning to Stukeley's "Medallic History of Carausius," we find coins of this type engraved as of silver in pl. i. 9, with the legend LEG . VIII . IN, and pl. xx. 3, with LEG . VIII . INV.; and as of brass, but with the ram to the left, pl. xxviii. 4, and the legend LEG . VIII . IN. Such a concurrence of testimony in favour of assigning Mr. Joseph Warren's coin to the Eighth Legion seems, at first sight, conclusive; but a farther investigation tends to prove that, instead of commemorating the Eighth Legion, it was struck in honour of the First.

At the time that I wrote the short observations that accompanied the exhibition of the coin, I had not by me that valuable storehouse of information respecting the coins of Carausius—C. Roach Smith's "Collectanea Antiqua." In that work, vol. iv. pl. xxx. 5, is engraved, from the collection of the late Lord Londesborough, a coin with the ram to the left, on the reverse, and the termination of the legend, of which only IN, and a part of a previous letter, remain. Mr. Roach Smith remarks, "A coin in the cabinet of Mr. Charles Hall, with a ram, reads—LEG. I. MI. I am therefore induced, by comparison with that in the cabinet of Lord Londesborough, to read the legend in full, as LEG. I. MIN—*Legio Prima Minervia*. Inscriptions show that the First Legion, surnamed Minervia, was stationed on the Rhine, over a considerable period of time. It is not improbable that some portion, at least, of this legion may have sided with Carausius. The few known examples of this type are in very bad preservation, with the exception of that referred to above."

This reading is fully borne out by another coin from the Rolfe Collection, also engraved in the "Collectanea Antiqua," vol. v. pl. xvii. 8, with the ram to the right, exactly as on Mr. Joseph Warren's coin, with the legend LEG. I. MI., and ML. on the exergue. The original, which is now in my own collection, but which, at the time of our last meeting I had not examined, I now have the pleasure of exhibiting. There is no doubt of the correctness of the reading LEG. I. MI., while at the same time, in a less perfectly preserved coin, it is evident that I.M.I. might easily have been mistaken for VIII., and until some more conclusive testimony than at present exists can be brought forward, I think that the claims of the Eighth Legion to these coins must stand in abeyance, and that they must be assigned to the First. There is no record of the title of Minervia ever having been given to the Eighth Legion, and its emblem on the coins of Carausius, is the bull rather than the ram.

Why the ram should have been assumed by a legion under the patronage of Minerva, is not, at first sight, so apparent; as this animal appears on coins to have been more the symbol of Mercury, at whose feet it is found on various Greek coins both autonomous and imperial. The ram was, however, a fitting emblem to be adopted by one of the Roman legions, as not only was it sacred to Mars,[1] but its Latin name of Aries has, by some,[2] been considered to have been derived from Ares—Mars. Its Greek name of κριος is allied with κρούω, *to strike*, and similar analogies are found in other languages. As a symbol of power, we find his horns upon the head of Ammon, who, by Diodorus Siculus, is said to have worn them as a sort of crest on his helmet. The constellation Aries, the first sign of the Zodiac, is said to have been so called in honour of Jupiter Ammon; but it seems to have been also regarded as sacred to *Minerva*, which may account for the ram being the symbol on these coins of a Minervian Legion. The "triste Minervæ Sidus" of Virgil (Æn., lib. ii. v. 258), is said by Servius to be this constellation. The reason being, that as Minerva was the goddess of counsel, this constellation, by her aid, was able to guide all the others which follow it, in their due course,

---

[1] Macrobius, lib. i. cap. 21.
[2] Wachter, Archæologia Numismatica, p. 65.

"Consilium ipse suum est Aries ut principe dignum est,"[3] says Manilius.

The ram being the first of the signs of the zodiac, may also have had some influence in causing it to be adopted as the device of the First Legion.

Let us now trace a portion of the history of this legion, or rather of the particular First Legion, which was known as Minervia; for it was the custom among the Romans, in some instances, to have several legions, each known by the same number, but distinguished by different appellations. There were, for instance, under Augustus,[4] three Third Legions, the Gallica, Cyrenaica, and Augusta; and two Sixth Legions, the Victrix and Ferrata. Of the various First Legions, we find the following on coins—LIB. MACRIANA, of Clodius Macer; ADIVTRIX of Severus and Gallienus; AVGVSTA and ITALICA of Gallienus; besides which there was the MINERVIA, of which I will now speak.

This legion was first formed under Domitian, in Lower Germany,[5] and was placed by him under the tutelage of Minerva, from the peculiar veneration in which he held that goddess,—as witness his numerous coins which bear her effigy. In fact, he intended this legion to bear her image on its ensigns, and this is the case on some of the coins which bear its name. Its first appearance upon Roman coins is under Severus, when both gold and silver were struck with the legend LEG. I. MIN. TR. P. COS. on the reverse, the type being a legionary eagle between two military ensigns, the same as on coins with the names

---

[3] Manilius Astron. 1, 2.
[4] Dion. Cass., lib. lv. p. 794, ed. 1752.
[5] Ibid., p. 797.

of other legions upon them. Its next appearance is under Gallienus, with the type of Minerva holding the palladium, and resting on a buckler, with a *hasta* on her left arm. There are two varieties of legend—the first LEG. I. MIN. VI. P. VI. F., and the other with VII. P. VII. F., showing that, in consequence of another victory under Gallienus, this legion had been hailed as Pia Felix for the seventh time.

It would appear as if some portion of this legion had taken part with Aureolus in Illyria, when he revolted against Gallienus, for among the extremely rare brass coins of this tyrant, one is said to bear the legend LEG. I. MIN. RESTITVTA, as if this first Minervian legion had been reconstructed by him. The type shows Minerva and Aureolus joining hands, with a palm branch between them. There is, however, some doubt as to the authenticity, and even the existence, of this coin—though the legend and type seem unlikely to be the mere result of a Paduan imagination. It appears to have been first published by Tristan, and derived from him by later writers. Eckhel terms it "nummus præclarus si modo certæ fidei," and it is regarded as dubious by Mionnet and modern authorities. This, if a genuine instance, is the last appearance of the name of the First Minervian Legion upon coins, until we find it on these of Carausius, and then with the novel type of the ram. I am not aware of its name having been found on any lapidary inscriptions in this country, and of its subsequent history I am unable to speak. It must be considered sufficient that we should be able to trace the existence of a legion still retaining its distinctive number and title for a period of upwards of two hundred years, extending from the days of Domitian down to those of Carausius.

J. E.

XXIII.

ON TWO CRETAN COINS IN THE BRITISH MUSEUM.

[Read before the Numismatic Society, March 22, 1860.]

THE coins of the Island of Crete form one of the most interesting and individual groups in the range of Greek Numismatics. They excel in all the characteristics that render coins attractive. They illustrate the history of one of the most ancient homes of Greek civilization, throwing no little light upon that early greatness which the general agreement of tradition attests, and giving us new facts for the reconstruction of its later annals which are imperfectly narrated by the classical writers. They preserve valuable records of the Cretan mythology, abounding in nature-worship like that of kindred Arcadia, and embracing strange legends either brought from Phœnicia or Cyprus, as the tale of Europa, or of native origin, as the story of Talos. Their bearing on art is not less interesting: they show that Crete had a special medallic school of its own, probably representing the style of its famous artists, of whose work we have no other certain remains. It is very usual to hear the art of Greek coins loosely spoken of, as though all such objects, of any one period, wherever struck, were of the same style. A careful study has, however, convinced me that there were three great styles. The coins of Greece Proper, Thrace, and Macedon, as well as those of the Æolian, Ionian, and Dorian settlements on the west coast of Asia Minor, show in the best period a pure and

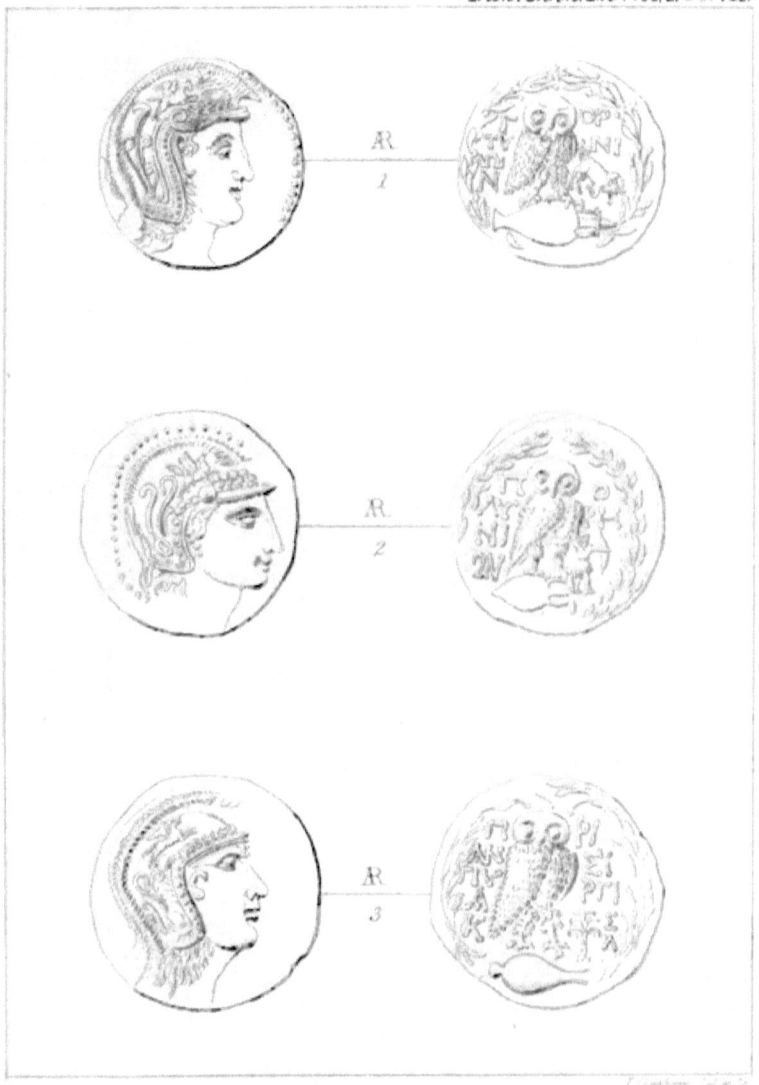

CRETAN TETRADRACHMS.

comprehensive art, rendering them worthy to be placed in the same class as the Elgin marbles, as works of the noblest Greek school. Further to the east, the coinage of the Greek cities is distinguished by a hardness and formality that may reasonably be ascribed to Persian or Lydian influence. In the west, the rich cities of Magna Græcia and Sicily produced an eclectic school, which, by aiming exclusively at the beautiful, overloaded its works with ornament, and so fell short of the severely-grand excellence of true Greek art. Crete had a school of its own. In style, its coins display the same love of truth and purity, and the same breadth of treatment, as the finest works of the great Hellenic school. They have, however, one peculiarity which markedly separates them from the coins of all other regions of the Greek world. They show, in very many cases, an entire want of knowledge of the forms proper for the surface of a coin, and of the fit method of representing them. It is a pictorial, instead of a sculptural, treatment. In illustration, a well-known didrachm of Gortyna (Æginetan standard) may be cited, as displaying extreme examples, in the types of both sides, of this distinctive peculiarity. The obverse of this piece is almost wholly occupied by the trunk and lower branches of an ancient tree. It represents the sacred plane at this town mentioned by Pliny (H.N. xii. 5), for upon it is seated Europa, in a dejected posture. On the reverse is a bull. He is stung by a fly, and starts, turning his head and thrusting out his tongue. In one specimen in the Museum, the bull is greatly foreshortened. The truth with which this subject is treated is almost unequalled in any similar representation, excepting those of the coins of Acanthus and Elis. While, at the first glance, we are delighted with the freedom and reality of these types, so strikingly contrasting with the almost necessary formality of numismatic art in general, we do not immediately see the utter unfitness of the objects chosen, and the positions preferred by the artist, for the form and surface of coins. To account for this peculiarity is not at present possible; but if a guess may be hazarded, it seems not unlikely that pictorial art especially flourished in Crete at that time, and that, therefore, when the artists of the country came to be employed to design the subjects of coins, they had in their minds painting rather than sculpture. Notwithstanding this grave fault as works of medallic art, if considered only as examples of Greek art, the Cretan coins are worthy of the first rank among the many records that have come down to us of this wonderfully-varied product of human genius.

The oldest known Cretan coins can scarcely be much anterior to the Expedition of Xerxes. Probably before this the commerce of the island was carried on in the staters of Cyzicus and the didrachms of Ægina and Ceos. The illustration of the primæval period of the island's history which they afford is, therefore, retrospective or inferential. We gain, however, some distinct evidence that is valuable in directing us to the selection of a correct theory from amidst the tangled mass of later-written statements. The Egyptian monuments, affording us the first historical glimpse of the Cretans, show that, in the twelfth or thirteenth century before the Christian era, as Greek tradition had already consistently told us, they were a great maritime power, closely allied with the kindred coast-peoples of the northern and eastern neighbouring shores of the Mediterranean. The coins so far confirm this evidence as to afford indications of the similarity of the religion of the island and that of the Phœnician coast, probably not of the Phœnicians themselves, but rather of the earlier people among whom they had settled.

The connection of Crete and Arcadia is more strongly brought out by the coins than by the evidence of history and geography. We knew already that Crete had a town called Arcadia, and that there was a Gortyna in Arcadia as well as in Crete. But the coins of both show us a far closer agreement in the strong prevalence of low nature-worship—the worship of animals, trees, and sacred mountains—which proves that the two countries were held by the same primitive race, driven inwards, in Greece, by the later Hellenic colonists, while the insular position of Crete seems to have kept the old population comparatively unmolested.

Among the most remarkable representations connected with mythology is that of the Cretan Jupiter, as a young man, with his native name, or title, ΓΕΛΧΑΝΟΣ, on a didrachm (Æginetan) of Phæstus. It is noticeable that the peculiarities of the Cretan dialect are chiefly seen in the names or titles connected with mythology. We have ΠΟΛΧΟΣ, as a title of Apollo, on tetradrachms (Attic) of Cnossus, and the title ΠΤΟΛΙΟΙΚΟΣ applied to a hero or divinity, on didrachms (Æginetan) of Aptera.

Of the special myths of the traditional period, that of the Minotaur receives the largest illustration from the coins. Not only is he portrayed on the oldest didrachms of Cnossus, but these and the later pieces of the same town bear representations of the famous Labyrinth, sometimes conventional, sometimes in the form of a plan. One of these coins, bearing on the obverse the Minotaur, and on the reverse the Labyrinth, is of about the time of the Expedition of Xerxes, or not much later, and thus affords evidence of the antiquity of the tradition of the Labyrinth, if not of its real existence; whereas Hoeck (*Kreta*, vol. i. p. 56, *seq*.), relying on the silence of Hesiod and Herodotus, and the assumed silence of Homer—though the Iliad contains what looks very like an allusion to the Cretan wonder (Il. xviii. 590, *seq*.)—has supposed it to have been an invention of the later poets, borrowed from Egypt.

For what we may term the earlier part of the strictly-historical period, ending with Philip, the coins do not afford us much information that is absolutely new as to their own times. They show the opulence of some towns already known to be famous, as Cnossus and Gortyna; and of at least one, Phæstus, of which we should not have imagined the greatness. Their weight is according to the Æginetan talent which was nearly universal, before Alexander's time, in Hellas and the islands; but by degrees they fall to the Persian standard, which, in the fourth century before Christ till near its close, dominated almost throughout Asia Minor. The latest coins of this weight cannot be brought down lower than the time of Philip of Macedon. After them there is a gap in the Cretan series, which must have been of many years, and the money of each town recommences on the Attic standard, with a far inferior art. This interval corresponds to the rule of Alexander, who suppressed everywhere the Æginetan standard, introducing the Attic in its stead, and some of whose coins bear symbols which have induced M. Müller, of Copenhagen, to assign them to cities of Crete. Of the later period, from Alexander's death until the island became a part of the Roman Empire, the historical records are extremely scanty, and the coins happily afford us valuable evidence to supply their deficiencies. The Greek writers had already given us indications of the close connection between Crete and the mainland of Greece, in the latest days of Greek independence. The island seems then to have been constantly torn by dissensions between the chief cities, which from time to time applied for aid to some ruler or power of the continent, and principally, it appears, to the kings of Macedon, at least to Philip V., and to the Achæan League. We already knew that when the Romans were in alliance with the League, 500 Gortynians joined Flamininus before the battle of Cynoscephalæ; but it was not until lately that a coin was found bearing the well-known types of the League, and struck at Gortyna. This coin was first published by my lamented colleague, Mr. Burgon, in a paper since printed in the Chronicle (xix. pp. 235-6). Mr. Burgon assigned it to the Arcadian Gortyna, but it has been ably shown, in his last work, by Colonel Leake, whose recent death has made another irreparable gap in the small body of Greek Numismatists, that it is of the Cretan town, and proves that cities beyond the continent were admitted into the League. (Supplement to *Numismata Hellenica*, European Greece, p. 110.)

Not less interesting than this connection with the Achæan League are the evidences of an alliance, political or commercial, of the chief Cretan towns with Athens in the same age. The coins of six of these—Cnossus, Cydonia, Gortyna, Hierapytna, Polyrhenium, and Priansus—comprise tetradrachms with exactly the types of those of Athens of the same period, but distinguished by having on the reverse the distinctive badges of the Cretan towns. The late tetradrachms of Athens which these imitate range from Alexander's death to the Roman period: from their style the Cretan pieces should probably be assigned to the most recent part of this age. They can scarcely be anterior to the fall of Lyttus, the rival of Cnossus, favoured by Athens (see the fragment probably of a treaty between the two towns in Rangabé's *Antiquités Helléniques*, ii. 273; Polyb. iv. 54), and were therefore more probably struck by the Cretan cities of the great alliance against Philip V., brought about by Cephisodorus (Paus. i. 36, § 5, 6) about B.C. 188.

Until lately this very interesting class was alone represented in the national collection by a coin of Gortyna. The sale of the Northwick Cabinet has, however, enabled the Museum to secure two other specimens, one of Polyrhenium and the other of Priansus, the former extremely rare, and the latter probably unique. The three coins may be described as follows:—

Obv.—Head of Pallas, to the right.
Rev.—ΓΟΡΤΥΝΙΩΝ. Owl, to the right, on amphora: in the field bull, butting, to the right: all within olive wreath.
Æ 7½, wt. 249·2 grs. Pl. vii. No. 1.

Obv.—The same type.
Rev.—ΠΟΛΥΡΗΝΙΩΝ. Owl, to the right on amphora: in the field Diana (?) drawing her bow.
Æ 8¼, wt. 248·6 grs. Pl. vii. No. 2.

Obv.—The same type.
Rev.—ΠΡΙΑΝΣΙ ΠΥΡΓΙ ΑΣΚΑ. Owl, to the right, on amphora: in the field a date-palm.
Æ 8¼, wt. 235·1 grs. Pl. vii. No. 3.

Here for the present I leave this subject, in the hope that fresh information may soon resolve the curious problem raised by these Athenian coins of Crete.

REGINALD STUART POOLE.

British Museum, February, 1860.

XXIV.

ON THE COINS OF THEODOSIUS I. AND II., WITH SOME REMARKS ON THE MINT-MARKS "COMOB." AND "CONOB.," AND ON THE COINS OF PLACIDIA, THE WIFE OF CONSTANTIUS (PATRICIUS).

In the last number of the NUMISMATIC CHRONICLE, I had the pleasure of calling the attention of the "coin-loving" public to the coins of the "Three Valentinians," and the various mint-marks occurring upon them, and on the coins of that period. I still find there is another point which does not seem ever to have been satisfactorily explained, and that is, what coins shall be assigned to Theodosius I. and what to Theodosius II.? I will now proceed to show that mistakes are impossible, and that it is just as easy to recognise to which of these two emperors a coin shall be attributed, as, I sincerely hope, for Numismatists now to attribute the coins of the Valentinians.

It is necessary to state that at this period of the coinage, *fabric* is the great and decisive guide, apart from many other minor points of indication; and it is only by a careful comparison of a large series, that one is able to discriminate between the Gallic, Italian, African, or Eastern fabrics.

On the death of Gratianus in A.D. 383, Arcadius is proclaimed Augustus by his father Theodosius I., and there are still three Augusti at the same time, viz., Valentinianus II., Theodosius I., and Arcadius. The following mint-marks, occurring also on the gold coins of Arcadius, are struck during his father's lifetime : ℞. TR. (Treves), Æ. LVG. (Lyons), N. COM. Æ. CON. (Constantina or Arles), MDOB. (Milan), N. TESOB. (Thessalonica), N. CONOB. (Constantinople—all those that have the diademed side-faced bust, and the three G's on the reverse), and most probably SM. COMOB. (Sirmium).[1]

After the death of Theodosius I., the empire is divided between his two sons Arcadius and Honorius, and the forms COMOB. for the *Western*, and CONOB. for the *Eastern* empire, become the adopted *exergual* mint-marks: the former with the slight distinction of M for N, so as to resemble CONOB., and yet to designate the western

---

[1] The following are the principal letters occurring in the *field*, from the reign of Valentinianus II. to the end of the Western empire :—

   A — Q.—Aquileia.
   A — R.—Arelate.
   L — D.—Lugdunum.
   M — D.—Mediolanum.
   R — M.—Roma.
   R — V.—Ravenna.
   S — M.—Sirmium.
   T — R.—Treviri.

The following (though I have seen but one, viz., RA.), if found, occur only on barbarous coins :—

Δ — R. = A — R.—Arelate.
L — P. = L — D.—Lugdunum.
M — B.
M — P.
N — B. } = M — D.—Mediolanum.
N — D.
R — A. = Ravenna, or more probably A—R. (inverted) Arelate.
R — D.
R — E. } = R — V.—Ravenna.

And there may be many others ; but the above *eight* mints are the only recognised mints of which we have letters in the *field*.

mints, and almost always accompanied by letters in the *field;* the latter *never*.[2]

Before I proceed further I must digress to remark that the OB. very probably stands for "72," and means that 72 "solidi" were coined from one pound of gold.[3] The figures LXXII on a "solidus" of Constans, are assuredly a mark of weight, and would seem of themselves sugges-

---

[2] On a coin of Leo I. in the British Museum, with R—V. (Ravenna), to the left and right in the *field,* there is in the *exergue* what some might read as COMOR. This is, of course, COMOB. Besides the fact that the bottom of this coin cuts by the very letter in question, no importance need be attached to it, as other coins of this emperor are found with RV. COMOB. The forms COMOB. and CONOB. continue as the Western and Eastern *exergual* mint-marks, till the time of Zeno and Anastasius, after which they are of no use as *distinctive* mint-marks.

[3] Messrs. Pinder and Friedlaender were the first to assert that OB. should be interpreted "72," and they state in proof that "a special law of Valentinianus I. ordered that 72 'solidi' should be coined from one pound of gold." The piece of Constans, however, seems to show that "72 solidi" were coined at the time of Constantine. This law, then, only confirms and enforces what had been the custom thirty years before. (See ***Rev. Num. Franc.***, 1849, p. 13.) The form CONOB., however, does not occur on the coins of Valentinianus I., as Messrs. Pinder and Friedlaender say, but is found, for the first time, under Gratianus, Valentinianus II., and Theodosius I. We find TROB. (Treves) on the coins of Valentinianus I. (See Num. Chron. N.S., vol. i. p. 124, and Table.) In the British Museum there is a gold coin of Valens, with to left and right the **letters OB.** in the *field,* and in the *exergue* CONS✱. What else can these letters OB. mean than 72, especially with the coin of Constans and this coin before our eyes? The Museum also possesses a gold coin of Valens with ANOB. (Antioch), as well as TROB. (Treves). The above coin of Valens, with OB. in the *field,* may be the commencement of the CONOB. mint-mark; and in consequence of our having this Antioch coin, it is very probable that the form CONOB. was adopted late in the reign of Valens (though at present I have not seen an example), as Valens, Gratianus, and Valentinianus II. were colleagues from A.D. 375 to A.D. 378, and we have the CONOB. mint-mark of the two latter.

tive of the above interpretation, yet there are, nevertheless, many Numismatists who cannot for one moment admit this extravagant explanation, and who think that OB. is far more likely to represent OBsignatus.[4]

To this I will state my principal objections. Is it likely that the Romans would adopt for their coinage, a word to which the very two letters that cause this discussion are *only prefixed?* And had they wished to have expressed the signification of "struck at," would not they rather have adopted the word "signatus?" The letters OB. are prefixed to all sorts of words, and their significations are various, and nothing seems to me more unlikely than that a compound word should be universally adopted for the Roman gold coinage. Apart from this, I think I am not far wrong in saying that we have no authority for using the word "obsigno," as applied to the "striking of money." Its proper meaning is "to seal up," or "to sign and seal as a witness," and it signifies "to stamp" or "impress," only in a figurative sense, and sometimes implies "to impress on the mind."[5] The word "signo," on the contrary, as well as "flo" and "ferio,"—which two latter occur on coins, A.A.A.F.F. (flando, feriundo)—is mentioned in Cicero and Pliny, especially with the signification of coining. With these facts before me, I must entirely repudiate the reading "OBsignatus."[6]

---

[4] In consequence of the form TROBS. being found, the OBS. is supposed to be the first letters of OBsignatus. But we also find TROBC. and TROBT. The last letters of each of these certainly indicate the number of the mint, C = 3rd mint; S = Secunda; and T = Tertia. (See Num. Chron. N.S., vol. i. p. 124, note.)

[5] Lucretius, iv. 569; ii. 582. See also "Codex Theodosianus," lib. xvii. Tit. i. Lex 56, and lib. xxii. Tit. i. Lex 7.

[6] If the letters OB. are not to be interpreted as numerical indications, the word OBryzatus, which has been also suggested,

One great argument brought forward in opposition to the "72" is, that the words COMOB. and CONOB. occur upon the so-called semisses and tremisses, the parts of the solidus; and that in consequence, if the meaning was 72, we should find K Δ. (24) on these small pieces, instead of OB. But it is the "solidus" that is struck at "72 to the pound;" and the "semisses" and "tremisses" are the parts of the "solidus," which latter is struck at "72 to the pound." The "solidus" is the coin, the "semisses" and "tremisses" its recognised fractional parts. In M. Sabatier's "Hôtels Monétaires," published in 1850, it is argued that these forms are found on the "medallions" of this period. The authorities quoted are Banduri, Tanini, Eckhel, and Mionnet. The Museum does not possess one, nor have I ever seen one. Granted that the forms are found on the medallions, it makes not the slightest difference to the explanation. The medallions are money not in general circulation (like our £5 pieces), and are the multiples of the "solidus," which is struck at "72 to the pound." As regards the silver and copper, I have seen specimens with these mint-marks, but they are, without any doubt, either *casts of the gold*, or *struck from the gold dies*. The form OB. positively only applies to the gold.[?]

---

is far preferable to "Obsignatus," and occurs often in the "Codex Theodosianus" to imply the "assaying of gold;" and these two letters, occurring, as they do, *only on the gold*, may have the signification that the coins are "made of standard gold," or they may have the double meaning of "72," and "obryzatus." This point really seems a "quæstio vexata," and after all is not of absolute importance, the mint-marks themselves being after a short time decidedly *conventional*.

[?] I think it right to state that Messrs. Pinder and Friedlaender have published nearly the same views on the reading OB. in their "Alteren Münzkunde" (pp. 1—25), as are here put forth.

In my paper on the "Three Valentinians," I remarked that COMOB. may be explained by "Constantinæ Moneta, 72—money of the standard of Constantina or Arles." This was because it superseded the mint-mark COM. (Arles) in the west. After the death of Theodosius I., however, in consequence of the barbarian invasions, there is no doubt that it may be interpreted "money of the standard of Constantinople — 72." This is still more likely from the fact that we have coins of the usurper Constantinus struck at Arles, with AR. in the *field*, and COMOB. in the *exergue*, a mint-mark which continues till the fall of the Western Empire.

I must now return to the subject from which I have somewhat digressed, and I think I have reduced to something like method, the means of attributing the coins of Theodosius I. and Theodosius II.

I.—The *helmeted full-faced bust*, though occurring on the gold coins of Constantius II., does not recommence till the reign of Arcadius and Honorius, and is generally, though not always, on the Eastern coins; consequently the gold coins reading D.N. THEODOSIVS. P.F. AVG. with the *helmeted full-faced bust*, belong to Theodosius II.[a]

II. The gold coins bearing the name of Theodosius, with the *helmeted side-faced bust*, belong to the second Theodosius; they are exceptional coins: the reverse—two helmeted figures holding a shield, on which is inscribed

---

This I did not know till after the paper was sent to the printers. That two persons should unconsciously publish the same views, is in itself a strong argument in favour of the principles advanced.

[a] There is no doubt that several coins were struck in Gaul from the time of Honorius downwards, and many bear the helmeted full-faced bust. The genuine Constantinople type is generally, though not always, accompanied by a Greek differential letter; and its absence, coupled by fabric, give reason for the above supposition.

VOT. XV. MVL. XX., and a star to left in the field—indicate the period to which they shall be assigned.[9]

III. The gold coins bearing the name of Theodosius with the *diademed side-faced bust*, and the mint-mark RV. COMOB. (Ravenna), belong to Theodosius II.[10] Ravenna was not made the seat of government till under **Honorius**, and "it was considered as such, and as the capital of Italy, till the middle of the eighth century."[11]

IV. The gold coins bearing the name of Theodosius, with the *diademed side-faced bust*, and on the reverse the mint-mark MD. COMOB. (Milan), belong to Theodosius II. The fabric and the style of head, when compared with the coins of the time, point to what period they should be assigned. Besides, the forms of the Milan mint of Theodosius I. are MD. COM.

---

[9] We find gold coins of Valentinianus I. and his brother Valens, both with the helmeted side-faced bust, and both struck at Treves. The helmets on these coins resemble those found on the coins of Honorius.

[10] M. Cohen has informed me that there is in Paris a coin of Theodosius II., with, on the obverse, the helmeted side-faced bust, and on the reverse, the emperor standing, right foot on lion, holding sceptre, on which is P, and two javelins. In field, left and right, R—V. (Ravenna). In exergue COB. The Museum possesses a coin of Honorius with similar obverse and reverse. The COB. is merely an abbreviated form of COMOB. The C. is put for COM., like we find C. put for CON. or CONS. at the Constantine period. No importance need be attached to these exceptions. In my paper on the "Three Valentinians" (Num. Chron. N.S., p. 123), I remarked that the form of CORMOB. occurred on a gold coin of Anthemius. The Museum also possesses a coin of the same emperor with CORVO. in the *exergue*. This should, no doubt, be CORVOB. The RM. and RV. signify respectively Rome and Ravenna, and the CO is affixed, and the OB prefixed to resemble as near as possible COMOB., and at the same time to designate a mint. The absence of the B. is easily accounted for by the lateness of the times and the ignorance of the artist. It is not of any importance.

[11] Gibbon, vol. iv.

V. The following small gold coins belong to Theodosius II.

 1. *Obv.*—D.N. THEODOSIVS. P.F. AVG. Bust to right, diademed, with paludamentum and cuirass.
 Rev.—VICTORIA. AVGG. Victory seated on cuirass to right, holding on left knee a shield, on which is inscribed XXXX. In field to left, a star. In field to right, ☧. In exergue CONOB. (Constantinopoli 72). Quin. N.

 2. *Obv.*—Same legend and bust.
 Rev.—VICTORIA-AVGVSTORVM. Victory walking facing, holding wreath and cross on globe. In field to right, a star. In exergue, CONOB. Trem. N.

 3. *Obv.*—Same legend and bust.
 Rev.—No legend. Trophy. On either side a star. In exergue, CONOB. Trem. N.

The star on the gold Constantinople coins first appears under Honorius and Theodosius II.

VI. The silver and copper coins are easily distinguishable by their style and fabric. The following are the silver coins I have seen :—

 1. *Obv.*—D. N. THEODOSIVS. P. F. AVG. Bust to right, diademed, with paludamentum and cuirass.
 Rev.—GLORIA . ROMANORVM. Emperor wearing paludamentum, and with the *nimbus*, standing to left, holding spear, and resting left hand on shield. In field to left, a star. In exergue, CON. (Constantinopoli). Ar (large).

 2. *Obv.*—Same legend and bust.
 Rev.—VOT. XX. MVLT. XXX. within wreath. In exergue, CONS✷ Ar.

 3. *Obv.*—Same legend and bust.
 Rev.—VOT. XXX. MVLT. XXXX. within wreath. In exergue, CONS✷ Ar.

Apart from the style of these coins, the numbers of the *rows* on one of the gold and on two of the silver coins clearly belong to Theodosius II., the elder Theodosius having only reigned sixteen years.

As to the copper coins, some have the full-faced helmeted bust, and some the side-faced; besides, there are others of small size, some with the monogram ℞E in a wreath, some with a cross in a wreath, some with two or three figures, and some with a horseman, to right: the two latter types occurring on the coins of **Arcadius and Honorius**, and none of them occurring at the time of Theodosius I. The following copper coin of Theodosius II. is exceptional:—

Obv.—D . N . THEODOSIVS . P . F . AVG. Bust, to left, diademed, with imperial robe, showing right hand, which holds a globe, and in left, a sceptre surmounted by an eagle.

Rev.—GLORIA . REIPVBLICAE. Gate of the prætorian camp. Above, ⳽. In exergue, TES. (Thessalonicæ). Æ.

There may be some doubts about those coins bearing the name of Theodosius, on the obverse the diademed bust, and on the reverse the emperor, in military dress, standing to right, placing left foot on captive, and holding in right hand the labarum, on which is the monogram of Christ, and, in the left, Victory on globe; in field, left and right, S—M. (Sirmium); in exergue, COMOB.[12] Firstly, the style and fabric is so superior to that found under Theodosius II.; and secondly, the total disappearance of Sirmium, as a mint, after Arcadius and Honorius, clearly indicate that these coins belong to Theodosius I.[13]

Before I conclude, I must call the attention of my readers to the coin usually attributed to Placidia, the wife

---

[12] The following are the mint-marks occurring on the gold coins of Theodosius I.:—TROB. TR. COM. (Treves), COM. (Arles), COMOB. (Rome? at any rate struck somewhere in Italy), MD. COM. (Milan), SM. COMOB. (Sirmium), TESOB. (Thessalonica), CONOB. (Constantinople). [See "The Table of Mint-marks," Num. Chron. N.S., vol. i., p. 126.]

[13] The mint of Siscia also ends under Arcadius.

of Olybrius, and which most certainly belongs to Placidia, wife of Constantius Patricius, as even yet there seem some doubts about the solidus with the obverse legend AEL. PLACIDIA AVG.[14] The obverse legend on the coins of Galla Placidia is usually the following:—D . N . GALLA PLACIDIA P. F. AVG.; and these coins, from their fabric, show two different epochs of her life—that, when her husband, Constantius (Patricius), was alive; and that, when as regent for her son, Placidius Valentinianus III., she was restored to her power, after the revolt of Johannes I., who had established himself at Ravenna, during the time that we know Placidia must have been at Constantinople. Aelia is evidently the *common* name of the empresses in the East at this period—for examples, Aelia Pulcheria, Aelia Eudoxia; and this coin being struck by her nephew, Theodosius II., while she was at Constantinople, fully accounts for finding the name *Aelia*. Were it not even for these facts, the style and fabric are so different to the coins of Olybrius, that it could not possibly belong to his period.

Dr. Friedlaender has also published some remarks, "Sur un Sou d'or d'Aelia Galla Placidia," in the *Revue Numismatique Belge*,[15] where he says that the reverses of all the coins of Placidia, with the legend VOT. XX. MVLT. XXX., have reference to the coins of her son, Valentinianus III. In this he is probably mistaken: they refer to the coins of her nephew Theodosius II., which bear the same legend.

FRED. W. MADDEN.

---

[14] In Akerman's "Roman Coins," this attribution is hinted at; and I have already published these remarks in my "Handbook to Roman Numismatics."

[15] 3ème Série, tome iv. p. 237.

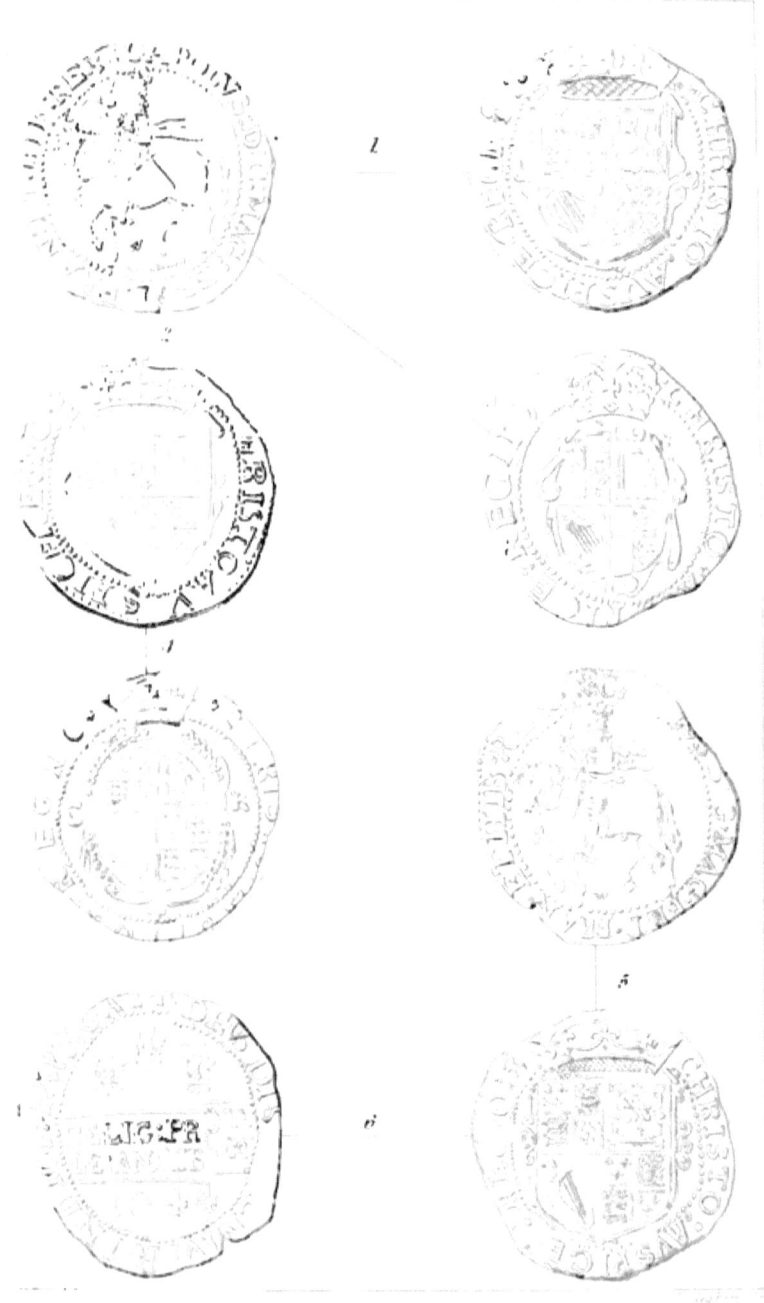

HALF CROWNS OF CHARLES I, WITH "W"
UNDER THE HORSE.

XXV.

ON THE HALF-CROWNS OF CHARLES I. WITH THE "W" UNDER THE HORSE ON THE FIELD OF THE OBVERSE.

[Read before the Numismatic Society, November 20, 1856.]

THE accompanying plate (No. viii.) comprises all the types of the half-crowns of **Charles I.** with W under the horse which have come under my notice. They are six in number, and the pieces themselves are, I believe, all of them in the British Museum, but the mint-mark on No. 5 is more distinctly visible on a specimen of my own.

Nos. 1—4 have a small castle for a mint-mark, and are all from the same obverse die. Nos. 5, 6 are likewise from one obverse die. The mint-mark is usually invisible, but on the specimen from which the drawing is made, it is evidently two lions.

The lions, the castle, the W, and the date of 1644 upon **No. 6** will, I think, together, serve to indicate the place from whence these half-crowns issued.

Under the article "Weymouth," in Lewis's "Topographical Dictionary," there are three representations given—of the arms of the town, of the Admiralty seal, and of the corporate seal. On the arms appears a lion rampant, in the second and third quarters; on the Admiralty seal is a ship bearing a small shield, in the first quarter of which is a lion rampant, in the second a small castle; on the corporate seal is a small shield, with three lions passant, and an embattled bridge.

I do not know upon what authority these drawings were made, but their correctness is in a great measure substantiated by the following extract from Hutchins' "History of Dorsetshire:"—

"Robert Cook, Clarenceux, &c., in 1592, granted to Weymouth and Melcombe Regis the following arms, *inter alia*. In the first a lion rampant, purpure; in the second, a castle, or;" for their common seal, *inter alia*, azure, a bridge embattled with three arches, &c., and three lions.[1]

It must be admitted that the lions on the coin No. 5 do not exactly correspond in attitude with the lions rampant on the arms and Admiralty seal, nor in number with the lions passant on the corporate seal; but we may easily account for this by supposing that a clumsy artist has made a confusion between the bearings of the two seals; and, on the whole, I am disposed to think that the lions, the castle, and the W sufficiently point to Weymouth as the place where these half-crowns were minted.

Further, the history of the place during the civil war

---

[1] The following are the arms of the united towns of Weymouth and Melcombe Regis, as given in Burke's "General Armory:"—Azure, on the waves of the sea, in base proper, a ship of three masts, tackled and rigged, all or; on the fore and mizen masts two square banners; on the first, per pale gules and vert, two lions passant guardant, or; on the second, quarterly, argent and gules; on the first and fourth a lion rampant, purpure; on the second and third, a castle, or; on the hulk of the ship an escutcheon, per fesse, or and gules; in chief, three chevrons of the second; in base, three lions passant guardant in pale of the first. The common seal represents, azure, a bridge of three arches, double embattled, argent, standing in the sea proper; in chief, an escutcheon, per fesse, or and gules; on the first, three chevrons, gules; on the second, three lions passant guardant in pale of the first.

makes the supposition probable. We read in Clarendon, that in September, 1643, the Earl of Carnarvon, General of the Horse, marched before Prince Maurice from Bristol, and "took Dorchester and Weymouth—both considerable places, and the seats of great malignity. The former was not thought necessary to be made a garrison, but the latter was the best port town of that country, and to be kept with great care." The government of the place was entrusted to Sir Anthony Ashley Cooper, but he was subsequently displaced for Colonel Ashburnham, who yielded it up to the Earl of Essex in June, 1644, and retired to Portland Castle.

Thus it appears that Weymouth was in the possession of the king's forces from September, 1643, to June, 1644. Subsequently in the latter year, in the end of January or beginning of February (the year not ending until the 25th of March), it was surprised by Sir Lewis Dives on the part of the king; but he only obtained possession of the forts and upper town, which, through the negligence of Lord Goring, were recovered again "by that contemptible number of the enemy who had been beaten into the lower town."

This last occupation of the place by the king's forces was so brief and partial, that it is not likely any coins were then struck; the coinage most probably took place between September, 1643, and June, 1644, and those pieces which bear the latter date must have been struck during the last three months of occupation.

There are other pieces[2]—half-crowns, shillings, and a

---

[1] The pieces alluded to are not all engraved, but for some of them consult Hawkins, 500, 528, 529, 534, and Snelling, xiv. 10, 16; also Ruding, G 1; others are described in Hawkins' letter-press.

sixpence—which evidently belong to the same family; they have no initial letter, but are of similar workmanship, and they bear the mint-mark of a lion rampant, a castle, a lis, a helmet, a bird, &c. If not minted at Weymouth, they were probably minted at some other place in the neighbourhood, and perhaps after its surrender. The shilling (Hawkins, 528), I am inclined to call a Weymouth shilling, as it bears both a castle and a lion rampant. One half-crown, and one or two shillings, have a lion rampant only, and these again are connected in type with other pieces with different mint-marks; but it would be rash, upon slight grounds, to venture upon their appropriation.

With respect to the W half-crowns, it would be desirable, if any members of our society have the opportunity, to ascertain whether there is any local tradition or proof of a mint having been established at Weymouth during the civil war.

T. F. Dymock.

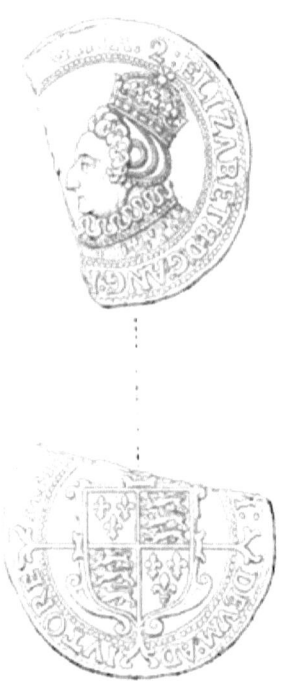

XXVI.

ON AN UNIQUE AND UNPUBLISHED PATTERN FOR A HALF-CROWN OF THE LAST YEAR OF THE REIGN OF QUEEN ELIZABETH.

The extreme sensitiveness of Queen Elizabeth as to the manner in which her portrait was represented is well known. Even so early as 1563 a proclamation was drawn up by Cecil,[1] prohibiting all manner of persons from drawing, painting, graving, or portraying her Majesty's personage or visage for a time, until, by some perfect pattern and example, the same might be by others followed. Increasing years did not by any means diminish this fastidiousness.

In Horace Walpole's "Catalogue of Royal and Noble Authors," vol. i. p. 126 of the first edition, and vol. i. pp. 141-2 of the second, is the following description of a fragment of one of the gold coins of this queen.

"Vertue, the engraver, had a pocket-book of Isaac Oliver, in which the latter had made a memorandum that the queen would not let him give any shade to her features, telling him, 'that shade was an accident, and not naturally existing in the face.' Her portraits are generally without shadow. I have in my possession another strongly presumptive proof of this weakness; it is a fragment of one of her last broad pieces, representing her horridly old and deformed. An entire coin with this

---

[1] "Archæologia," vol. ii. p. 169.

image is not known; it is universally supposed that the die was broken by her command, and that some workman of the mint cut out this morsel, which contains barely the face.[2] As it has never been engraved, so singular a curiosity may have its merit in a work which has no other kind of merit."

The fragment here referred to was purchased at the Strawberry Hill Sale in May, 1842, by the British Museum, for the sum of £36 15s., and is engraved in Ruding, Suppl. part ii. Pl. iii. No. 7. It has been much tooled; but the present specimen of the half-crown, or rather the pattern for the half-crown of the same coinage, shows that the portrait on the gold coin has been most correctly restored, as the impression on that portion of the half-crown which has been preserved is almost as it came from the die. The coin is engraved in Pl. ix., and it will be observed that the mint-mark is 2, showing that these patterns were intended for a coinage of the last year of Elizabeth. The bust of the queen is large, and she is attired in an ermine mantle, and with a full ruff. She is without the orb and sceptre, and the crown is rather more open and arched than on the generality of her silver coins. The legend of the obverse appears to be the same as on the ordinary half-crowns of Elizabeth, and the reverse seems to have been struck from the usual die. The same appears to have been the case with the reverse of the gold pattern-piece.

Any one comparing the portrait on these pattern-pieces with that on the actual coins of the same date, will readily acquiesce in Walpole's suggestion that its " horridly old "

---

[2] This piece was purchased from the cabinet of the Earl of Oxford.—*Ruding.*

look was the cause of the suppression of this coinage. Had it been issued, her Majesty's loving subjects would have found her portrait aged at least forty years in one short twelvemonth between 1601 and 1602. There can, however, be but little doubt of the accuracy of the likeness on these pattern-pieces. It carries the impress of truth upon it. The expression of the mouth, and, indeed, the whole face, bears out to the letter the description of Paul Hentzner, the German, who visited England in 1598, and saw Elizabeth at "Greenwidge." "Her oblong and white, though wrinkled, face; her small, though black and gracious, eyes, her rather hooked nose, her compressed lips (compressed to hide her sooty teeth), and her light brown hair, which in point of fact was a wig,"[3] are all represented to the life.

But although she had attained her seventieth year—an age unto which, says Camden, no King of England had ever attained before—and although this was no doubt an accurate likeness of her, still Elizabeth retained until the very last her old anxiety to have her "person, favor, and grace" placed in an advantageous manner before the public; and accordingly every specimen of this coinage was defaced, and but these two mutilated pieces have been allowed to survive to our times. Those who take an interest in the subject of the portraits of Elizabeth, will find a valuable article upon them by Sir Frederic Madden, K.H., in *Notes and Queries*, vol. vi. p. 237.

R. WHITBOURN.

---

[3] Hentzner, "Itinerarium," 1612, p. 135.

NOTICE OF RECENT NUMISMATIC PUBLICATIONS.

DESCRIPTION GENERALE DES MEDAILLONS CONTORNIATES, PAR J. SABATIER. *Paris*, 1860, 4to. pp. 148, with 19 plates.

This account of the mysterious but interesting class of medals known as Contorniates is in all respects worthy of the author whose name it bears. The plates, which are numerous, are admirably engraved by Dardel, and the description of them by M. Sabatier not only comprises almost all the information that can be gathered from other authors upon the subject of contorniates, but throws much additional light upon their history. It was, indeed, only by collecting together the whole of the known types, so as to be able to compare each member of the series with the others in one comprehensive review, that anything was likely to be effected which would materially add to our knowledge of this class of medals; and the amount of labour that must have been bestowed by M. Sabatier, and those who in this country and elsewhere aided him in the collection of his materials, must have been enormous, before he could have been in possession of a sufficient number of specimens to commence the still more arduous labour of systematic arrangement and historical description. One reason assigned for his undertaking the task, is that it was the only branch of Roman Numismatics which had been hitherto forgotten or neglected, except by Eckhel, and that, possibly, not unintentionally, on account of the difficulties it presents.

There is of course no question as to these medals having received their name of "contorniates" from the *contorno* around them—a groove, having in all cases been turned by means of a lathe, just within their outer edge, so as to form a sort of border. The main questions concerning them are, and always have been, for what purpose were they intended? and at what period were they struck?

The number that is at present known to exist is by M. Sabatier estimated at from 700 to 800; but this estimate is probably rather below the mark, as about 400 are divided between the English and French national collections, and there are about 160 in the museum at Vienna, while contorniates are to be found in greater or less abundance in numerous other cabinets. The varieties engraved by M. Sabatier are about 240; but as many of the reverses are accompanied on different specimens by two, three, or even four different obverses, the total number of types including these various combinations, may be estimated at 300. Though the heads of many of the earlier Roman emperors are found upon them, especially those of Nero and Trajan, there can be no doubt that they belong to a much later period, as the same reverse is occasionally found combined at one time with the head of Nero, and at another with that of Valentinian III., and various similar anachronisms have been observed. The inaccuracies and barbarisms in the legends also point to the period of the decay of the Roman empire, and M. Sabatier fixes the date of the emission of these pieces between the reign of Gratian and that of Anthemius, or from A.D. 375 to 472.

From the character of the devices, and the appearance of the names, not only of charioteers and athletes, but even of horses upon them, it would appear that the greater number of them bore some reference to the games of the circus and amphitheatre, and the monogram EP or PE, which is found upon so many of them, may bear reference to their having been given as rewards or badges of distinction—*Præmii Ergo*, or *Palmâ Emeritâ*.

Regarding them in this light, a portion of the book is devoted by M. Sabatier to an account of the principal events in connection with the circus at Constantinople during the lower empire, and he shows the important part played by the factions of the hippodrome and amphitheatre, which had in fact become political bodies. Of the names of the four factions of the circus, which had originally been four—the white, red, green, and blue (*alba, russata, prasina*, and *veneta*)—only two remained when Constantinople became the capital of the empire, and both are found upon these medals, on one of which EUSTORCHIUS appears as the winner of a chariot race, IN PRASINO, and DOMININVS on another, as AN VENETO (*sic*).

But it would be endless to attempt to enter into the various topics of interest suggested by this class of medals. We can only refer our readers to M. Sabatier's book. Besides those which are connected more immediately with the circus, there is another division, with mythological and allegorical subjects, as well as a third of those with heroic and historical subjects and personages, and a fourth of those of unknown or difficult interpretation—all of which are treated with great felicity of conjecture and of apposite illustration.

The third number (May and June) of the *Revue Numismatique* for 1861 contains the following articles:—

1. Letter XIII. of M. de Sauley, addressed to M. Adrien de Longpérier, on the "Numismatique Gauloise," being an interesting essay on the coins of the Lexovii.

2. Letter of M. Vasquez Quiepo, addressed to M. A. de Longpérier, on the "Nummus Tullianus."

3. "On some 'ideal' coins, viz., on those of (1) Victorina, (2) Lotharius, and (3) L. Ælianus," by J. de Witte.

The coin that has been attributed so often to Victorina is here shown to be none other than one of the coins of the Gothic kings of the fifth and sixth centuries, struck in Italy. The legend is altered, and instead of INVICTA . ROMA, that of IMP . VICTORIA . AVG. has been substituted. The coin of Lollianus is no doubt a Gordianus Pius, and the L. Ælianus is either a Maximian or Diocletian. These two names, Lollianus and L. Ælianus, may be safely identified with that of Lælianus, who was also one of the so-called thirty tyrants, and of whom there are coins extant.

4. "Essay on the Monetary History of the Counts of Flanders of the house of Burgundy, and a description of their gold and silver coins," by M. L. Deschamps de Pas.

In the *Nécrologie* is a tribute of respect to the distinguished Numismatist, M. Joachim Lelewel, who died in Paris on the 29th of May, at the age of sixty-six.

In the fourth number (July and August) of the *Revue Numismatique* there are the following articles:—

1. "Leaden Money of Alisia," by M. Adrien de Longpérier.

2. "An Essay on the coins of the family of Gallienus," by M. A. Deville.

This interesting article demands a few words, and we proceed to make a short extract of its principal points. The family of Gallienus, according to many historians and many Numismatists, consisted of two sons—one named Saloninus, the other, Q. Julius Gallienus; of two daughters, Julia and Galla; and a brother, Valerianus Junior. According to Eckhel, all the coins which have ever been attributed to Valerianus Junior, belong to Saloninus. Let us follow M. Deville's arguments. Valerianus I., on ascending the throne, associated in the empire Gallienus and his eldest son—the first with the title of Augustus, the second with that of Cæsar, and the name of the son of Gallienus, as given by Aurelius Victor, is *Cornelius Valerianus*. He was killed by Postumus in A.D. 260. From the same source we learn that Gallienus had another son, *Salonianus* (he is afterwards, by the same writer, called *Saloninus*), and that he was substituted by Gallienus in the place of the one he had lost. The names of the two sons occur also on an inscription found at Sétif, in Algeria. (See Léon Renier, "Inscriptions de l'Algérie," p. 393.)

When **Valerianus I.** was engaged in the expedition against Sapor, the senate, confident of his success, struck coins with the legend VICTORIA . PARTHICA. Coins with the same legend were also struck for Gallienus and his *eldest* son, and could not belong to the *youngest*, as he was not made Cæsar till after the defeat and capture of Valerianus I. The coins, therefore, with a *young* head and the "Parthian Victory" reverse belong to *Cornelius Valerianus*, the *eldest* son of Gallienus. "Consecration" coins, in large and second brass, with the designation DIVO, belong to the *eldest* son, for the senate would not have commemorated the younger, whom it had ordered to be killed after the death of Gallienus, though it struck them for Gallienus at the express wish of Claudius. (See Aurelius Victor.) The names of the *eldest* son, gathered from coins and inscriptions, are, "Caius, Publius, Licinius, *Cornelius*, Saloninus, Valerianus;" and those of the *younger*, "*Saloninus*, Valerianus," and the coins with these latter names belong to *Saloninus*. The "consecration" coin with these names, and without DIVO, belong to him, for his mother did not dare to give him that title. An inscription in Gruter (p. cclxxv) affords further proof of this. There was a third son, by name Q. Julius Gallienus, known only by inscriptions (Gruter, p. cclxxv); but of him there are *no coins*. And now a few words about **Valerianus Junior**. Eckhel says that there are no coins, for he was never Augustus or Cæsar. Trebellius Pollio says the contrary, and mentions a tomb near Milan, on which is the inscription VALERIANVS . IMPERATOR. This could not apply to Valerianus I., whose remains were left in Persia, where he was killed. (See Trebellius Pollio and Julius Capitolinus.) Valerianus Junior never received the names of *Cornelius* and *Soloninus*. M. Deville enters at length into the question whether Valerianus Junior was Augustus and Cæsar. The results of his paper may be summed up as follows:—Valerianus I. ascended the throne at the age of seventy, and died when seventy-six. We should therefore expect to find on his coins an *elderly* head; on those of his grandson, *Cornelius Valerianus*, a *young* head; and on those of his son, Valerianus Junior, the portrait of a *middle-aged* man. M. Deville attributes coins in the following manner to the family of Gallienus:—

1. Cornelius Valerianus. [Elder son of Gallienus.]

Obs.—P . C . L . VALERIANVS. }
P . LIC . COR . VALERIANVS. }

Rev.—VICTORIA . PART.

Obvs.—C.P.L.VALERIANVS.
C.P.LIC.VALERIANVS.
DIVO.VALERIANO.
DIVO.CORN.SAL.VALERIANO.
C.P.LIC.COR.SAL.VALERIANO.

Rev.—CONSECRATIO.

2. Saloninus. [Second son of Gallienus.]

Obvs.—SALON.VALERIANVS.
SAL.VALERIANVS.

3. Q. Julius Gallienus. [Third son of Gallienus.]   No coins.
4. Valerianus Junior. [Brother of Gallienus.]

Obv.—P.LIC.VALERIANVS.
Rev.—IOVI.CRESCENTI.

We have now given our readers an abstract of the principal points of M. Deville's paper, and will briefly state our own views. In the first place, the coins attributed by him to Saloninus and Valerianus Junior are of much too good a metal to be of the late period of Gallienus. In the second place, the attribution of the "consecratio" coin without the word DIVVS to Saloninus, as having been struck by his mother, is excessively improbable. Is it likely that Salonina, a *private person*, would dare to commemorate her son, who was killed by order of the senate, after the death of her husband?—besides, we have coins of the elder son also without the word DIVVS. In the third place, the coin attributed by him to Valerianus Junior was struck in the East, and belongs to Saloninus Valerianus, the eldest son of Gallienus, and the legend IOVI.CRESCENTI could never apply to a man of thirty. Apart from this, were there any of his coins, they would probably bear the title of *Augustus*, and not that of *Cæsar*. Space does not permit us to enter into all the "minutiæ" of our objections, and, in conclusion, we quote the same objection as that given by Mr. de Salis to M. Cohen's attribution of coins to Valerianus Junior, viz., "that should any coins have been struck, either of Saloninus (the second son of Gallienus), or of Valerianus Junior (the brother of Gallienus), they would necessarily be of the base metal of the later years of Gallienus." M. Deville's article is likely to do a great deal of harm, and we state that we continue to recognise the attribution of the coins to the family of Gallienus only as follows:—

Valerianus I. . . . . *Coins.*
Gallienus . . . . *Coins.*
Saloninus Valerianus [Elder son of Gallienus]. *Coins.*

Saloninus [Second son of Gallienus] . . . *No coins.*
Q. Julius Gallienus [Third son of Gallienus]. *No coins.*
Valerianus Junior [Brother of Gallienus] . . *No coins.*
F. W. M.

3. "Description of some Merovingian coins of Limousin," by M. Max. Deloche, (eighth article.)

4. "Unedited *denier* of William **IV.**, Prince of Orange," by M. R. Géry.

5. "Numismatique Lorraine," by M. Ch. Robert.

In the *Nécrologie* is a tribute of respect to M. Rethaan Macaré.

The following articles are in the 2d livraison of the *Revue Numismatique Belge* for 1861 :—

1. "On an unedited coin of Charlemagne," by M. de Coster.
2. "On some unedited mediæval coins," by M. Chalon.
3. "On some unedited coins of the collection of M. de Jonghe," by M. Camille Picqué.
4. "Documents pour servir à l'histoire des monnaies et des monnayeurs, XIVème et XVème siècles," by M. de la Fons-Méliocq.
5. "Order of Philip the Good, Duke of Burgundy, for the fabrication of money at Amiens and St. Quentin," by M. L. Deschamps de Pas.
6. "Biography of the Belgian engravers—Georges Mivelt, Henri Noël, Jerome Noël, Jean le Noire, Humbert Pierron, and Josse de Halle," by M. Alexandre Pinchart.

In the *Nécrologie* there are notices of Messieurs P. C. Q. Guyot, and C. A. Rethaan Macaré.

MISCELLANEA.

THE COINAGE.—Nine years have elapsed since the discovery of gold in Australia, and a comparison may now be drawn between the amount of that most precious metal which has been coined at the Royal Mint between the equal periods comprised between 1843 and 1851, and 1852 and 1860 inclusive :—

Year.	Gold Coinage.	Year.	Gold Coinage.
1843	£6,607,849	1852	£8,742,270
1844	3,563,949	1853	11,952,391
1845	4,244,608	1854	4,152,183
1846	4,334,911	1855	9,008,663
1847	5,158,440	1856	6,002,114
1848	2,451,999	1857	4,859,860
1849	2,177,955	1858	1,231,023
1850	1,491,836	1859	2,649,509
1851	4,400,411	1860	3,121,709

These figures exhibit a total coinage of £86,151,680—viz., £34,431,958 in the first nine years, and £51,719,722 in the second. The yearly average between 1843 and 1851 was £3,825,773, and between 1852 and 1860, £5,746,635, showing an increase of, as nearly as possible, 50 per cent. The fact must also be taken into consideration that a very large number of sovereigns have been coined at the mint established in Sydney. The value of the silver coined has undergone considerable fluctuations, having reached its *maximum* in 1853, when it was £701,544, while in 1848 it was only £35,442. The copper coin struck fluctuated between £448 in 1850 and £61,538 in 1854. The total value of the silver coinage in the eighteen years was £5,982,461, and of the copper coinage £241,449, the aggregate metallic issues of all descriptions having been £92,377,590.—*Times*, May 28, 1861.

SALE OF COINS, 2ND–10TH AUGUST, 1861.—The collections of the late Baron de Chaudoir, of St. Petersburg ; the late Rev. Dr. Bandinel, of Oxford ; and Count Torelli, of Modena, by Messrs. Sotheby and Wilkinson. Lot 514. Cyzicene stater, N, size 4 by 3 ; figure seated on a tunny-fish, to left; rev., quad. incus. Fine—£13. Lot 524. Ptolemy Soter and Berenice, N, size 7½ ; rev., ΑΔΕΛΦΩΝ ; busts of Ptolemy Philadelphus and Arsinoe. A rare tetrastater, but not fine—£11. Lot 526. Ptolemy III. N, size 7 ; bust, with radiated diadem, chlamys, and a trident-shaped sceptre ; rev., cornucopia, with tæniæ, &c. A rare tetrastater, but not fine—£8 8s. Lot 755. Domitian, 1 Æ ; rev., JOVI VICTORI ; usual type. Highly preserved, and finely patinated—£7 2s. 6d. Lot 761. Galerius Antoninus, 1 Æ ; rev.,

Faustina, Sen. Perfectly genuine, and a most desirable specimen
—£25 10s. This coin formerly belonged to the Prince Gagarin.
Lot 948. Mithradates VI.; an extremely fine tetradrachm, with
a splendid portrait; rev., stag, grazing; date, EKΣ, = year 225 of
the Pontic æra—£29 10s. Lot 851. Lycia, Æ, 5½; wt. 142 grs.;
boar, to right; rev., a triscelium, the ends forming cocks' heads,
within a sunk beaded square. (Cf. the drachm in Fellows'
"Lycian Coins," Pl. ix. No. 7.) Unpublished—£10. Lot 857.
Seleucus I., King of Syria; the drachm; head and neck of a
bridled horse, with bull's horns in the place of ears; rev.,
ΒΑΣΙΛΕΩΣ.ΣΕΛΕΥΚΟΥ; anchor and flower. Fine - £5 17s. 6d.
Lot 908. Pescennius **Niger**; rev., JUSTITIA AVGVSTI; Equity,
standing—£5. Lot 969. Charles I., Oxford penny, as Hawkins'
553—£22 10s. This coin sold (1824) for £9 15s. 6d. Lot 992.
George III., Pistrucci's **pattern for** a five-sovereign piece, 1820;
rev., St. George and the Dragon—£17. Lot 1081. Tiridates,
Satrap of Persia, minted in Cilicia, Æ, 6; **Hercules** and the king,
standing; **rev.**, Baal-Tars, seated. In good condition—£12.
Lot 1083. Cyzicus, Æ; ΣΩΤΕΙΡΑ, above the head of Proserpine;
rev., ΚΥΖΙ; lion's head, tunny-fish, &c. A fine tetradrachm—
£8 8s. Lot 1089. Aenianes Thessaliæ, Æ; head of Pallas, with
decorated helmet; rev., ΑΙΝΙΑΝΩΝ. ΝΙΚΑΡΧΟΣ; slinger, javelins,
star, &c. An excellent specimen—£5. **Lot** 1193. Argos, Æ,
6¼; **head** of Juno, to right, **with low crown**, encircled with Ionic
ornaments; rev., wolf (the **symbol of Apollo** Lycius) between
two dolphins—£15 15s. Lot 1194. Ptolemy (?), Æ, 6½; wt.
216 5/10 grs.; draped busts of **Jupiter and Juno**; rev., ΠΤΟΛΕ-
ΜΑΙΟΥ . ΒΑΣΙΔΕΩΣ; eagle, ΣΩ mon. and date ΣΙ between its legs.
Very fine—£29 10s. A similar specimen was bought in the
Thomas sale for £21. Lot 1359. Naxos, Æ; bearded head of
Bacchus, crowned with ivy, the back-hair tied in a knot; rev.,
NAXION; Silenus, seated, holding a two-handled wine cup. A
splendid tetradrachm, of early work—£13 5s. Lot 1361. Athenæ,
Æ, 6; full-faced mask; rev., a sunk square, containing the full-
faced head and fore-paws of a lion. (*Vide* Beulé, "Monnaies
d'Athènes.") Fine, but perforated—£16 16s. Lot 1366. Ha-
liartus Bœotiæ, Æ, 5½; trident on a Bœotian buckler; rev.,
ΑΛΙΑΡΤΙΩΝ; Neptune, **with trident, to right**. Perfectly genuine,
but much oxydised—£10. Lot 1368. Epirus, Æ; heads of
Jupiter and Juno, to right; rev., ΑΠΕΙΡΩΤΑΝ; a furious bull,
butting, to right, within a garland. A fine tetradrachm—
£17 10s. Lot 1396. Pescennius Niger; **rev.**, FORTUNÆ REDUCI.
See Cohen, p. 216, No. 19. Very fine—£11.

SALE OF COINS, 12TH AUGUST, 1861.—The valuable cabinet
of Greek and Roman coins, formed by Octavius Borrell, Esq., of

Smyrna. The following pieces merit special notice. Lot 8. Pæonia. Eupolemus Rex, Æ, 3; three highly ornamented circular shields; rev., ΕΥΠΟΛΕΜΟΥ; sword and belt. Very fine —£1. Lot 36. Bithynia. Prusias I., Æ, 10½; head, diademed and bearded, to right; rev., ΒΑΣΙΑΕΩΣ . ΠΡΟΥΣΙΟΥ; Jupiter, standing, attired, in the pallium; in the field, a thunderbolt and two monograms, Mt. 28 and 755. Fine,—£14 5s. Lot 52. Troadis. Gentinos, Æ, 2½; Head of Apollo, to right; rev., ΓΕ ΝΤ, with a bee in the centre, the whole within a wreath. Fine —£5 7s. 6d. Lot 58. Ephesus of Gordian III., Æ, 8; rev.. ΑΠ[ΗΜ mon.] Η . ΙΕΡΑ . ΕΦΕCΙΩΝ; carpentum of mules, to right. Extra fine — £5 5s. Lot 61. Caria. Aphrodisias of Caius Cæsar, Æ, 3; ΓΑΙΟΣ . ΚΑΙΣΑΡ; bare head of Caius, to right; rev. ΑΦΡΟΔΙΣΙΕΩΝ; head of Aphrodite, to right. Unpublished and very fine—£6. Lot 68. Lycia. Æ, 3 by 4; forepart of a wild boar, to left; rev., ΤΙΧΧΕΦΙΕΒΕ, and a four-pronged grapnel within a sunk square—£7 15s. Lot 102. Phrygia. Acmonia, of Poppæa, Æ, 3½; ΠΟΠΠΑΙΑ . CΕΒΑCΤΗ; a beautiful head of Poppæa, to right, with a diadem of wheat-cars; rev., ΑΚΜΟ-ΝΕΩΝ . CΕΡΟΥΗΝΙΟΥ . ΚΑΠΙΤΩΝΟC . CΕΟΥΗΡΑC . ΚΑΙ . ΙΟΥΛΙΑC; Diana, to right; in the field, monogs. ΕΠΙ . ΑΡΧ . ΤΟ. A perfect specimen—£16. Lot 113. Phrygia. Eucarpia, Faustina, jun., Æ, 4½; ΦΑΥCΤΕΙΝΑ . CΕΒΑC; head of the empress, to right; rev., ΕΠΙ . Γ . ΚΛ . ΦΛΑΚΚΟΥ . CΥΚΑΡΠΩΝ; Fortune, standing, to left. Fine — £3 13s. Lot 119. Phrygia. Siblium, of Caius Cæsar, Æ, 3½; ΓΑΙΟΣ; bare head of Caius, to right; rev., ΚΑΛΛΙΚΛΗΣ . ΚΑΛΛΙΣΤΡΑΤΟΥ . ΣΙΒΛΙΑΝΩΝ, in five lines. Unpublished, and very fine—£20 5s. Lot 126. Syria. Antiochus II., Æ, 9; with a wing attached to the diadem of Antiochus; rev., Apollo, seated; in the field, a monogram, exergue, a monogram and a horse. Very fine—£13 5s. Lot 128. Syria. Antiochus (?), Æ, 9; youthful diademed head, to right, within a circle of pellets; rev., ΒΑΣΙΛΕΩΣ . ΑΝΤΙΟΧΟΥ; the usual seated Apollo; in the field, a stag's head and monogs. ΑΡ and ΠΑ. Fine—£8. Lot 129. Syria. Antiochus (?), Æ, 8½; a very unusual style of head, diademed, and with close-cropped hair, to right; the usual seated Apollo, exergue ΔΙ, the whole within a circle of pellets. Fine—£8. Lot 154. Pulcheria, Ν; rev., VOT . XX . MVLT . XXX . Є; Victory, with a long cross, above, a star; exergue CONOB. Fine—£6 2s. 6d.

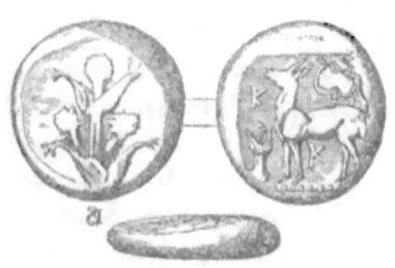

XXVII.

ON A COIN FROM THE CYRENAÏCA, PRESENTED TO THE BRITISH MUSEUM BY THE LATE F. H. CROWE, ESQ., H. M. CONSUL AT CAIRO.

[Read before the Numismatic Society, October 24th, 1861.]

At the time of the arrival at the British Museum of the Cyrene marbles, the presentation of a very rare coin struck in the Cyrenaïca is extremely opportune; especially as it is one that raises questions of a more general character than are usually suggested by ancient money. This coin I should thus describe:—

    Obv.—Silphium plant.

    Rev.—Gazelle, to the left; in front, silphium plant; above, fruit of silphium; in the field and under gazelle, K: all in a sunk square.

    Æ 5¾, wt. 264·7 grs.

The silphium plant is the well-known symbol common to the coins of Cyrene, Barca, and Hesperides. The fruit of the silphium occurs on early coins without inscriptions, probably of the kingdom of Cyrene, and the gazelle is common to Cyrene and Hesperides. Into the meaning of these types I shall not here inquire; it is sufficient to remark their common character.

The date of the coin, judging from its style, which is slightly hard, must be about B.C. 450; perhaps somewhat earlier, but I think certainly not later. It is an Attic tetradrachm, having the heavy weight of the earlier coins of Cyrene or the Cyrenaïca, and Barca, which are of the same or of archaic style. The inscription is certainly K K. There can be no reasonable doubt that one of these letters stands for KYPANAION; the other would seem to correspond to the KOINON which occurs singly on coins of the Cyrenaïca of the Ptolemaic period. This opinion is strengthened by the circumstance that Sestini published a silver didrachm of the period before the Ptolemies with the legend KOIN KYPA, which has been suspected. The word KOINON is known to indicate a community, and to have been frequently used under the Roman emperors by Greek cities, similarly to OMONOIA, and the like. It was one of those fictions by which the Roman emperors contrived to keep their Greek subjects in good humour by giving them a semblance of independence. The community is either that of a city, or of several cities in a province, as KOINON BYZANTIΩN, KOINON KPHTΩN. In the present instance, it would intend either the community of Cyrene, or that of the Cyrenaïca; but the evidence in favour of the latter is overwhelming when it is remembered that all the inhabitants of the Cyrenaïca were generally under the government of Cyrene, and were called Cyrenians. At Cyrene alone we find this term used before the Roman rule, and it was probably granted as a matter of policy by the Egyptian sovereigns. As the example cited by Sestini is anterior to the Egyptian dominion, we may reasonably infer that the term was employed under the republic; and this gives a special interest to our yet earlier coin. If it be rightly read it would indicate that at the time when it was struck the republic was already established, for kings would not have *originated* the use of this term. The history of the latest period of the kingdom of Cyrene and of the foundation of the republic is extremely obscure. We only know that the last king was Arcesilaus IV, who gained a victory in the chariot race at the Pythian Games, B.C. 460, which Pindar has celebrated. (Pyth. iv. v.) He is supposed to have died or been dethroned about B.C. 450. We have no information, however, as to the existence of the republic before B.C. 401. The evidence of our coin is, therefore, probably a great help to history, for if the explanation of the inscription which I have ventured to give be correct, it would more nearly fix the age of the establishment of the republic, since, as already shown, its style forbids our placing it after about B.C. 450.

This coin is of extreme rarity. In the excellent work of MM. Falbe and Lindberg, completed and edited by M. Müller, "Numismatique de l'Ancienne Afrique," vol. i. pp. 11, 12, No. and Fig. 24, the only other specimen of which I know is engraved from the French collection, where but one letter—that beneath the gazelle—is given; and it seems incorrectly, for it here resembles a Xί and not a Καππά. The form of the letters on our specimen would explain this mistake, if it be one.

REGINALD STUART POOLE.

XXVIII.

ADDITIONAL VARIETIES OF SHORT-CROSS PENNIES OF HENRY III. TO THOSE PUBLISHED IN THE FIRST AND SECOND VOLUMES OF SAINTHILL'S "OLLA PODRIDA."

In February, 1858, a hoard of 1,115 coins, said to have been found at Newry, came to Dublin, and, fortunately, were first submitted to Dr. Aquilla Smith, from whom a detailed report of the coins is anxiously expected. Part of the lot were 534 English pennies of Henry III., short cross, and five cut half pennies. Of these, the five cut half pennies and 431 pennies came to Cork, and on examination gave the following results:—

	Coins.
Canterbury	56
Carlisle	7
Cari (?)	1
Chichester	3
Durham	2
Exeter	6
Lincoln	10
London	202
Northampton	9
Norwich	17
Oxford	2
Rhudlam	8
Winchester	45
Worcester	4
Wilton	2
York	19
Illegible	38
	431

The cut half pennies were, two of London, two of Canterbury, and one of Oxford, being halves of five different coins.

Five of the pennies had the cross *pommée* mint-mark, ✤, WILLELM ON LU, FULKE ON LUN, NICOLE ON DU, ADAM ON WIN, SIMUND ON RULA.

I had previously, of this rare mint-mark, COLDWINE ON C, NICOLE ON CAN, TOMAS ON RULA.

A very rude penny of FULKE ON LUND has on the reverse a plain, broad, solid cross, with the usual cross *pommée* in the quarters, and usual cross MM. It is most probably from a carelessly engraved, unfinished, or worn-out die (?) but the result renders it probably an unique reverse of Henry III.'s short-cross coinages.

NEW READINGS, 43.

CANTERBURY.
MEINIM ON CANT.
RENALD ON CA.
RENAUD ON CA.
ROINARD ON CA.
SAMUEL ON C.

CARLISLE.
ALAIN ON . ARD.
ALEIN ON CARD.

CHICHESTER.
WILLELM ON CIC.

DURHAM.
ADAM ON DUR.
NICOLE ON DU.

EXETER.
ROGER ON EXEC.

LINCOLN.
EDMUND ON NICOL.
LEFWINE ON NIC.
WILLELM ON NICO.

LONDON.
DAVI ON LUNDE.
FILAMER ON LUN.
FULKE ON LUN.
GOLD—E ON L—.
JOHAN ON LUNDE.
RANDUL ON LUND.
STIEVENE ON LUND.
WILLELM P. ON LU.
WILEM ON LUND.
WILLELM ON LUND.
VI. ON . ON . LUNDE (*Blundered?*).

NORTHAMPTON.
SIMUN ON NORH.
RAUL ON NORH.
RAUL ON NORHT.

NORWICH.
RANDUL ON NO.
RANDUL ON NOR.
RENALD ON NOR.
ROBERD ON NOR.

OXFORD.
OWEIN ON OXENE.
SWEIN ON OXE.

RHUDLAM.
SIMUN ON RULA.

WINCHESTER.
ADAM ON WIN.
CLEMENT ON WIN.
GOCELM ON WI.
HENRI ON WINC.
REINIER ON WINC.

WORCESTER.
EDRIC ON WIRIC.

YORK.
NICOLE ON EVER.

R. Sainthill.

XXIX.

SHORT-CROSS PENNIES OF HENRY II. OR III.

The following list of the varieties of short-cross pennies of Henry II. or III. in a hoard of these coins lately discovered, has been communicated by the Rev. Assheton Pownall, M.A., and forms a fitting sequel to the preceding article by Mr. Sainthill.

The necessity of careful observation of the names of the various moneyers, as connected with the different mints, both on these and on the long-cross coins, is obvious, as in the case of the more uncommon names they are among the most important means of throwing light upon the still unsettled question as to whether the coins with the short cross are to be attributed to Henry II. or III., respecting which so many communications have appeared in former volumes of the NUMISMATIC CHRONICLE.

LIST OF SHORT-CROSS PENNIES.

CANTERBURY.

	No.
ARNAUD ON CA. *CAN.*	12
HUE ON CANTE.	8
JOHAN ON CAN. CANT.	8
JOHAN B. ON *CA.* CAN.	2
JOHAN M. ON CA. *CAN.*	9
SAMUEL ON CA. CAN.	4
SIMON ON CANT.	3
ROBERT ON CA. CAN. } ROBER. }	8
COLDWINE ON C. CA.	6
ALISANDR ON C.	2

WINCHESTER.

RAUF ON WINC.	2
MILES ON WINC. WINCE.	4
BARTELME ON W. } BERTELME. }	3
ADAM ON WIN. WINCE.	4
JOHAN ON WINC.	1
ANDREU ON WIN.	1
LUKAS ON WINC.	2

LINCOLN.

HUE ON NIC. NICOL. NICOLE.	8
RAUF ON NICOL.	2
RAUF ON NIC	1
RICARD ON NICOL.	1 ✠
NICOLE ON LEN.	1

YORK.

NICOLE ON EVE. EVER.	2
NICOLE ON *EVER.*	1 ✠
RENAUD ON EV.	1
DAVI ON EVER.	2

	No.
DAVI ON EVERW.	2 ✢
TOMAS ON *EVR.*	2
EVERARD ON EV.	1

OXFORD.

AILWINE ON OC.	1
HENRI ON OCSE.	1

EXETER.

JOHAN ON ECCE.	2
GILEBERD ON EC.	2

NORTHAMPTON.

ADAM ON NORH.	1

NORWICH.

RENAUD ON NO.	2
JOHAN ON NOR.	1

CHICHESTER.

PIERES ON CICE.	1
WILLELM ON CIC.	1
RAUF ON CICE.	1

CARLISLE.

TOMAS ON CAR.	1

DURHAM.

PIERES ON DVRE.	1

LONDON.

ABEL ON LVN. LVND. LVNDE.	60
ADAM ON LVND. LVNDE.	5
BENEIT ON LVN. LVND.	3
FULKE ON LVND.	1
ILGER ON *LV. LVDE.* One reads *ILGIER.* ILGER ON LVN. LVND. LVNDE.	67
RAUF ON LVN. LVND. LVNDE.	74
WALTER ON LV. LN. LVN.	89
RICARD ON LVND.	2
RICARD B. ON LV.	4

ABSTRACT.

	No.
RENER ON *LVN.* LVND.	4
WILLELM ON LV. LVN.	4
WILLELM B. ON LV. LW.	4
WILLELM L. ON LV. LW.	4
WILLELM T. ON L. LV. LW.	8
Illegible	27

ABSTRACT.

	Moneyers.	Varieties	No. of coins.
Canterbury	10	17	60
Winchester	7	10	17
Lincoln	5	7	13
York	5	8	10
Oxford	2	2	2
Exeter	2	2	4
Northampton	1	1	1
Norwich	2	2	3
Chichester	3	3	3
Carlisle	1	1	1
Durham	1	1	1
London	15	36	357
	54	90	472

2 DAVI ON EVERW.
1 NICOLE ON EVER.
1 RICARD ON NICOL.

} These four have the rare mark of the cross *pommée* ✤ instead of a cross *patée*.

Unpublished varieties (so far as I know) are twenty-six in number. The following are the new moneyers of their respective mints:—

LUKAS ON WINC.
✤RICARD ON NICOL.
EVERARD ON EV.
AILWINE ON OC.
HENRI ON OCSE.
GILEBERD ON OC.
RAUF ON CICE.
TOMAS ON CAR.
NICOLE ON LEN.

Weights of 149 of these Pennies.

Above	19½ g	...		2 [1]
,,	20 ,,	...		3
,,	20½ ,,	...		3
,,	21 ,,	...		6
,,	21½ ,,	...		12
,,	22 ,,	...		42
,,	22½ ,,	...		44
,,	23 ,,	...		34 [2]
,,	23½ ,,	...		3 [3]
				149

Mem. Their weight does not generally seem determined by their condition.

These coins, of which 472 came into my hands, are said to have been found in Yorkshire. They are all of the type which has two locks of hair right and left of the face, and in each lock a pellet; the type approximating most nearly to that of the "long-cross" penny; and many of them are so fresh that the bloom is still upon the silver, and the edges are quite sharp.

The names of unpublished varieties, and of those with the cross *pommée* or *botonée* instead of the usual cross *patée*, are printed in italics.

ASSHETON POWNALL.

---

[1] Together weighing 1 dwt. 15½ grs.
[2] Altogether 1 oz. 12 dwt. 19 grs., being only 25 grs. short of full weight on the 34 pieces.
[3] These together were 3 dwt. all but half a grain.

XXX.

A FEW WORDS ON BYZANTINE NUMISMATIC ART.

During the middle reigns of the members of the Heraclian dynasty, Byzantine art, as illustrated by its numismatics, had somewhat languished and deteriorated. After, however, the return of Justinian Rhinotmetus from exile, A.D. 705, the coins of this series record a marked and decided stimulus for the better, both in the design and vigour of their representations. The solidus of Fileppicus Bardanes, on which he holds the eagle sceptre, is the best type of this phase of revival; nor, in our opinion, can this beautiful coin be surpassed in the whole length and breadth of the Byzantine series. The gold pieces which occur of Theodosius Adramytenus are principally of barbaric, and probably Italian fabric; but one tremissis, the only coin in our national collection worthy to have issued from the mints of the capital, shows no great perceptible degeneration from the improvement of the previous reign; nor do the solidi of Artemius Anastasius, the next in order, which are fine and well-spread pieces, of a bold and artistic design.

The troubles of these emperors' reigns would not have led us to expect any progressive movement for the better in their monetary art, which, under most conditions, may be accepted in its renewed epochs of vitality as no unfair test of national prosperity. But it has been remarked with some justice, that a worthless generation often may acquire by an undeserved inheritance the slowly matured improvements of a preceding age. Yet many are the instances in which the arts of a nation are susceptible of revival and decay at intervals sufficiently near each other to prevent us tracing any correspondent analogy of disturbance or variety in the history of their times.[1]

We may thus perceive that it would be highly erroneous to assume that the degeneration of Byzantine art, any more than of the Byzantine empire, continued in one steady downward course from Anastasius to the last of the Paleologi, although the convenience of such a generalisation has tempted the carelessness of some writers into kindred statements.

We have next to notice a second phase, or rather modification, of style in numismatic art, inaugurated by, and contemporaneous with, the accession of Constantine Copronymus. We shall find that this period attains its maximum of excellence in the solidi of Michael the Stammerer as emperor, in association with his son Theophilus as Despotes or Cæsar. The excellence of these coins consists rather in their elaboration and finish than in any originality of design, and, although of considerable beauty in their way, they have lost the freedom of execution and freshness of the solidi of Fileppicus, nor is this compensated by their somewhat superior accuracy in the treatment of details.

Under the Macedonian dynasty the commencement of a third phase is not less clearly distinguishable. The

---

[1] Mr. Finlay, in his "History of the Byzantine Empire," illustrates the vicissitudes of art in a short period by a comparison of a guinea of George III. with a coin of Cromwell, or even Anne, or by the National Gallery as contrasted with Whitehall.

coinage of this style is inferior from its first appearance, and, indeed, throughout its continuance to the productions of our two previous epochs. Yet, though we must not compare the typical coins of this period with the delicacy of execution observable on the pieces of the two first emperors of Armorian family, we shall not be disposed to deny to the coinage of the Macedonian dynasty a decided impress and character of its own. Nor does it lack at times the rough quaint vigour of a somewhat stern and religious cast, offering us certain peculiar, and even realistic, motives of its own, which stamp and distinguish its products. This tendency of expression becomes intensified, but at the same time somewhat improved, towards the end of this dynasty, and numismatic art continues to develop its above-mentioned characteristics in an even course of slow, but what we may still call appreciable, progress until the early part of the reign of Alexius Comnenus; from and after which period the deterioration is gradual, but uninterrupted, till the decay of all representative art on the coinage culminates in the *aspers* of Trebizond, and the ungainly *manueluti* of the last centuries of the empire. It is interesting to observe that, after the time of Manuel I., Comnenus, a depreciation of the currency also ensued.[2] This, inasmuch as nearly contemporaneous in commencement with the decay in the fabric and art of the coinage, may have progressed in some sort of proportion therewith.

In the above general view of the phases of improvement in numismatic art, I must be understood as speaking merely with reference to the coinage of the capital; thus the element of barbarism must be carefully considered

---

[2] Finlay, "Greece under the Romans," p. 543.

and eliminated before we should venture to generalise upon the comparative excellence of coin-art at any two given periods. Examples vary from the coinage of some great mint, to all appearance little inferior to that of the capital, to the clumsiest copy by a barbarous tribe, sometimes many years after the original piece was struck; thus are we perplexed, in some reigns, by the puzzling alternations of rudeness and comparative excellence displayed by coins often inscribed with the name of one and the same emperor; and it is only by a careful study of barbarism in its effects upon, and relations with, numismatic art, that we are ever likely to arrive at even an approximate chronological arrangement of the series of ancient Greek cities—a most interesting field of research, where the materials and descriptive notices are abundant, but the attempts at generalisation comparatively few.

To return to Byzantine art, the real importance of which, as to Byzantine history, is contained in the fact of its supplying us with the link between the ancient and the mediæval world. Nor must we forget that this Eastern Empire was the channel through which the civilization of Rome, and of the Roman Cæsars, was slowly ingrafted upon the different nations who had overrun the provinces of the Western Empire.

Nor was Byzantium less instrumental in handing down to our times much which, but for the comparative security of the East during the confusion that succeeded the invasions of Odoacer and Theodoric, must have been inevitably swept away and forgotten.

It would be no uninteresting task to trace the influence which Byzantine art exercised upon the first revival of the Italian schools of painting, as exhibited in the works of Giotto, Cimabue, and their disciples. Analogies are more than frequent, both in the choice of subjects and in the treatment of such subjects—the same grim realistic conceptions of saints and kings, the same stiff limbs and draperies, the same heavy and cumbrous ornamentation.

Yet, even long before the time of these Italian artists, the different barbarians of the West had, like the Saracens in the East, taken the Byzantine type as models for their coinage.

We have only to select, perhaps, the best-known instance of this process, to convince ourselves of the frequency and closeness of such copies.

The series of the dukes of Benevento had branched immediately from the solidi of Justinian II. At first, the prototype was exactly and servilely reproduced; gradually the initial letter of the ducal name for the time being was inserted; and, lastly, we read on such coins the substitution of the duke's name and title in full for those of Justinian, though they never venture to discard the original and typical effigy of that emperor for any closer resemblance to the portrait of their living dukes.

J. L. W.

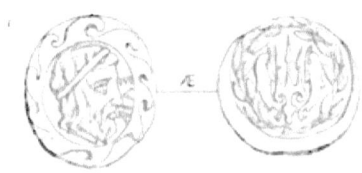

XXXI.

A COIN OF HELIKE.

[Translated from the "Berlin Archæologische Zeitung," 1861.]

THE perfectly preserved brass coin, the drawing of which I send herewith, has been bought recently by a German traveller at Chani Makarù, near Helike, and with it this ancient Ionic capital of Achaia, mentioned so early as the "Iliad," appears for the first time in the series of the towns which struck coins. Perhaps the coin hands down to us, in the head of Poseidon, surrounded by a circle of waves, a copy of the brass statue of Poseidon Helikonios. This idol was considered so sacred, that the partaking of foreigners in the service of the temple was forbidden. Even the permission to copy the statue for another temple, when the Ionians of Asia Minor came to ask for it, was withheld. This refusal provoked the god so that he destroyed his own sanctuary. The town was demolished in the year 373 A.C. (Ol. 101, 4) by an earthquake, and swallowed by the ocean.

The inscription can only be read from right to left, ΚΙΛΕ, for read from left to right, turning the coin, it would give EVIK. But the second letter is not Λ: and even V, this ancient form of Lambda had ceased too soon for it to be found on a Greek *brass* coin, especially on a coin of so beautiful a style. This piece was certainly not coined long before the destruction of the town.

Besides Corinthus and Sicyon, there are but few towns of Achaia which had mints—Ægira, Ægium, Patræ, Pellene, Phlius; and, under the domination of the Romans, Ægira, Ægium, Bura, Patræ, Pellene. Recently, some silver and brass coins, with the inscription ΔΥ, have been attributed to Dyme, as well as a dubious one coined under Augustus with C.I.A.DYM. (perhaps instead of C.I.A.DIVM.?) The coins Payne Knight attributes to Peiræ, are of Amisus; those given to Rhypæ, of Rybastini in Apulia. The coin described in the Magnoncour Catalogue, No. 281, as one of the Achaei, with the inscription ΑΧΑΙΩΝ, is now in the royal cabinet at Berlin. It bears the inscription ΑΧΑΙΩΝ ΕΥΜΕΝΕΩΝ; consequently, it is of Eumenia, in Phrygia.

Julius Friedlaender.

Berlin.

XXXII.

UNPUBLISHED GREEK AUTONOMOUS AND IMPERIAL COINS.

I have much pleasure in laying before the Numismatic Society a notice of many hitherto unpublished Greek Autonomous and Imperial coins in copper and silver; some of which are of extreme rarity, and remarkably fine.

Caria.

Aphrodisia of Caius Cæsar. Æ 3. ΓΑΙΟΣ. ΚΑΙΣΑΡ. Bare head of Caius, to right. *Rev.* ΑΦΡΟΔΙ-ΣΙΕΩΝ. Head of Aphrodite, to right.

*** This is the first coin known of Caius, of this town.

———— of Gordian III. Æ 10½. ΑΥ.Κ.Μ.ΑΝ. ΓΟΡΔΙΑΝΟC.CΕ. Radiated head of Gordian, to right, with the *paludamentum*. *Rev.* ΔΗΜΟC. ΕΛΕΥΘΕΡΙΑ ΑΦΡΟΔΙCΙΕΩΝ. Nude Genius of the People, standing by an altar, holding a patera in his right hand, and a long branch in his left, with a mantle depending from his left arm; to his left, the goddess Aphrodite, standing with her right hand raised above his head, and with a bird perched on her left.

Apollonia. Æ 2½. Head of Apollo, to right. ΑΠΟΛ-ΛΩΝΙΑΤΩΝ, in two lines, divided by a four-stringed lyre.

Astypalea, insula. Æ 1½. Helmeted head of Perseus, to right. *Rev.* ⋝ A (*sic*). The *falx*,' or pruning-knife.

Eriza. Æ 3. Head of Jupiter, to right. *Rev.*—ЄΡΙ-ΖΗΝΩΝ, in two lines, divided by an eagle perched on a thunderbolt.

Paleopolis of Elagabalus. Æ 10½. ... ΑΥ. ΑΝΤΩ ... ΝΟC. Radiated head of the emperor, with draped bust, to right. *Rev.*—ΠΑΛΕΟΠΟΛΕΙΤΩΝ. Three athletes, standing, one to right, and one to left, whilst the other, or centre one, is anointing his right arm by thrusting it into a vase; above, a prize vase; *exergue*, ΘΕΜΙC.

Rhodus, insula. Æ 4. Radiated head of the sun, three-quarter face. *Rev.*—ΜΕΛΑΝΙΠΠΟΣ, around a full-blown rose, the whole within a circle of pellets.

Telos, insula. Æ 1½. Head of Mercury, with *petasus*, to right. *Rev.*—ΤΕ and a fly, within a sunk square.

LYCIA.

Lycia in genere of Claudius. Æ 4. ΤΙΒΕΡΙΟΣ. ΚΛΑΥ-ΔΙΟΣ [ΚΑΙΣΑΡ. ΣΕΒΑΣΤΟΣ]. Bare head of the emperor, to left. *Rev.* — ΓΕΡΜΑΝΙΚΟΣ. ΑΥΤΟΚΡΑΤΩΡ. Germanicus, on horseback, galloping, to right.

——————————— Æ 6. *Legend wanting.* Bare head of the emperor, to left. *Rev.*—ΓΕΡΜΑΝΙΚΟΣ. ΑΥΤΟΚΡΑΤΟΡ. [ΠΑΤΗΡ] ΠΑΤΡΙ-ΔΟΣ. Diana, standing, holding a torch in her right hand, and a victory in her left; at her feet, a stag.

——————————— Æ 6. ΤΙΒΕΡΙΟΣ. ΚΛΑΥ-ΔΙΟΣ. ΣΕΒΑΣΤΟΣ. Bare head of the emperor, to left. *Rev.*—ΓΕΡΜΑΝΙΚΟΣ. ΑΥΤΟΚΡΑΤΩΡ. ΠΑΤΕΡ. ΠΑΤΡΙΔΟΣ. Germanicus, on horseback, armed, to right; behind, Pallas, on a pedestal.

Apollonia of Geta. Æ 7. *Rev.*—ΑΠΟΛΛΩΝΙΑΤΩΝ. ΑΥ. Fortune, standing, to left.

————— of Gallienus. Æ 11. *Rev.*—ΑΠΟΛΛΩΝΙΑΤΩΝ. A river-god, seated; *exergue*, ΟΡΑΚ.

Araxa. Æ 4½. Head of Diana, to right; in front, ΛΥΚ. mon. *Rev.*—A stag, to right; *exergue* ΧΑ. mon. ΡΑ.

Caunus. Æ 2. Sphinx, squatting, to right. *Rev.*—Bull, butting, to right.

Choma. Æ 2. Head of Jupiter, to right. *Rev.*—ΧΩ, divided by a club, within a wreath.

Corycus. Æ 2. Two bearded heads, side by side, to right. *Rev.*—ΚΟ. Lion, running, to right.

Cragus and *Xanthus* (*in alliance*). Æ 3. Head of Diana, to right. *Rev.*—ΚΡ . ΞΑΝ. A quiver.

Cyaneae. Æ 2⅓. Head of Medusa. *Rev.*—ΚΥ. mon. ΑΣΜΙ, separated by a rose.

Heraclea and *Phaselis* (*in alliance*). Æ 4. Bearded head, to right. *Rev.*—ΗΡΑΚΛΕΑΤΩ . ΦΙΑΣ (*sic*), and a club within a wreath.

Limyra. Æ 1½. Head of Apollo, to right. *Rev.*—ΛΥΚΙΟΝ . Λ. Bow and club transversed.

———— Æ 2. Head of Diana, to right. *Rev.*—ΛΥ and a quiver within a sunk square.

Patara. Æ 1½. ΠΑΤΑ. Female head, to right. *Rev.*—Female head, to right.

Tlos. Æ 3. Head of Apollo, with the attributes of Diana, to right. *Rev.*—ΛΥΚΙΩΝ . ΤΛ. Head of Diana, to right, within a sunk square.

Tlos and *Cragus* (*in alliance*). Æ 3½. Head of Diana, to right. *Rev.*—ΤΛ . ΚΡ. Stag, to right.

Xanthus. Æ 1. Head of Apollo, to right. *Rev.*—ΞΑΝ-ΘΙΩΝ, in two lines, separated by a lyre.

PAMPHYLIA.

Ariassus of Gordian III. Æ 9. *Rev.*—ΑΡΙΑССΕΩΝ. A nude figure, standing, receiving a branch from a draped figure, seated.

Magydus of Gallienus. Æ 9. ΑΥΤ.ΚΑΙ.ΠΟ.ΑΙ.ΓΑΛ-
ΛΙΗΝΟ.СЄΒ. Laureated head of the emperor,
with *paludamentum*, to right; below, a globe.
Rev.—ΜΑΓΥΔΕΩΝ. Fortune, standing; in the
field, MA and I.

Pisidia.

Antiochia Colonia. Æ 2. ANTIOCH. Bare juvenile
head, to left; behind, a caduceus. *Rev.*—AN.
mon. COLONI. Cock, to right.

Apollonia. Æ 3. Helmeted head, to right. *Rev.*—ΑΠΟ.
Slinger, to right.

Claudio-Seleuceia of **Caracalla.** Æ 6. *Rev.*—ΚΛΑΥΔΙΟ-
СЄΛЄΥΚЄΩΝ. Apollo, discharging an arrow
from his bow.

——————— of Claudius Gothicus. Æ 9. *Rev.*—
ΚΛΑΥΔΙΟСЄΛЄΥΚЄΩΝ. Jupiter, seated, to
left, holding a victory in his right hand.

Conane of Julia Mamæa. Æ 6½. *Rev.*—ΚΟΝΑΝЄΩΝ.
Bacchus, standing, to left; at his feet, a panther.

Cremna. Æ 3. Head of Diana, to right; behind, a
spear-head. *Rev.*—ΚΡΗ. Forepart of lion, to
right; above, Γ; the whole within a dotted
circle.

——————— of Aurelian. Æ 9. IMP.C.S.L.
DOM . AVRELIANO. Laureate head of
Aurelian, with *paludamentum*, to right. *Rev.*—
COL.IVLI.AV.CREMNE. A semi-draped
male figure, seated, to left, with *hasta*; at his
feet, a bird.

Pednelissus of Antoninus Pius. Æ 4. *Rev.*—ΠЄΔΝΗ-
ΛΙССЄ.Ν. Female head to left.

Pogla. Æ 1½, 2, 4. [O] on a round buckler. *Rev.*—Tri-
quetra.

Sagalassus of Marcus Aurelius. Æ 6. *Rev.*—ΣΑΓΑ-
ΛΑССЄ[ΩΝ, *mon*]. Lion, springing to left;
in *exergue*, a branch.

Sagalassus of Claudius Gothicus. Æ 9½. *Rev.*—CAΓA-
ΛACCEΩN. Hercules destroying the hydra.

——————————————— Æ 10. *Rev.*—
. . OYΛH . ΔHMOC . CAΓAΛACCEΩN. The
Genius of the People hand-in-hand with the
emperor.

Lydia.

Blaundos of Otacilia Severa. Æ 9. M . ΩTAK . CEBHPA .
CE. Head of the empress, to right. *Rev.*—EΠ .
AYP ΓΛYKONOC . Γ . NIΓP . APX . A . BΛAYN-
ΔEΩN . MAK. Amazon, on horseback, to right,
armed with a bipennis.

——————— of Volusian. Æ 8. *Rev.*—BΛAYNΔEΩN .
MA . ET . PAYΠATNIAE. Amazon, on horseback, to right, armed with a bipennis.

Phrygia.

Acmonia of Poppæa. Æ 3½. ΠΟΠΠΑΙΑ . ΣΕΒΑΣΤΗ.
Head of Poppæa, to right, dressed with a diadem
of wheat-ears. *Rev.* — ΑΚΜΟΝΕΩΝ . ΣΕ-
POYHNIOY . ΚΑΠΙΤΩΝΟΣ . ΣΕΟΥΗΡΑΣ . ΚΑΙ .
ΙΟΥΛΙΑΣ. Diana, to right, holding a bow in her
extended left hand, and with her right drawing
an arrow from her quiver; in the field, *mons*.
ΕΠΙ . APX . TO.

Cotiaeum of Domitia. Æ 5½. ΔΟΜΙΤΙΑ . ΣΕΒΑΣΤΗ.
Head of the empress, to right. *Rev.*—ΕΠΙ .
ΜΕΤ . Φ . ΣΩΣΘ(?)ΕΝΟΥΣ . ΚΟΤΙΑΕΩΝ. Female,
seated on a high-backed chair, to left, holding a
patera in her right hand.

——————— of Otacilia Severa. Æ 6. *Rev.*—EΠΙ . Γ .
ΙΟΥΛ . ΠΟΝΤΙΚΟΥ . ΑΡΧΙΕΡΕΩΣ . ΚΟΤΙΑΕΩΝ.
Hercules despoiling the Ceryneian stag of its
golden antlers.

Eucarpeia of Faustina Jun. Æ 4½. ΦΑΥCTEINA .
CEBAC. Head of the empress, to right. *Rev.*—
EΠI . Γ . KΛ . ΦΛΑΚΚΟΥ . ΕΥΚΑΡΠΕΩΝ.
Fortune, standing, to left.

Prymnessus. Æ 4½. Head of Serapis, to right. *Rev.*—ΠΡΥΜΝΗCCЄΩΝ. Æsculapius, standing.

Siblium of Caius Cæsar. Æ 3½. ΓΑΙΟΣ. Bare head of Caius, to right. *Rev.*—ΚΑΛΛΙΚΛΗΣ. ΚΑΛΛΙΣΤΡΑΤΟΥ. ΣΙΒΛΙΑΝΩΝ, in five lines across the field.

⁎⁎ This is the first coin known of Caius of this town.

W. Webster.

XXXIII.

A SELECTION OF INEDITED COINS OF THE EGYPTIAN SERIES.

Cairo, Sept. 11, 1861.

SIR,

I enclose an account of a few inedited coins of the Egyptian series, together with sketches and impressions of some of the more remarkable among them, in the hope that you may think them of sufficient interest for insertion in the NUMISMATIC CHRONICLE.

I am, Sir,

Yours faithfully,

H. C. REICHARDT.

To the Editors of the Num. Chron.

KINGS OF EGYPT.

1. PTOLEMY VI. (?) PHILOMETER.

Obv.—Diademed head of Ptolemy VI. (?) to the right.

Rev.—. . . . . . ΟΛΕΜΑΙ . . ΦΙΛΟΜΗΤ . ΘΕΟΥ . L . Δ.   A flying eagle on a thunderbolt, to the left; in the field the monogram ₰.

Æ 6½.

IMPERIAL COINS OF ALEXANDRIA.

CAIUS CÆSAR.

Obv.—Laureate head, to the right.

Rev.—Γ . . ΟΥ, written above a half-moon.

Æ 1½.

ALEXANDRIAN COINS.

Faustina, Sen.

2. *Obv.*—L . KB. (an. 22 of Ant. Pius, *i. e.* 138 A.D.) ΦΑΥϹΤΙΝΑΝ . ΘΕΑΝ. Veiled head of Faustina Senior, to the right.

   Rev.—ΑΝΤⲰΝΙΝΟϹ . ϹΕΒ . ΕΥϹΕΒ. Laureate head of Antoninus Pius, to the right.
   Pot. 6.

Crispina.

3. *Obv.*—ΚΡΕΙϹΠΕΙΝΑ . ϹΕΒΑϹΤΗ. Head of Crispina, to the right.

   Rev.—L . KB. (an. 22). Victory in a chariot, drawn by two horses.
   Pot. 6.

Pescennius Niger.

4. *Obv.*— . . . . . . ΝΙΓΡΟϹ . ΔΙ. Radiated head of the emperor, to the right.

   Rev.—L . B. (an. 2). A naked figure, standing, holding a cornucopiæ in the left arm, which rests on a pillar, and stretching out the right arm.
   Æ 6.

Pertinax.

5. *Obv.*—ΑΥΤ . ΚΑΙ . Π . ΕΛΟΥΙΟϹ . ΠΕΡΤΙΝΑΞ . ϹΕ. Laureate head of the emperor, to the right.

   Rev.—L . A. (an. 1.) Jupiter, seated on a chair, to the left, holding a thunderbolt in his right hand, and the left arm resting on a simple staff.
   Pot. 7. (Pl. x. No. 1.)

Septimius Severus.

6. *Obv.*—ΑΥΤ . Κ . Λ . ϹΕΠΤ . ϹΕΟΥΗΡΟϹ . ΠΕΡΤ . ϹΕΒ. Laureate head of the emperor, to the right.

   Rev.—L . B. (an. 2). Roma Nicephora, seated, to the left.
   Pot. 6½.

7. *Obv.*—ΑΥΤ.Κ.Λ.CΕΠ.CΕΟΥΗ.ΠΕΡΤ.CΕΒ.ΑΡΑΑΒΙ?
Laureate head of the emperor, to the right.

Rev.—L..Δ. (an. 4). An eagle, standing, to the right, but having its head turned to the left, holding in its beak a garland.

Pot. 6.

8. *Obv.*—ΑΥΤ.Κ.Λ.CΕΠ.CΕΥΗ.ΕΥCΕ.ΠΕΡΤ.CΕΒ.Α...
Laureate head, to the right.

Rev.—L..Δ. (an. 4). Victory, to the right, resting her left foot, which is lifted up, on a helmet, and placing on a pillar a shield, on which is drawn the head of Serapis.

Pot. 6. (Pl. x. No. 3.)

9. *Obv.*— .... Κ.Λ.CΕΠ.CΕΥΗ.ΕΥ.... Laureate head, to the right.

Rev.—L.Δ. (an. 4). Equity, to the left, holding a pair of scales in her right, and a staff in her left hand; behind her stands Mercury, on an estrade, holding a purse in his right hand.

Pot. 6. (Pl. x. No. 2.)

10. *Obv.*— .... CΕΠ.CΕΥΗ.ΕΥCΕ.ΠΕΡΤ.CΕΒ.
Laureate head of Sept. Sev., to the right.

Rev.—L.Ε. (an. 5). Eagle, to the right, as No. 7.

Pot. 6.

JULIA DOMNA.

11. *Obv.*—ΙΟΥΑ....ΔΟΜΝΑ.CΕΒ.ΜΗΤΡΙ CΤΡΑ. Head of Julia Domna, to the right.

Rev.—L.Θ. (an. 9). Laureate heads of her two sons, Caracalla and Geta, facing each other; both with the *paludamentum*.

Pot. 6. (Pl. x. No. 4.)

CARACALLA.

12. *Obv.*—Α.ΚΑΙCΑΡ.ΜΑ.ΑΥ.C.ΑΝΤѠΝΙΝΟC. Laureate head to the right.

Rev.—L.Γ. (an. 3). Head of Serapis, to the right.

Pot. 6.

13. *Obv.*—AVT . K . M . AYPHA . ANTⲰNINOC......Laureate and bearded head, to the right.
   Rev.—L . IΘ. (an. 19). Equity, standing, to the left.
   Pot. 6½.

? ? ? 14. *Obv.*— ..... AYP . CЄ . ANTⲰN ...... As before.
   Rev.—L . KΓ. (an. 23). A triumphal arch, on which the emperor sits between two figures, to the right; Serapis, from behind, offers him a crown; within each of the three gateways of the arch there is a divinity.
   Æ. 10.

Diadumenian.

15. *Obv.*—MA . OII . AN ΔIAΔOYMЄNIANOC . K . CЄ. Bare head of Diadumenian, to the right.
   Rev.—L . B. (an. 2). A military figure, to the left.
   Pot. 6. (Pl. x. No. 5.)

Orbiana and Alexander.

16. *Obv.*—CAΛΛ . BAPBIA OPBIANA . CЄB . L . ΠЄMΠ. (an. 5). Head of Orbiana, to the right.
   Rev.— ..... AYP . CЄOYHP . AΛЄΞANΔPOC . ЄYCEB. Laureate head of Severus Alexander, to the right.
   Pot. 6½.

XXXIV.

NOTE ON THE ἘΝ ΤΌΤΟ ΝΊΚΑ AND ἈΝΑΝΈΟΣΙΣ TYPES OF THE HERACLIAN DYNASTY.

Since writing a description of a hoard of coins discovered in Cyprus, I have found the views I there advocated singularly confirmed by the following passage in Mr. Finlay's "Greece under the Romans." This historian, in speaking of the wholesale emigrations effected by the imperial caprice of Justinian Rhinotmetus, says:—

"Three years after the conclusion of peace with Abdal Melik, he (Rhinotmetus) resolved to withdraw all the inhabitants from the half of the Island of Cyprus, of which he remained master, in order to prevent the Christians *from becoming accustomed to the Saracen administration.* The Cypriote population was transported to a new city near Cyzicus, which the emperor called after himself, Justinianopolis."[1]

Such testimony evidences the ready disposition of the Greek population to amalgamate with their Saracenic masters, and speaks volumes for the equitable administration of the latter. We submit, with the greatest respect for the authority of M. de Saulcy, that such a passage is at variance with his reason for the attribution of the coin of Cyprus, engraved, Pl. viii. No. 3, in his excellent work on the Byzantine series. He says, at p. 71:—

---

[1] P. 476.

"Cette île (Chypre) étant tombée au pouvoir des Sarrazins dans l'année VII. du règne de Constant II., comme le rapporte Cedrenus, la pièce est nécessairement d'Heraclius, Martine et Heraclius-Constantin."

M. de Saulcy is right in this attribution, but wrong in the reason he assigns for it, since the monogram of the elder Heraclius—only indicated in his engraving above the monetary M on the reverse of the coin, but perfectly distinct in a British Museum example—settles the point.

Mr. Finlay's hypothesis for the origin of the types under consideration is well worthy of attention.

"Heraclius, in the early part of the seventh century, first introduced a Greek legend, ἘΝ ΤΟ͂ΥΤΟ ΝΊΚΑ, on the copper coins of rude fabric, which were probably coined for the use of the troops and the provincials during his Persian campaigns."[2]

The only modification to be suggested in this extract is to omit the words "of rude fabric;" for certainly the coins of this type are no ruder in general workmanship than the rest of the copper currency of the period. The sentence, as it reads above, would almost give one the impression of this having been issued as a *pièce de nécessité*, and the fabric would be accordingly inferior, as that of the siege-pieces of later times. The idea, however, of connecting the appearance of the ἘΝ ΤΟ͂ΥΤΟ ΝΊΚΑ pieces with the Persian campaigns of Heraclius for paying the army and passing current among the provinces contiguous to the military operations, deserves a conspicuous place among the theories propounded on the origin of this type. Such a type would be peculiarly appropriate in a war against the crescent and the infidels, thus

---

[2] P. 545, Appendix I.

re-adopting the labarum motto—translated, however, and thereby showing how essentially Greek the Empire had become. This supposition only disposes of half the difficulty, since the ΑΝΑΝΕΟΣΙΣ part of these types does not agree well with Mr. Finlay's ingenious suggestion, and would seem rather to indicate some fresh era inaugurated by the accession of a new dynasty, than the commencement of a war in the thirteenth year after that event.

J. L. W.

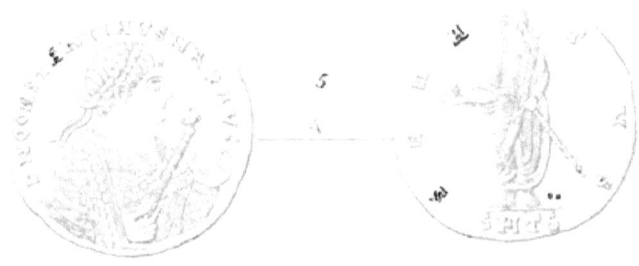

XXXV.

ON THE IMPERIAL CONSULAR "DRESS."

[Read before the Numismatic Society, November 21, 1861.]

It is doubtful whether in the following remarks there may be anything that is really new; yet, notwithstanding, I am inclined to think that there will be found some things that the generality of my readers do not know. My attention was principally called to the subject before you by the indiscriminate manner in which the form of the "garment," as represented on the coins of the later emperors, is described in M. Cohen's work, "Les Médailles Impériales." Either it is "the emperor's bust, covered with the *paludamentum* and cuirass," or it is varied by "bust with the imperial robe." It is my object here to lay before you an account of the various dresses used in the imperial period, and to show that the bust is not always covered with the *paludamentum* or the imperial robe. Besides, the term "imperial robe" is very indefinite, and an appropriate name ought to be found for it.

I may notice the extreme fondness, in ancient times, for fine and gaudy robes. The following passages, extracted from Homer, will illustrate this:—

ἡ δὲ μέγαν ἱστὸν ὕφαινε
Δίπλακα πορφυρέην, πόλεας δ'ἐνέπασσεν ἀέθλους
Τρώων δ' ἱπποδάμων καὶ Ἀχαιῶν χαλκοχιτώνων.
Il. lib. iii. 125.

.........ὐ πέπλοι παμποίκιλοι, ἔργα γυναικῶν
Σιδονίων.
Il. lib. vi. 289.

'Αλλ' ἥγ' ἱστον ὕφαινε μυχῷ δόμου ὑψηλοῖο
Δίπλακα πορφυρέην, ἐν δὲ θρόνα ποικίλ' ἔπασσεν.
Il. lib. xxii. 440.

The first ancient author who mentions silk is Aristotle.[1] It was manufactured at Cos as early as the fourth century B.C. Under the empire, the rage for silk garments was immense, and Tiberius was obliged to enact a law, "ne vestis serica viros fœdaret."[2] The beautiful material and fineness of the silk in use, as also the flowered texture, is mentioned by an author supposed to be contemporary with those of the Augustan age.[3] Afterwards, measures were adopted to restrict its use, but it was again revived by Caligula for both males and females.[4] In the year A.D. 176, M. Aurelius sold his wife's silks in the forum of Trajan.[5]

Among the various names for the dresses, and parts of the dresses, in use during the reigns of Elagabalus, Severus Alexander, Aurelianus, Claudius II., and Carinus, I may mention the following:—

1. Toga prætexta.[6]   2. Toga picta.

---

[1] H. A. lib. v. cap. 19.—'Εκ δὲ τούτου τοῦ ζῴου καὶ τα βομ-
βύκια ἀναλύουσι τῶν γυναικῶν τινες ἀναπηνιζόμεναι, κἄπειτα ὑφαί-
νουσιν.—Βομβυξ is a silkworm.

[2] Tac. Ann. ii. 33.

[3] Diony. Perieg. 755:—

"Εἱματα τεύχουσιν πολυδαίδαλα, τιμήεντα
Εἰδόμενα χροιῇ λειμωνίδος ἄνθεσι ποίης.
Κείνοις οὔτι κεν ἔργον ἀραχνάων ἐρίσειεν.

[4] Suet. Cal. 52.

[5] In foro divi Trajani auctionem ornamentorum imperialium fecit vendiditque .... et vestem uxoriam sericam et auratam.—(Capit. Aur. 17.)

[6] The ordinary dresses, viz., the *toga*, *tunica*, *pænula*, *la-*

3. Tunica palmata.
4. Serica vestis.
5. Subserica vestis.
6. Holoserica vestis.
7. Subarmalis profundus.
8. Paragaudæ.
9. Clavus latus.
10. Clavus angustus.
11. Interulæ dilores.
12. Interulæ paragaudæ.
13. Monolores vestes.
14. Dilores vestes.
15. Trilores vestes.
16. Pentelores vestes.

The *toga prætexta*[7] had a broad purple border.

The *toga picta* was ornamented with Phrygian embroidery, and usually worn by generals in triumph, and, under the emperors, by the consuls when they triumphed.

The *tunica palmata* was a flowered tunic, and was also called *tunica Jovis,* because it was taken from the Temple of Jupiter Capitolinus.[8] This robe was also worn at triumphs, and by the consuls.

The *serica* and *subserica vestis* were partially or half silk, and *holoserica* entirely silk.

The *subarmalis profundus* was a long unembroidered tunic, worn by the consuls.

Paragaudæ, were the borders or trimmings of a garment.

---

cerna, &c., I need not allude to. The first may be seen on the coins of Trajanus, Hadrianus, Antoninus Pius, &c., where the type is generally "the emperor, wearing the *toga,* sacrificing before an altar."

[7]. The *toga prætexta,* under the emperors, probably superseded the *trabea* under the republic. The latter was worn by the consuls in public solemnities, such as opening the Temple of Janus:—

"Ipse, Quirinali *trabed* cinctuque Gabino
Insignis, reserat stridentia limina consul."
Virg. Æn. vii. 612.

Claudian, in speaking of the consulship of Probinus and Olybrius (l. 178), mentions robes interwoven with gold (auratas trabeas), made for them by their mother Proba. The word *trabea* at this period is used to express the consular robe. There are many other allusions to the consular dress in the same author, but space does not permit me to quote them.

[8] See Liv. x. 7, Juv. x. 38. This robe was also called *Capitolina.*—(Vopisc. Prob. 7.)

These were among the presents given by Furius Placidus in A.D. 313, when he was made consul.[9] By a law of Valentinianus and Valens, their use was forbidden, excepting in the emperor's private gynæcea.

The *clavus latus* was a broad stripe, of purple colour, in the middle of the tunic, in front, running down from the neck, and was a distinctive badge of the senatorial dignity.

The *clavus angustus* was a narrow stripe of purple.

Interulæ dilores, under-garments with two stripes.

Interulæ paragaudæ, under-trimmings.

Vestes monolores, &c., robes with one, two, three, and five stripes of embroidered silk.

The following are the passages in which Nos. 1, 2, 3, and 7 are alluded to:—

Prætextam et *pictam togam* nunquam nisi consul accepit, et eam quidem quam de Jovis templo sumptam alii quoque accipiebant, aut prætores aut consules. Accepit *prætextam* etiam quum sacra faceret, sed loco Pontificis Maximi, non Imperatoris.—(Lamprid. Alex. Sev. 40.)

Palmatam tunicam et *togam pictam*, primus Romanorum privatus suam propriam habuit, cum ante Imperatores etiam de Capitolio acciperent vel de Palatio.—(Capit. Gord. i. 4.)

Cape igitur tibi pro rebus gestis tuis......*togam prætextam, tunicam palmatam, togam pictam, subarmalem profundum*...... nam te consulem hodie designo.—(Vopisc. Aur. 13.)

In the above passages it is plainly stated what the *consular* robes consisted of.

The following quotations allude to Nos. 4, 5, 6, 8, 9, 11, 12, 13, 14, 15, and 16.

Primus Romanorum *holosericâ veste* usus fertur; quum jam *subserica* (*subsericæ?*) in usu essent.[10]—(Lamprid. Elagab. 26.)

Vestes sericas ipse raras habuit; *holosericas* nunquam induit, *subsericam* nunquam donavit.—(Lamprid. Alex. Sev. 40.)

---

[9] Quum darentur tunicæ *subsericæ*, lineæ *paragaudæ* . . . . . —(Vopisc. Aur. 15.)

[10] This can only apply to its adoption for *men*, as mention is

Albam *subsericam* unam ...... *Interulas*, puras duas; ...... *latum clavum* quem refundat, unum.—(Treb. Poll. Claud. 14.)

Albam *subsericam, paragaudem* triuncem unum.—(Treb. Poll. Claud. 17.)

Interulas dilores duas.—(Vopisc. Bonosus.)

Interulas paragaudas duas.—(Vopisc. **Prob. 4.**)

See passage already quoted.—(Vopisc. Aur. 15, p. 234, note.)

Vestem holosericam neque ipse in vestiario suo habuit, neque alteri utendam dedit.[11]—(Vopisc. Aur. **45.**)

Paragaudas vestes ipse primus militibus dedit...... et quidem aliis *monolores*, aliis *dilores, trilores*, aliis usque ad *pentelores*, quales hodie lineæ sunt.—(Vopisc. Aur. 46.)

Holosericam **vestem** viris omnibus **interdixit.** — (Vopisc. Tac. 10.)

Græcis **artificibus** ...... **donata et** *vestis serica*.—'(Vopisc. Carin. 19.)

It seems rather doubtful what the *lora* were; one would be inclined to see an allusion to the garment *lorum* in the following sentence, "Vestis subtegmine serico aureis filis insignior;"[12] yet that the *lora* were rather stripes than mere threads woven in, seems more probable. The word *lora*, of which *monolores, dilores*, &c., are compounds, has been suggested to signify **trimmings**, and to be the same as *paragaudæ* or **segmenta,** the latter of which words occurs in Juvenal[13] and Ovid.[14] Whatever the word

---

made by Varro, in Nonius, of a *holoserica stola mulierum*.—(Varro Fragmenta, 8vo. Dordrecht, 1619, p. 93.) Lampridius also mentions that Elagabalus had prepared a rope made of purple, silk, and scarlet, with which, if it was necessary, he might hang himself! (c 33.) What a pity he did not!

[11] At the time of Aurelian a pound of gold was the price of a pound of silk.—(Libra enim auri tunc libra serici fuit. *l. c.*)

[12] Capit. Pert. viii.

[13] *Segmenta*, et longos habitus.—(Lib. i. Sat. ii.)

[14] Quid de veste loquar? nec vos, *segmenta* requiro;
   Nec quæ bis Tyrio murice lana rubes.
   (De Arte Amandi, iii. 169.)

lorum may mean, I think there can be no doubt that, later, it was used to express *a whole consular robe*; i. e., *a scarf*, worn over the other consular robes.

And now to see if we can find any traces on the coins of the dresses above alluded to. The first appearance of a robe differing from the ordinarily worn *paludamentum* may be found represented on a coin of Augustus, without his head. It may be thus described :—

> *Obv.*—S . P . Q . R . PAREN[T.] CONS . SVO. (Senatus Populusque Romanus Parenti Conservatori (?) suo.) On the left, the Roman eagle; in the middle, the *tunica palmata*, over which is the *toga picta*, and, on the right side, a wreath.
>
> *Rev.*—CAESARI . AVGVSTO. Quadriga, to right, on the top of which are four horses. Æ. (Pl. xi. No. 1.)

Eckhel has suggested the word CONSERVATORI, but why should not CONS. represent CONSVLI? In B.C. 2, not only was Augustus made *Pater Patriæ*, but he entered also on his thirteenth consulship (Suet. Aug. c. 26). The *ornamenta* here, though triumphal, are equally applicable to the consular office, as the crown and sceptre were granted to the consuls when they triumphed. No mention, indeed, is made of a triumph in B.C. 2; but new honours were continually given to Augustus, and it is likely that a coin would be struck when he was made *Pater Patriæ*, bearing the titles of *Parens* and *Consul*, commemorating the two events of the year B. c. 2, and at the same time recalling his threefold triumph in B. c. 29.

The *toga picta* seems to have been the same as the *toga purpurea*, and was, as I have before remarked, generally, if not always, worn at triumphs.[15] Representations of

---

[15] Livy evidently uses *toga picta* and *toga purpurea* quite promiscuously.—(See lib. x. 7, xxx. 15, xxxi. 11.) Dionysius Halicarnassus (lib. iii.) — χιτῶνα τε πορφυροῦν χρυσοσήμον, καὶ

the emperors in a triumphal quadriga, probably wearing the dress, may be found on several of their coins.[16] The first time that we find a difference in the treatment of the bust is (as far as I am aware) under Gordianus Pius (Cohen, No. 192). Here is represented the *tunica palmata*, and, above it, the *toga prætexta*. These dresses may also be seen on the bronze medallions of Treb. Gallus (Cohen, 80), Volusianus (Cohen, 85), and other emperors. Some of the emperors are represented *togati* on the reverses of their respective coins down to the reigns of Diocletianus and Maximianus, on whose coins the word CONSVL appears on the reverse. On a coin of Maximinus II. (Daza) we first notice in the representation of the emperor on the reverse an addition to the usual *toga*. It is in the shape of an ornamental border over the left shoulder, which probably represents the *toga prætexta*. This is further increased on a coin of Constantine the Great with the legend CONSVL. P. P. PROCONSVL., engraved at Pl. xi. No. 6. Here we have a representation something similar to that on the diptych of Flavius Felix (which I will mention presently), viz., the under tunic, or *subarmalis profundus*, the *tunica palmata*, and the *trabea* (or *toga prætexta*), which is afterwards the *lorum*.

It seems to me that the representation of the bust on coins of the Lower Empire may be divided into three classes :—1, Ordinary, or civil ; 2, Military ; 3, Consular. First, the usual honours of the Augusti — the laurel wreath, the diadem, *paludamentum*, cuirass, and spear, &c.;

περιβόλαιον πορφυροῦν ποικίλον—the *tunica purpurea* and *toga purpurea picta*.

[16] See Germanicus (Cohen, No. 5); Titus (Cohen, No. 237); and others.

second, the helmet,[17] shield, cuirass, spear, globe—on which is sometimes a Victory—&c.; and third, the laurel wreath, the diadem, the *tunica palmata*, the *lorum*, cuirass,[18] *mappa*,[19] globe—on which is sometimes a Victory —and staff, on which an eagle.

As an example of this I may quote three *aurei* of the Emperor Probus, representing him in Ordinary, Military, and Consular dress, which are engraved at Pl. xi. Nos. 2, 3, 4.

On the famous gold medallion of Constantine the Great there is an excellent illustration of our subject; it may be described as follows:—

> *Obv.*—D.N.CONSTANTINVS.MAX.AVG. Bust of the emperor, to right, laureate, showing half the body, which is clothed in the *subarmalis profundus* (under-tunic), over which is the *tunica palmata*, above all is the *lorum*; both hands are represented, the right holding sceptre, on which is an eagle, and the left holding a globe.
>
> *Rev.*—SENATVS. The emperor, laureate, standing, to left, wearing the *toga*, which is edged with an ornamented band, holding in right hand a globe, and in left a sceptre. Round his waist is an embroidered belt. In exergue, S.M.TS. (Signata Moneta Thessalonicâ.) *N*. (Pl. xi. No. 5.)

The best idea of what the consular dress really was, can be formed from what we find represented on the diptychs, which extend from A.D. 428 to A.D. 541.

---

[17] The helmet occurs for the first time on the coins of Gallienus.

[18] In the 3rd number of the NUMISMATIC CHRONICLE, N.S., vol. i. p. 161, there is a denarius of Carausius engraved, representing the *lorum* over the cuirass.

[19] The *mappa* was a napkin thrown into the circus by the person presiding, for the games to commence.—(See Suet. Nero, 22; Mart., Ep. xii., xxix. 9.) The Circensian games are called by Juvenal, *spectacula mappæ*.—(Sat. xi. 190.)

Amongst the more important, I may mention the four following:—

1. Diptych of Flavius Felix, consul in the West, Flavius Taurus holding the same office in the East, in A.D. 428, the third year of the Emperor Valentinianus III., Theodosius II. being emperor in the East.

2. That of Boethius, consul in the East, **without a colleague**, in A.D. 487, the **Western** Empire having been destroyed four years before **by Odoacer**.

3. That of Anastasius, grand-nephew of **the Emperor** Anastasius, consul in A.D. 517.

4. That of Philoxenes, consul in the reign of Justinus, A.D. 525.[20]

On these we can clearly distinguish three distinct dresses:—1. A tunic without any ornaments (*subarmalis profundus*). 2. A tunic richly embroidered (*tunica palmata*). 3. A robe cast over the tunic. The question now is, what is this third robe? That seen on the diptych of Boethius represents more exactly the ancient *trabea*, or *toga prætexta*; the *trabea* on the diptych of Flavius Felix is nearly reduced to what is afterwards the *lorum*, though not forming the usual shape of Y; whilst the dress of Anastasius shows us the *trabea*, or *toga prætexta*, actually reduced to the *lorum*, and in the exact form of Y. From this it would seem that the *clavus latus*, gradually getting larger and larger, at last formed a dress of itself, which dress was the *lorum*.[21]

I may remark that the *lorum* on the coin of Constantine

---

[20] For fuller particulars concerning the diptychs, I refer my readers to "An Essay on Antique Ivories," by F. Pulszky, Liverpool, 1856.

[21] The similarity of the pontifical dress of the Popes is probably traditional from the imperial times.

the Great, described above, is quite different in arrangement to that represented on the diptychs; instead of it "coming under the right arm, then crossing the chest and left shoulder, round over the right shoulder, and *beneath* the fold across the chest," it comes "*above* the fold across the chest," seeming, as it were, joined to the embroidered robe, so that the hand of the emperor comes out from under it.

Having now mentioned the various dresses, and various manners in which they are employed, there is left to determine which of all these embroidered robes was the most important. This I cannot do, from the absence of authorities.[22] At any rate, from the various questions I have considered in this paper, I think some results can be drawn, and that I shall not be wrong in saying that the following were the consular dresses of the Lower Empire:—

1. *Subarmalis profundus* (under tunic, not embroidered).
2. *Tunica palmata* (embroidered tunic).
3. *Lorum* (first the *trabea*, the *toga prætexta*, or the *clavus latus*.)

My object has been to show my reasons for disagreeing with the description of M. Cohen in the case of the medallions of Gordianus Pius, Treb. Gallus, and Volusianus, their busts being described by him as "avec paludament," or "paludament richement orné."

The subject might be much enlarged, but I have here merely treated it numismatically.

FRED. W. MADDEN.

---

[22] "Pinge vastos humeros vario colore *palmatæ*, &c.—(Cassiodor. Variar. lib. vi.) Unfortunately, he does not say whether it is the *toga* or *tunica*, or what, that is embroidered. Cassiodorus was "comes rerum privatarum" and "sacrarum largitionum" under Odoacer, who was King of Italy from A.D. 476 to 493.

MEDALS

XXXVI.

NOTICE OF THREE CHINESE SILVER MEDALS.

[Read before the Numismatic Society, Nov. 20, 1856.]

During the recess, the three Chinese Medals in silver which I now exhibit have come into my hands, having been lent me by a gentleman who has a large and extremely curious collection of Chinese coins, which may possibly ere long be offered for public sale. Similar pieces to two of them were also brought me by another gentleman. These last were very inferior in condition, and much disfigured by countermarks and deep indentations, made in them apparently for the purpose of ascertaining whether they were of silver throughout, as very many dollars have been fabricated for circulation in the East, which are formed of copper with a thick plating of silver.

The last-mentioned specimens were evidently struck on Spanish dollars, as the ornamental edge was untouched. I am unable to lay them before you, as they were returned as soon as I had examined them.

The first of the medals (Pl. xii. No. 1) has simply inscriptions on both sides. That on the obverse is—

足 Tsuh
紋 Wan
通 Tung
行 Hing

The first word, "Tsuh," gives ideas of sufficiency or

competency. The second word, "Wan," although its general meaning is "fine silk," relates also to silver; and the phrase "Tsuh wan" is used to imply that the silver is as pure as the standard requires. The third word, "Tung," means precious, universal, and is applied to the currency in general. The fourth word "Hing," gives ideas of action or doing a thing. Read "Hang," or as it is frequently pronounced, "Hong," it is used for a mercantile house or factory. From this I infer that the inscription implies, "Standard silver for mercantile purposes."

The reverse has—

Chang
Chow
Keun
Heang

The word "Chow" is applied to certain districts in the various provinces of China. It answers in some measure to our words Hundred or Tything, which are employed in the same manner. It is also applied to cities and towns. Thus, then, "Chang Chow" signifies the district, city, or town of Chang. "Keun," the third word, is applied to military affairs, and also means an army. "Heang" means "food," "provisions," and also money raised for the support of the army. From this I infer that pieces of this description have been struck as money for the army; and in this particular instance, for the use of the troops of the district or city of Chang Chow, which, upon reference to an original map of China, I find to be situated in the province of Tahkun, the neighbouring province to that in which Canton is situated. In corroboration of this supposition I may mention that a similar piece, one of those to which I have before alluded, was stamped with various countermarks, one of which was "Heĕ," the designation of the military officer of a district. The word "Ho" also appeared as a countermark, and was very frequently repeated. This word means to agree, to suit, harmonise with. Some of its compounds are rendered "to answer the purpose completely." It may therefore have been used to imply that this piece would fully answer the purpose for which it was intended.

The second of these medals (Pl. xii. No. 2) presents, on that which I shall call the obverse, a magnificent dragon, holding clouds in his talons. Beneath is 十五 Shih-woo, the number 15. On the reverse the Sun appears in the centre, with the four following characters—

明 Ming
命 Ming
通 Tung
寶 Paou

The first of these words, "Ming," is composed of the characters signifying the sun and the moon, and signifies "bright," "glorious." The second "Ming" implies fate, destiny, lot, and the like. Together, they form the appellation of the monarch striking the money. The remaining words, "Tung Paou," are the usual designation of money on Chinese coins. I am informed that this is a coin of Annan, where I presume it is current. Coins of this description, however, appear to be common in China, where, although forming no part of the authorised currency, they are frequently given as reward medals to children in schools. Another specimen which came under my observation was full of countermarks, and as it was much worn, it had possibly been in circulation rather as bullion than as a recognised coin. With respect to Chinese countermarks, I may mention that I have been informed that a gentleman had a Spanish dollar so full of them that scarcely any trace of the original devices could be made out. They were accounted for by supposing that each person through whose hands this dollar had passed had stamped his peculiar mark upon it. I have, however, been unable to ascertain whether this is a general custom in China or not.

The third piece (Pl. xii. No. 3) presents us, on the obverse, with the half-length figure of an old man with a long beard, holding a staff in one hand. This represents the god of riches. There are three inscriptions, one on each side of this figure, and one in two lines in front. One of these is—

錢 Tseen
夀 Fung
聖 Shing
宰 Chae

the name of this divinity. The opposite one is—

足 Tsuh
串 Chuen
文 Wan
銀 Yin
餅 Ping

relating to the value of the piece as of fine or standard silver; and the lower inscription is—

庫 Koo
平 Hoo
柒 Pei
弍 Urh

relating to its weight; but I have not been able to make

these inscriptions out satisfactorily, so as to give them in English denominations. The characters in which they are written approach to the form termed "seal letters," which adds considerably to the difficulty of reading them.

On the reverse is a kind of tripod, or vessel on three feet, with inscriptions in the Mongolian character, which I have been informed imply the name of the Mongolian chief Jin Sung. There are also countermarks, but I have not been able to make them out satisfactorily.

With respect to the values or Chinese designations of these pieces I have hitherto been unable to procure any information. Two of them appear to be coins of States bordering upon China; and, as those I have seen were procured either in Canton or the immediate neighbourhood, and were said to be not uncommon, they may possibly circulate as bullion among the Chinese. Those now before you appear to have been struck on blanks, in the usual manner. Those of the other lot I have mentioned, were, as I before stated, evidently altered Spanish dollars.

JOHN WILLIAMS.

MISCELLANEA.

Finds of Coins.

A small hoard of silver coins of Edward VI., Philip and Mary, Elizabeth, and James I. was recently discovered at Barrow, in Leicestershire. The numbers and denominations are as follows:—

Edward VI.

Shillings, full face.　Tun M.M.　.　.　.　.　2

Philip and Mary.

Shilling, usual type, 1554　.　.　.　.　.　1

Elizabeth.

Shillings (hammered): —	Martlet	M.M.		2	
	Cross crosslet	,,	.	2	
	Bell	,,	.	2	
	A	,,	.	2	
	Escallop	,,	.	1	
	Tun	,,	.	4	
	Woolpack	,,	.	2	
	Key	,,	.	2	
	1	,,	.	1	
	2	,,	.	1	
					— 19
Sixpences (hammered):—	Pheon	M.M. 1561	.	2	
	Lion	,, 1566	.	1	
	Coronet	,, 1567	.	1	
	,,	,, 1569	.	2	
	Cinquefoil	,, 1574	.	2	
	Uncertain	,, 1574	.	1	
	Cross	,, 1574	.	2	
	,,	,, 1580	.	3	
	Escallop	,, 1585	.	2	
	Hand	,, 1591	.	1	
	Tun	,, 1593	.	1	
					— 18
					— 37

James I.

Half-crown,　2nd coinage.　Quæ Deus, &c.
　　　　　　　　Trefoil　M.M.　.　.　1

　　　　　　　　　　　　Carried forward　.　1–40

		Brought forward	.	1–40
Shillings, 1st coinage.	Exurgat, &c.			
	Thistle	M.M. .	. 2	
	Lis	„ .	. 1	
			—	3
Shillings, 2nd coinage.	Quæ Deus, &c.			
	Thistle	MM. .	. 1	
	Lis	„ .	. 2	
	Rose	„ .	. 1	
	Grapes	„ .	. 1	
	Coronet	„ .	. 3	
	Bell	„ .	. 1	
	Uncertain	„ .	. 2	
			—	11
Sixpences, 2nd coinage :—Lis		„ .	. 1	
	Rose	„ .	. 1	
			—	2
			—	17
		Total coins .	.	57

The whole were in bad preservation, the half-crown being, however, somewhat better than the rest. The sixpence of Elizabeth, with cross, MM., and date 1574, is not in the list of Snelling or Hawkins.

J. B. BERGNE.

The following is a list of coins found at Idsworth, near Horndean, Hants :—

Elizabeth.	Shillings . . .	.	18
	Sixpences . . .	.	43
James I.	Shillings, English .	.	14
	„ Irish .	.	2
	Sixpences . . .	.	8
Charles I.	Half-crowns, English	.	73
	„ Scotch	.	1
	Shillings . . .	.	73
	Sixpences . . .	.	8
			240

The half-crowns of Charles I. are all of the ordinary type, with the oval shield. The shillings are also of ordinary types, chiefly with the square-topped shield, excepting one struck at Exeter, dated on reverse, 1644.

A. W. FRANKS.

February, 21, 1861.

NOTICE OF RECENT NUMISMATIC PUBLICATIONS.

CELTIC INSCRIPTIONS ON GAULISH AND BRITISH COINS, BY BEALE POSTE. J. Russell Smith, 1861, pp. 180, and 11 plates.

WE have here another volume upon the Ancient British Coinage, by the indefatigable author of "The Coins of Cunobeline and of the Ancient Britons," published in 1853. It may, however, be said to be *alter et idem*, as the present work contains many of the same speculations, and precisely the same illustrations as those in the former volume.

Still, it must be confessed that there are some points of novelty about it, and one of these is a glossary of Celtic words, found, or supposed to be found, on Gaulish and British coins, which contains much curious matter, and displays a considerable amount of varied reading and much etymological ingenuity, in some cases exercised with surprising boldness. The main object of the work seems to be to prove that the names and inscriptions on British coins are all merely titular. And, indeed, there is no doubt that the Celtic proper names, the same as those of all other nations, had originally some inherent meaning, and in some cases were derived from the personal attributes of those who bore them, or were even possibly, to a certain extent, titular or significant of different public functions —like the originals of many of our English surnames. But it by no means follows that these meanings can now be traced, nor that because any given name had originally some significance when applied to a person, the same of necessity held good in all subsequent cases where the name was used. It is not every Abraham who has been the father of a multitude, nor has every Philip been attached to horses, nor every Robert been famous in council. Still less is it likely that the same prince would apppear under a multitude of different names upon his coins as suggested by Mr. Poste; and when we inform our readers on his authority, that "Caractacus had eight distinct and different names, as it appears from history, inscriptions, coins, chronicles, and triads" — (among which the supposed KERATIK and CEARATIC are included)—that Togodumnus had three (one of which was DVBNOVELLAVNOS), and Adminius had four (among which were AMMINVS and

AEDEDOMAROS); we think that we have said enough on this head.

It is almost needless to enter into the question of the attribution of the various classes of British coins as propounded in this book, as they are much the same as those which have already been advocated by Mr. Poste in his former volume, and also in his communications to the NUMISMATIC CHRONICLE—but one of his recent discoveries may be taken as a specimen.

It is that Cunobeline honoured Huiccum, the capital city of the Huiccii, by striking coins with their name — the tribe of the Huiccii being, as Mr. Poste *naïvely* remarks, only mentioned by Bede and the later chroniclers, and not by Ptolemy and Antoninus. We have, therefore, not only a new mint, but a new tribe, restored by numismatic evidence as interpreted by Mr. Poste. Luckily, we have the means of judging of the value of this interpretation. The whole theory rests on a small gold coin of Cunobeline, engraved by Pegge, with the legend AM . CV, or possibly CAM—CVN, on the obverse, instead of the ordinary CAMV, which is read as WICV by Mr. Poste, and all this superstructure built upon it.

There is one other question raised in the present work, which it will be well to notice; it is as to the forgery of ancient British coins. There is unfortunately but too good reason for caution in accepting some types as genuine, but we cannot in any way understand why the beautiful little coin in the British Museum, inscribed ANDO (Num. Chron., vol. xv. p. 80, No. 2) should be placed among those of doubtful authority, as it is beyond all question authentic. Why, too, should the gold coin of Epaticcus (Num. Chron., vol. xx. p. 1) have doubts cast upon it, unless it be because it cannot be made to read CEARATIC, so as to refer it to Caractacus? But though Mr. Poste seems to be thus fastidious as to the coins which he thinks worthy to be admitted among the British series, we must confess our surprise at finding the indisputably false coins with the legend VER BOD TASCI, or, as he prefers to read it, VREIS BOD TASCIA, not only treated as genuine, but forming the principal basis for hypotheses opposed to nearly all previous writers. That the authenticity of these coins was by no means above suspicion, was pointed out in the Num. Chron., vol. xx. p. 175, but this is entirely ignored in the present work. There is now no doubt whatever of their having been fabricated at or near the place of their pretended discovery in Suffolk. We need not enter into the circumstances under which this successful forgery was perpetrated. Its success induces us to express a hope that the future theories of any writer on British coins may rest on a surer foundation.

UEBER DIE SO-GENANNTEN REGEN-BOGEN-SCHÜSSELCHEN. ERSTE ABTHEILUNG, VON FRANZ STREBER. *Munich*, 1860. Pp. 112, and 9 plates.

THIS treatise upon the curious ancient gold coinage of Southern Germany is reprinted from the "Transactions of the Royal Bavarian Academy of Sciences," and will be read with interest by all students of the early Gaulish and British coins. The name *Regen-bogen-Schüsselchen* "Rainbow-dishes," (*Patellæ Iridis*), applied to these ancient German coins, originates in the popular tradition current in so many countries that a hoard of treasure or a crock of gold may be found if dug for at the exact spot where a rainbow touches the earth. Indeed, so firm was the belief that this was the case, or that the coins themselves had actually fallen from heaven, that in the earlier works which treat of these coins, pains are taken to prove that the *Regenbogen* or *Himmel-Schusselchen* are not of heavenly but of earthly origin.

The bow-like figure which most of them bear on their concave side, may also have been supposed to prove their connection with the rainbow; while their peculiarly dished shape fully justifies their name of *Schüsselchen*, and shows their capability of receiving and retaining celestial influences. Coins of this class have been preserved as "lucky" for many years, and have gone down as heir-looms in peasants' families from generation to generation; but their special value was for medicinal purposes when used as an ingredient in draughts for fevers, by simply placing them in the cup.[1]

The immediate subject of the work now before us is a find of upwards of a thousand gold coins which lately took place in the neighbourhood of Ingolstadt, a town on the Danube, a little above Ratisbon. A detailed account is, however, given of numerous other discoveries which have been made, principally to the south of the Upper Danube, between the Lake of Constance and the River Inn, but also in the tract of country between the Danube, the Rhine, and the Maine, and occasionally in Bohemia. Unfortunately none of the finds appear to have comprised any Greek or Roman coins, by which a definite age could be assigned for their deposit. M. Streber is inclined to regard them as having been struck by the Vindelici to the south of the Danube, and by Keltic tribes to the north; but would ascribe them to the fourth, or even, in some cases, to the fifth century B.C.—a degree of antiquity which we cannot by any means con-

---

[1] The gold coins of Akber the Great are still so used by the natives of the Pánjáb.

cede to them without further proof. We can hardly believe that any coinage originated in this highly dished form and with these barbarous devices; and if the coinage were derived from some civilised source, its antiquity cannot be nearly so great as Dr. Streber supposes.[1]

The engravings of the coins are remarkably well executed. They are divided into seven groups, each containing numerous varieties, the total number of coins engraved being 116. The devices of the obverse include serpents, heads of birds, wreaths, lyres, triquetræ, and occasionally heads in profile, very much like those on some of the Gaulish series. The reverse has usually the semicircular torc (?) upon it, with from three to six large pellets arranged within it. Their general resemblance in character to some of the more barbarous of the Gaulish and British coins is such, that German *Regen-bogen-Schüsselchen* have been engraved in works professing to treat of the first-mentioned coinage only. Examples of this will be found in " Lambert," pl. i. 26, and pl. xi. *bis.* 1; in " Lelewel," pl. iii. 34; the Numismatic Journal, vol. i. pl. i. 3, and " Ruding," pl. A. No. 76; but those who wish to become thoroughly acquainted with this class of coins must study Dr. Streber's work.

The fifth number (September and October) of the *Revue Numismatique* contains the following articles:—

"On the Coins of the Salassi," by M. A. de Longpérier. The tribe of the Salassi, mentioned by Livy, Appian, Strabo, and others, occupied the long valley extending from the Great St. Bernard to Ivrea, and comprising within it the ancient city of Aosta (Augusta Prætoria). From time to time a few gold coins have been found in this district, bearing on their obverse trellised triangles and symbols, which have been variously interpreted, and on their reverse inscriptions in characters allied to the Etruscan. These inscriptions have by some been regarded as Punic or Celtiberian, and led to the conclusion that these were Carthaginian or Spanish coins, relics of Hannibal's passage of the Alps. M. de Longpérier shows them, however, to have been in all probability struck by the Salassi, whose country was once noted for its abundance in gold, and whose gold-

---

[1] M. de Longpérier's remarks with regard to the coins of the Salassi are worth quoting here. " Les pièces d'or dont nous nous sommes occupé ici appartiennent, comme les monnaies d'or de la Germanie, de la Grande Bretagne et des Gaules, au système Grec. On ne pourrait faire de querelle qu'à celui qui prétendrait que les médailles d'or des Salasses sont antérieures aux statères de Philippe de Macédoine."

washing operations frequently led to wars with the neighbouring tribes. It has been asserted that similar coins have been found in England and elsewhere; but to this we can give, as M. de Longpérier does on the part of Lusatia and Poland, an unqualified denial. It is to be hoped that future discoveries may throw some light on the derivation of the type and the meaning of the legends, which are at present in the highest degree enigmatical.

2. "Description of some Merovingian coins of Limousin," by M. Max. Deloche (ninth article).

3. "On the *regalis aureus* of St. Louis," by M. A. de Longpérier. We may recognise in the name of this nearly unique coin the original of our own "gold rial."

4. "On the coins of the Counts of Tonnerre," by M. A. de Barthélemy.

5. "Jettons commemorating the Siege of Arras by the French in 1640," by M. J. Rouyer.

In the correspondence is a letter from M. de Saulcy, "On a discovery of twelfth-century coins," and an answer from M. Robert.

The following articles are in the 3rd livraison of the *Revue Numismatique Belge*:—

1. "On a *denier* of Charles le Chauve, struck at Famars," by M. R. Chalon.

2. "Numismatic *souvenirs* of the Crusades," by J. M. Dirks.

3. "On the famous *écu* of Mayence, 1438," by M. H. Helbig.

4. "On a Jetton on which is represented an eye-glass," by M. E. Vanderstraeten.

5. "Sur un Mérau inédit de laiton," by M. le Bon. Chaudruc de Crazannes.

6. "On a Mexican medal of Ferdinand VII.," by M. R. Chalon.

7. "Documents pour servir à l'histoire des monnaies," by M. de la Fons-Meliocq.

In the *Mélanges* are reviews of new numismatic publications, &c.

INDEX.

A.

Abdera, coin of, 106
Alexander the Great, **coins struck by his generals**, 137
Alexandrian coins, 224
'ΑΝΑΝΕΟΣΙΣ, remarks on the legend, 47, 228
Anglo-Gallic coins, unpublished English and, 17
Anglo-Hanoverian copper coinage, **144**
Anglo Saxon Coins:—
 Alfred, large coin of, 66
 Coenwlf, 19
 Eadgar, **20**
 Edward **the** Elder, coin of, 67
 Eric, 20
 Ethelstan, King of East Anglia, 85
 Harold II., 20
 St. Eadmund, 20
Anglo-Saxon ornaments **found with looped coins in Kent**, 58
Autedrigna, coins of, 4
Antoninus, coins of, 99
Augustus, coins of, 91
Azes, double-struck coins of, 72

B.

Bactrian coins, 72
Bactrian King, Azes, double-struck coins of, 72
Barrow, coins found at, 246
BAYLEY, E. C., Esq., H.E.I.C.S.:—
 Observations on some double-struck coins of the Bactrian King, Azes or Azas, 72
BERGNE, J. B., Esq., F.S.A.:—
 On a hoard of coins discovered at Hounslow, 140
British coins found near Frome, 1
British coins found with Romans, 8, **79**, 133
British coins **found at Lightcliffe, near Halifax**, **79**
British coins, Poste's inscriptions on, 248
Bronze coinage, **modern art and the new**, 38
Bronze coinage, **proclamation relating to**, 26

Brunswick, coins of, 159
Burgundian coins found at Hounslow, 140
Byzantine coins, 42, 58, 228
Byzantine numismatic art, 211

C.

Caracalla, coins of, 100
Carausius, silver coins of, 36, 161; legionary coin of, 163
Caria, coins of, 218
CATTI, coin inscribed, 4
Celtic inscriptions on Gaulish **and British coins, by Beale Poste**, 248
Charles I., unpublished coins **of, 27; halfcrowns of, with "W,"** **185**
Chinese medals, 241
CHRISTMAS, REV. H., F.R.S., **M.R.S L., F.S.A.**:—
 Unpublished English and Anglo-Gallic coins, 17
 On the Anglo-Hanoverian copper coinage, **144**
Claudius, coins of, 92
Clotaire II., coin of, 58
Coinage, statistics of, 63, 198
Coins, finds of:—
 Abingdon, 161
 Barrow, 246
 Cyprus, 42
 Goldborough, 65
 Hounslow, 140
 Idsworth, near Horndean, 24
 Lightcliffe, near Halifax, 79
 Newry, 204
 Nunney, **near Frome**, 1
 Sarre, 58
 Scotland, 56
 Verulam, 36
 Yorkshire, 206
Commonwealth, unpublished **coins of, 28**
"COMOB" and "CONOB," remarks on, 173
Constans II. and his sons, coins of, 42
Constantine the Great, medallion of, 238
Constantine Pogonatus, coins of, 52
Contorniates, M. Sabatier's description of, 192
Cretan coins, 168

INDEX.

Cufic coins, 67
Cyprus, coins of Constans II. and his sons found at, 42, 228.
Cyrenaica, coin of the, 201

D.

Delphi, coin of, 108
Domitian, coin of, 95
Domna, coin of, 100
Dress, imperial consular, 231
DYMOCK, THE LATE REV. T. F. :—
  On the half-crowns of Charles I. with the "W" under the horse on the field of the obv., 185

E.

Edward I., York halfpenny, 21
Edward III., Anglo-Gallic coins of, 29
Edward IV., unpublished coins of, 21; coins found at Hounslow, 140
Edward VI., unpublished coins of, 24
Egyptian coins, 224
Elis, coin of, 107
Elizabeth, unpublished coins of, 26; pattern for a half-crown of, 189
EN TSTO NIKA on coins, 228
English coins, unpublished, 17
EVANS, JOHN, ESQ., F.S.A. :—
  An account of a hoard of ancient British coins discovered in the neighbourhood of Frome, 1
  Silver coins of Carausius, 36
  An account of British gold and Roman silver coins found at Lightcliffe, near Halifax, in the year 1827, 79
  On an English jetton, or pattern-piece, 109
  Unpublished coin of Carausius, 116
  On a legionary coin of Carausius, 163
EVANS, SEBASTIAN, M.A. :—
  Modern art and the new bronze coinage, 38

F.

Faustina Senior, coin of, 99
Foreign and English sterlings found in Scotland, 56
FRIEDLAENDER, DR. JULIUS :—
  A coin of Helike, 216
Frome, ancient British coins found in the neighbourhood of, 1, 133

G.

Gallienus, coins of the family of, 194
Gaulish coins, Poste's inscriptions on, 248
George I., Hanoverian coins of, 146
George II., Hanoverian coins of, 148
George III., Hanoverian coins of, 150
George IV., Hanoverian coins of, 156
Goldborough, Yorkshire, coins found at, 63
Gortyna, coin of, 174
Greek coins, some remarkable ones lately acquired by the British Museum, 104
Greek unpublished coins, 218
Grey, Lady Jane, 111

H.

Hadrian, coins of, 96; medallion of, 97
Hanover, copper coinage of, 144
Helike, coin of, 216
Henry I., unpublished penny, 20
Henry II. or III., short-cross pennies of, 204, 206.
Henry IV., V., and VI., unpublished coins of, 21
Henry V. or VI., coins found at Hounslow, 140
Henry VII., unpublished coins of, 23; coins found at Hounslow, 140
Heraclius, coins of, 52, 58
Hildebrand, Swedish medals, 130
Hounslow, coins found at, 140

I.

Ilsworth, coins found at, 247
Imperial consular dress, 231

J.

James I., unpublished coins of, 26
Jetton, English, 109
Jetton of Perkin Warbeck, 32

L.

Lancaster, coins of Henry Duke of, 28
Legionary coin of Carausius, 163
Looped coins found with Anglo-Saxon ornaments in Kent, 58
Lycia, coins of, 219
Lydia, coins of, 222

M.

Macedonian coins, 104
Macrinus, coin of, 103
Madden's Handbook to Roman Numismatics, 128
MADDEN, FRED. W. ESQ. M.R.S.L. :—
  On an unpublished variety of the coins of Ethelstan, King of East Anglia, 85
  The three Valentinians, 112
  On the coins of Theodosius I. and II., with some remarks on the mint-marks "Comob" and "Conob," and on the coins of Placidia, the wife of Constantius (Patricius), 175
  On the imperial consular dress, 231
Mallus, unpublished coin of, 87

INDEX.

Mary, penny, 25
Mauricius Tiberius, coins of, 58
Medals, Chinese, 241; Swedish, 130.
Mints, Roman, 126

N.

Nero, coins of, 92
Nerva, coins of, 95
Nunney, near Frome, British coins found near, 1, 133

P.

Pamphylia, coins of, 220
Pattern-piece, 109
Philippus V. of Macedon, 105
Phrygia, coins of, 222
Pisidia, coins of, 221
Placidia, coins of, 175
Polyrrhenium, coin of, 174
POOLE REGINALD STUART, ESQ., M.R.S.L.
  On a coin of Mallus, in Cilicia, 87
  On a copper coin of the class struck after the death of Alexander the Great by his generals before they assumed regal titles, 137
  On two Cretan coins in the British Museum, 168
  On a coin from the Cyrenaica, &c., 201
Poste's Gaulish and British coins, 248
POWNALL, THE REV. ASSHETON, M.A.:—
  Short-cross pennies of Henry II. or III., 206
Prisucus, coin of, 174
Proclamation relating to bronze coinage, 62
Ptolemy VI., coin of, 224

R.

Regen-bogen-Schüsselchen, 250
REICHARDT, REV. H. C.:—
  Egyptian and Alexandrian coins, 224
Revue Numismatique, notices of, 60, 131, 193, 251
Revue Numismatique Belge, notices of, 60, 132, 197, 252
Richard III., coins of, found at Hounslow, 140
Roman coins found with British, 8, 79, 133; unpublished, 91; the three Valentinians, 112
Roman mints, 126
Roman mint-marks, 175
Roman numismatics, Handbook to, 128

S.

Sabatier's description des médailles contorniates, 192

SAINTHILL, R., ESQ.:—
  Additional varieties of short-cross pennies, 204.
Salassi, coins of the, 251
Sales of coins, 63, 198, 133
SALIS, J. F. W. DE, ESQ:—
  On some looped coins found with Anglo-Saxon ornaments in Kent, 58
Soloninus, coins of, 194
SIM, GEORGE, ESQ.:—
  English and foreign sterlings found in Scotland, 36
Streber's Regen-bogen-Schüsselchen, 250
SUEI, coins inscribed, 6
Swedish medals, 130

T.

Theodosius I. and II., coins of, 175
Tiberius, coins of, 52
Titus, coins of, 93
Trajan, coins of, 95

V.

Valentinians, the three, 112
VAUX, W. S. W., ESQ., M.A., F.S.A.:—
  An account of a find of coins in the parish of Goldborough, Yorkshire, 65
  On some remarkable Greek coins lately acquired by the British Museum, 104
VEP. CORF., coins inscribed, 80
Verus, coins of, 99
Vespasian, coins of, 92

W.

Warbeck, Perkin, Jetton of, 32
WARREN, HON. J. LEICESTER, M.A.:—
  Jetton of Perkin Warbeck, 32
  On some coins of Constans II. and his sons, discovered in the Island of Cyprus, 42
  Byzantine numismatic art, 211
  Notes on the EN TSTO NIKA and ANANEOΣIΣ types, 228
WEBSTER, WILLIAM, ESQ.:—
  Unpublished Greek coins, 218
Weymouth, half-crowns attributed to, 185
WHITBOURN, R., ESQ., F.S.A.:—
  On an unique and unpublished pattern for a half-crown of the last year of the reign of Queen Elizabeth, 189
William III., unpublished sixpence of, 28
William IV., Hanoverian coins of, 157
" W," half-crowns of Charles I. with, 185
WILLIAMS, JOHN, ESQ. F.S.A.:—
  Notice of three Chinese medals, 241

LONDON:
PRINTED BY JAMES S. VIRTUE,
CITY ROAD.

PROCEEDINGS OF THE NUMISMATIC SOCIETY.

SESSION 1860—61.

November 22, 1860.

W. S. W. Vaux, Esq., President, in the Chair.

Mr. Madden read a paper "On some Unpublished Roman Coins." The paper will be found in the Numismatic Chronicle, Vol. I. p. 91, N.S.

Mr. Vaux read a paper, "On the Coins of Carthage," in which he showed that certain coins which have hitherto been attributed to Panormus, though upon no sufficient grounds, may, from the character of their workmanship and their Punic legends, be ascribed with some degree of certainty to Carthage.

December 13, 1860.

W. S. W. Vaux, Esq., President, in the Chair.

The following present was announced, and laid on the table:—

A Bronze medal from the Royal University of Norway.

Mr. Evans read a paper descriptive of a hoard of British

coins discovered in the neighbourhood of Frome, which will be found in full, Numismatic Chronicle, Vol. I. p. 1, N.S.

Mr. Madden read a paper upon the late popular discussion whether BRIT. or BRITT., as it appears upon the new bronze coinage, is the correct abbreviated form for the name of her Majesty's dominions. The paper is printed in the Numismatic Chronicle, Vol. XX. p. 195.

Mr. Madden also communicated some remarks upon a rare medallion of Hadrian in the Museum collection, of gem-like workmanship, and with the figures of Hygeia and apparently Antinous on the reverse. This paper will be found incorporated with the "Unpublished Roman Coins," Numismatic Chronicle, Vol. I. p. 91, N.S.

JANUARY 24, 1861.

W. S. W. VAUX, Esq., President, in the Chair.

William Allen, Esq., of Winchmore Hill, Southgate, was elected a member of the Society.

Dr. A. Namur, Secretary of the Archæological Society of Luxembourg, was elected an honorary member.

A short paper was read, "On Modern Art and the New Bronze Coinage," communicated by Sebastian Evans, Esq., M.A., in which the grave artistic defects of the new issue were pointed out and commented upon. The paper will be found in the Numismatic Chronicle, Vol. I. p. 38, N.S.

Mr. C. Roach Smith exhibited casts of some ancient British coins in gold, found in a field called the Golden Piece, near Ryarsh, Kent, and now in the possession of the Rev. L. B. Larking. Mr. Roach Smith remarked that he suspected that prior discoveries, of the same nature in the same field, gave it the name of the Golden Piece. The coins are as follows—

1. *Obv.*—Portion of laureated head, with an approach to a face.

   Rev.—Disjointed horse, to the right, with **pellets**, &c., above. (See "**Coll. Ant.**," Vol. I. Pl. VI. 5.) One specimen.

2. *Obv.*—Plain.

   Rev.—Disjointed horse, to the right, with pellet below. The exergue ornamented with semicircles, each containing a central **dot**, and placed alternately. **Pellets**, &c., above the horse. (See "Ruding," Pl. I. 3.) Three specimens.

3. *Obv.*—Plain.

   Rev.—Similar to the last, but **of coarser work** and wider spread. See Numismatic Chronicle, Vol. I. Pl. II. 2. One specimen.

Coins similar to the first have been found near Maidstone and Elham, in Kent, and the other varieties are of frequent occurrence through the whole of the southern part of England, and are found occasionally on the Continent.

The Rev. Professor Henslow exhibited **the impression of a** small gold coin **of Panormus** (*Obv.* Head of Ceres, to left. *Rev.* Horse, standing, to right), said to have been found at Felixstow, Suffolk, where Roman coins and other antiquities are constantly being found. If, as there appears good reason to suppose, the coin was really discovered there, it was probably brought thither by one of the Roman soldiers or colonists, at a period considerably posterior to that in which it was struck.

Mr. Evans exhibited a drachma of **Philip Aridæus**, struck at Mitylene, in Lesbos, which had been given to him at Aldborough, Suffolk, and which was stated to have been found beneath the roots of an oak on its being grubbed up in Rendlesham Park, a few miles from Aldborough. There was little doubt that it had been found in the manner stated, but how the coin came into such a position it was impossible to say.

Mr. J. Y. Akerman, exhibited a photograph of a silver coin of Carausius, found in digging for the railway at Abingdon, and in the possession of Henry B. Godwin, Esq.

Obv.—IMP. CARAVSIVS. P.F.AVG—Bust, to left, with sceptre.

Rev.—CONCORDIA MILITVM—Two right hands joined, on exergue R.S.R. See Numismatic Chronicle, Vol. I. p. 161, N.S.

Mr. Vaux read a short account of four barbarous imitations by Merovingian kings of Byzantine solidi, found with a Saxon brooch at Sarre, in Kent. This notice, which was communicated by Mr. de Salis, will be found in the Numismatic Chronicle, Vol. I. p. 58, N.S.

Mr. Bateman communicated an account of the discovery of some ancient British coins at Light Cliffe, near Halifax, in the year 1827. They comprised three gold coins of the ordinary Yorkshire type, with the legends VOLISIOS and DVMNOCOVEROS, and one with the legend VEP (retrograde) CORF. The remarkable feature of this find was the discovery in the urn with them of a large number of Roman family denarii, and a few imperial, including one of Caligula, thus affording an approximate date for the deposit. See Numismatic Chronicle, Vol. I. p. 79, N.S.

Mr. Webster exhibited a remarkable silver jetton, having on the obverse the full-blown rose of England, surrounded by lions, &c., and with the legend SI DEVS NOBISCVM QVIS CONTRA NOS. On the reverse are three crowns, arranged one above another, with the legend IVSTITIA VIRTVTVM REGINA. He was inclined to consider this curious piece to have been struck by the supporters of Lady Jane Grey. An account of it, by Mr. J. Evans, will be found in the Numismatic Chronicle, Vol. I. p. 109, N.S.

FEBRUARY 21, 1861.

W. S. W. VAUX, Esq., President, in the Chair.

The Rev. H. J. B. Nicholson, D.D., F.S.A.; Augustus W. Franks, Esq., M.A., Dir. Soc. Ant.; Samuel Birch, Esq., F.S.A.; and Sebastian Evans, Esq., M.A., were elected members.

Mr. J. J. Mickley, of Philadelphia, communicated a drawing of a *denier* of John III., Duke of Brittany, differing slightly from that engraved in the *Revue Numismatique*, Vol. XII. Pl. XVIII. No. 7.

The Hon. J. L. Warren communicated an account of a remarkable jetton of Perkin Warbeck, of which an engraving has lately been given in the *Revue Numismatique* by M. A. de Longpérier. It will be found described in the Numismatic Chronicle, Vol. I. p. 32, N.S.

Mr. Franks communicated an account of a find of silver coins at Idsworth, near Horndean, Hants. They were two **hundred and forty** in number, and consisted of half-crowns, shillings, and sixpences of Elizabeth, James I., and Charles I.; among the latter was a **shilling struck at Exeter, with the date 1644** on the reverse.

Mr. Madden read an account of an unpublished variety **of** the pennies of Ethelstan, King of the East Angles, A.D. 825 to 852. The paper is printed in the Numismatic Chronicle, Vol. I. p. 85, N.S.

MARCH 21, 1861.

W. S. W. VAUX, Esq., President, in the Chair.

James Sprent **Virtue**, Esq., was elected a member of the Society.

The following **presents were** announced, **and laid on the** table :—

1. Bulletin de la Société des Antiquaires de Normandie. 1 An. 2 and 3 trimestres. Paris, 8vo. 1860. From the Society.
2. Monnaies Austrasiennes inédites } by M. Roberts.
3. Monnaies de Mâcon }

Mr. Lockhart exhibited a barbarous third-brass coin (struck

in imitation of those of Tetricus the Younger, with the sacrificial instruments on the reverse), which he had lately picked up with some other relics of the Roman period in an excavation made for a sewer at the corner of Blomfield Street, Finsbury.

Mr. Lockhart also exhibited a number of Chinese medals, some of which were used as tokens for interchange between lovers during their courtship. These were of brass, some four or five inches in diameter, highly ornamented, and like bracteates in their character, the work being *repoussé*. Other specimens exhibited the manner in which collections of medals were preserved among the Chinese, and the method in which the "cash" or brass coins of that nation are cast. Some Buddhist medals, with Sanskrit inscriptions, usually placed in the foundations of houses, were also exhibited.

Mr. Evans read a short paper on the medallions of Commodus, which exhibit his head with the attributes of Hercules on the obverse, and the Emperor (also in the character of Hercules) ploughing with a yoke of oxen on the reverse, which presents the legend HERC. ROM. CONDITORI, with the year of the consulate and tribunitian power. Mr. Evans remarked on the causes which led Commodus to assume the character of Hercules, and gave some account of the gladiatorial exploits which he had performed in justification of this assumption. He then proceeded to comment on the reverse, which commemorates the insane desire of Commodus to be regarded as the founder of Rome, a city to which he gave the name of Colonia Commodiana: its *pomœrium* he is represented, on these medallions, as ploughing out with a yoke of oxen. We learn from history of a golden statue of Commodus ploughing with a yoke of oxen, from which, possibly, the design was taken.

April 25, 1861.

W. S. W. Vaux, Esq., President, in the Chair.

Sir Henry Dryden, Bart., was elected a member of the Society.

The following presents were announced, and laid on the table:—

	Presented by
1. La Coniazione delle Monete Antiche, by Dr. Friedlaender.	
2. Un Sou d'or d'Aelia Galla Placidia, by Dr. Friedlaender.	Mr. Webster.
3. Monnaie de Gregorius, exarque d'Afrique, by Dr. Friedlaender.	
4. Denkmäler und Forschungen, No. 136, Ap. 1860.	Dr. Friedlaender.
5. Revue Numismatique Belge, Parts I., III., IV.	The Society.
6. Annuaire de l'Académie Royale de Belgique, 1861.	The Academy.
7. Bulletin de l'Académie Royale de Belgique, 29 année, 2 Sec. tom. IX., X.	
8. Minnespenningar öfver enskilda Svenska Män och Quinnor—Medals of Private Swedes, by E. B. Hildebrand. Stockholm.	The Author.

Mr. R. Stuart Poole communicated an account of a copper coin of the class struck after the death of Alexander the Great, and before the assumption of regal titles by his generals. The account will be found in Numismatic Chronicle, Vol. I. p. 137, N.S.

Mr. Warren, of Ixworth, exhibited a cast of a third-brass legionary coin of Carausius. The device on the reverse is a ram, standing, to the right, and it bears on the exergue the letters M.L., showing that it was issued from the London mint. Of the legend only the final N is visible; but it would appear from specimens published by Stukeley and others, that when complete it stood LEG. VIII. IN. There is some doubt whether this IN was not preceded by some other letter; if so, it was probably an M, and the title of the legion MINERVIA, and not INVICTA, as would be suggested by IN.

May 23, 1861.

W. S. W. VAUX, Esq., President, in the Chair.

The Right Hon. the Earl of Enniskillen, Lieut.-Gen. Fox, and the Rev. C. Weatherley, were elected members.

Mr. Evans read the following communications:—

From Mr. G. Sim, "On the Lee Penny," which is formed of a groat of Edward IV. of the London Mint, and not, as is described in the edition of Sir Walter Scott's Novels of last year, a *shilling* of Edward I.

From Dr. Friedlaender, "On a Coin of Helike," bearing the head of Poseidon, surrounded by a circle of waves, which may be a copy of the brass statue of Poseidon Helikonios. This is the first coin that has been attributed to this town, which was destroyed, in B.C. 373, by an earthquake. See Numismatic Chronicle, Vol. I. p. 216.

From Mr. Webster, "On some Unpublished Roman Brass Coins," including a rare medallion of Antoninus Pius.

Mr. Evans read a paper "On a Legionary Coin of Carausius," with a ram, r., on the reverse, and in the exergue M.L. (Londinium), with the legend LEG. I. MIN(ervia). Mr. Evans's paper is printed in the Numismatic Chronicle, Vol. I. p. 163, N.S.

Mr. Bergne gave a list of Coins found at Hounslow, which will be found in full, Numismatic Chronicle, Vol. I. p. 140, N.S.

Mr. Madden read a paper "On an Aureus of Licinius I.," lately brought from the East by Mr. G. Macleay, and of great rarity, there being only two others known, one in the Vienna

Museum (Mionnet), and the other, though very badly preserved, in the Cabinet des Médailles, at Paris. It may be described as follows :—LICINIVS.AVG. OBDV.FILII.SVI. Full-faced bust of Licinius I., with paludamentum and cuirass; *rev.* IOVI.CONS. LICINI.AVG. Jupiter, seated on an estrade, on which is inscribed, SIC.X.SIC.XX. At his feet an eagle. In field, r., a star. In exergue, S.M.AN.E. (Signata Moneta Antiochiâ 5). The British Museum already possesses the full-face coin of Licinius II., with the same reverse, excepting the exergual letters, which are S.M.N.Δ. (Nicomediâ 4). The letters OBDV. have been variously explained: "Ob Decennalia Vota," "Ob Duplicem Victoriam," &c., but all are improbable and without meaning. Mr. de Salis suggests OB. D (iem) V. (Quintum) (natalem understood),—struck on the fifth birthday of his son. This seems the most probable explanation.

Mr. Madden contributed a paper "On the three Valentinians," with remarks on the mint-marks of the period. It may be found in full, Numismatic Chronicle, Vol. I. p. 112, N.S.

June 20, 1861.

ANNIVERSARY MEETING.

W. S. W. VAUX, Esq., President, in the Chair.

The Rev. Frederick K. Harford, Samuel Sharp, Esq., of Dallington Hall, Northampton, and W. H. Coxe, Esq., F.Z.S., of the British Museum, were elected members of the Society.

The minutes of the last Anniversary Meeting were read and confirmed, and the following Report of the Council was read to the meeting :—

GENTLEMEN,—According to the usual custom of the Society, the Council have the honour to lay before you the following

Report of the state of the Numismatic Society at this, another Anniversary Meeting. And in the first place, the Council must congratulate the Society on the flourishing condition it presents to-day, both with respect to the new members it has added to its books, and with respect to its loss, which is less than usual during this year.

The only member whom we have lost by death is John Hampden, Esq., of Leamington, while we have the satisfaction of recording the election of the following gentlemen:—

The Right Hon. the Earl of Enniskillen, Hon. D.C.L., F.R.S., F.G.S.

Sir Henry Dryden, Bart.

Rev. H. J. Boone Nicholson, D.D., F.S.A.

Lieut.-Gen. Fox, re-elected May 23, 1861.

Augustus W. Franks, Esq., M.A., Dir. S.A.

Sebastian Evans, Esq., M.A.

Samuel Birch, Esq., F.S.A., formerly an honorary member—elected February 21, 1861.

William Allen, Esq.

J. Sprent Virtue, Esq.

Rev. C. Weatherley.

Rev. Frederick K. Harford, F.S.A.

Samuel Sharp, Esq.

W. H. Coxe, Esq., F.Z.S.

If, therefore, we have lost by death one member, we have, on the other hand, to congratulate the Society on the election of thirteen new members, some of whom are well known as men interested in, if not eminent for, the study of Numismatic Science.

According to our Secretary's report, our actual numbers are as follows; it will be seen that the term "Associates" has been abolished, and that the associates and honorary members are all under the one heading of "Honorary:"—

	Original.	Elected.	Honorary.	Total.
Members, June, 1860	10	51	48	109
Since Elected	—	13	1	14
	10	64	49	123
Deceased	—	1*	—	1
Resigned	—	2†	1‡	3
Total, June, 1861	10	61	48	119

We will now proceed to give a short notice of **Mr. Hampden's** life, for which the Society is indebted to Mr. Dickinson, who obtained it from his brother, the Bishop of Hereford.

The late John Hampden was a resident for many years, indeed, all the last years of his life, at Leamington, where, from the continual ill-health of his wife, he led a life of comparative retirement. Having received an excellent classical education, he devoted his time to the cultivation of those literary tastes in which he greatly delighted, especially interesting himself in the study of pictures, and of ancient coins and medals. Of these he had formed a considerable collection. Among his pictures is a valuable authentic one, by Walker, of John Hampden. In regard to history, proud as he was of the connection of his family with that of the patriot, he had particularly acquainted himself with that portion in which that illustrious man was so conspicuous a leader, and had collected a mass of materials illustrative of that period. But his own infirm health, aggravated by continual anxious care for his wife, prevented his turning these materials to account by any work of literary labour. He entered the University of Oxford when about eighteen years of age, as member of University College, and passed the first examination for the degree of B.A., but having occasion to leave Oxford for a short time, he did not

---

* J. Hampden, Esq.

† Lieut.-Gen. Fox, and C. T. Newton, Esq., M.A.

‡ Samuel Birch, Esq., F S.A.

return there to complete his academical course. Afterwards he married Mary Georgina, one of the sisters of the late Sir Edmund Filmer, Bart., of East Sutton Park, Kent, by whom he had two sons and one daughter. One of the sons, and the daughter, now a widow, survive him. During the sojourn of the present Emperor of the French at Leamington, Mr. Hampden became acquainted with him, and had the honour of receiving him and his suite at his house. In political feeling, holding at the same time sound Conservative principles, he belonged to the Liberal party. In religion, he was a firm and consistent member of the Church of England, yet of a spirit tolerant and kind towards those of other communions. His own death was probably much hastened by his affliction at the death of his wife in the year preceding. Most affectionate as he was to those with whom Providence had especially connected him by the ties of nature, he was kind and courteous to all with whom he was in any way associated, so that he has passed from among us, not without leaving to many a pleasing, to some a grateful remembrance of his gentle and unostentatious virtues. He died when he had but just attained the sixty-second year of his age, on the 13th of November, 1860. His remains were placed by the side of his departed wife in a vault in the catacombs under Leamington parish church, and a monumental slab, with a Latin inscription, is erected to his memory on the walls of the church.

The Council have the honour of recording the election of Dr. Namur, Secretary of the Archæological Society of Luxembourg, as an honorary member.

The Council cannot conclude their report without calling the attention of the Society to the new base on which it has been placed during the present session. The rules have been revised, the subscription has been reduced from £1 10s. to £1 1s. per annum, which entitles the subscriber to the Publications of the Society for that year; and a New Series of the Chronicle has been commenced. The Council earnestly hope that all members will help it by contributions, as, without their cordial co-operation, it will be impossible for the Chronicle to be issued with due regularity, or to represent, as it ought, the state of Numismatic Science in **Great Britain**.

A complete index of the twenty volumes of the Old Series has been made, including names of contributors and titles of papers.

The New Series is edited by W. S. W. Vaux, Esq., M.A., F.S.A., and by the Secretaries, John Evans, Esq., F.S.A., and Fred. W. Madden, Esq., M.R.S.L., Mr. J. Yonge Akerman being compelled, through increasing ill-health, to retire from those pursuits he loved so well.

The balance sheet of the Treasurer showing the financial condition of the Society is annexed :—

Statement of the Receipts and Disbursements of the Numismatic Society, from June 21, 1860, to June 20, 1861.

Dr. THE NUMISMATIC SOCIETY IN ACCOUNT WITH G. H. VIRTUE, TREASURER. **Cr.**

1860-61.	£	s.	d.	1860-61.	£	s.	d.
To Cash paid to Secretary and Treasurer for Stamps, Stationery, &c.	3	17	0	By Balance brought forward	88	15	4
To Cash paid for Petty Expenses	0	7	6	By Subscriptions and Fees	64	13	0
To Cash paid to Wertheimer and Co. for Chronicle, Nos. 79 and 80	30	0	0	By Cash received of Mr. Smith for back Nos. of the Chronicle	0	9	4
J. S. Virtue for Chronicle, No. 1, New Series	18	10	3	By Dividend (July) on £305 17s. 10d. 3 per Cent. Consols	4	8	0
To Cash paid ditto for Circulars	0	10	0	By ditto, January	4	8	0
To Cash paid to Collector for Commission	3	6	0				
To Cash paid to Mr. Swain for Drawing and Engraving	1	0	0				
Expenses of Meetings	2	0	0				
To Cash paid to Mr. Curt for "Cohen's Médailles Consulaires"	2	6	0				
Balance brought forward	100	16	11				
	£162	13	8		£162	13	8

G. H. VIRTUE, TREASURER.

J. B. BERGNE
JOHN EVANS } *Auditors.*

A list of the papers contributed to the ordinary meetings was then read.

The meeting then proceeded to ballot for the Officers of the ensuing year, when the following gentlemen were elected:—

President.
W. S. W. VAUX, ESQ., M.A., F.S.A., F.R.A.S.

Vice-Presidents.
J. B. BERGNE, ESQ., F.S.A.
EDWARD HAWKINS, ESQ., F.S.A., F.L.S.

Treasurer.
GEORGE H. VIRTUE, ESQ., F.S.A.

Secretaries.
JOHN EVANS, ESQ., F.S.A., F.G.S.
FRED. W. MADDEN, ESQ., M.R.S.L.

Foreign Secretary.
JOHN YONGE AKERMAN, ESQ., F.S.A.

Librarian.
JOHN WILLIAMS, ESQ., F.S.A.

Members of the Council.
S. BIRCH, ESQ., F.S.A.
W. BOYNE, ESQ., F.S.A.
F. W. FAIRHOLT, ESQ., F.S.A.
JOHN LEE, ESQ., LL.D., F.R.S.
CAPTAIN MURCHISON.
REV. H. J. B. NICHOLSON, D.D. F.S.A.
REV. ASSHETON POWNALL, M.A.
J. F. W. DE SALIS, ESQ.
HON. J. LEICESTER WARREN, M.A.
R. WHITBOURN, ESQ., F.S.A.

The Society then Adjourned till October 24, 1861.

THE RULES

OF THE

NUMISMATIC SOCIETY

OF

LONDON.

LONDON:
PRINTED BY J. DAVY & SONS, 137, LONG ACRE.

1861.

THE RULES

OF THE

NUMISMATIC SOCIETY

OF

LONDON.

I.—OBJECT.

THIS Society is established for the encouragement and promotion of Numismatic Science.

II.—CONSTITUTION.

1. The Society shall consist of Members and Honorary Members.

2. The affairs of the Society shall be under the management and direction of a Council, consisting of a President, two Vice-Presidents, one Treasurer, one Librarian, two Secretaries, and ten other Members of the Society.

III.—ELECTION OF THE COUNCIL.

3. The President, Vice-Presidents, Treasurer, Librarian, Secretaries, and other ten Members of the Council, shall be elected by Ballot at every Annual General Meeting.

4. Six only of the ten Members of the Council shall be eligible in the same capacity for the ensuing year.

IV.—Election, Admission, and Expulsion of Members.

5. Every person desirous of admission into the Society as a Member, must be proposed and recommended agreeably to the form No. 1, in the Appendix hereto; which must be subscribed by, at least, three Members, one of whom must certify his personal knowledge of such candidate.

6. Every recommendation of a proposed Member must be read at one of the ordinary Meetings of the Society; after which it shall be placed in some conspicuous part of the room where the Society meets, and shall remain until the candidate be balloted for.

7. The ballot shall take place at the first ordinary Meeting after that on which the candidate is proposed.

8. No person shall be considered as elected a Member, unless he have in his favour at least three-fourths of the Members voting.

9. When a person shall have been elected a Member, one of the Secretaries shall inform him thereof by letter, at the same time forwarding to him a copy of the Rules of the Society, with the card announcing the days on which the Meetings are held.

10. Every person so elected shall be requested to pay his admission-fee and first annual contribution within two calendar months after the day of his election; and, shall, thereby, become a Member of the Society, and entitled to have his name inscribed in the Register of Members.

11. Should there appear cause in the opinion of the Council for the expulsion of any Member, the same shall be communicated to the Society at one of their Meetings, and, at that next ensuing, if three-fourths of those voting agree that such Member or Associate be expelled, the

President, or other Member in the chair, shall declare the same accordingly. Whereupon his name shall be erased from the list of Members.

V. — CONTRIBUTIONS OF MEMBERS.

12. Each Member hereafter to be elected shall pay the sum of two guineas, *i. e.* one guinea as an admission-fee, and one guinea as his first year's Subscription; and shall pay one guinea for every subsequent year, on the first of January, which shall entitle him to the Publications of the Society for that year.

13. Any Member may, at his entrance, compound for his contributions by the payment of twelve guineas, exclusive of his admission-fee; or he may, at any time afterwards (all sums then due being first paid), compound for his subsequent annual contributions by the like payment of twelve guineas.

14. Every Member desirous of resigning, shall be liable to the payment of his annual contributions until he shall have signified such desire in writing to the Treasurer of the Society, and shall have discharged his arrears.

15. Whenever a Member shall be more than one year in arrear in the payment of his annual contributions, the Treasurer shall write a letter of the form No. 2, in the Appendix hereto, and address and forward the same to such Member, accompanied by copies of this and the following Rule.

16. If the arrears shall not be paid within six months after the forwarding of such letter, the name of the Member so in arrear shall be placed in some conspicuous part of the room where the Society meets, with the amount of the contributions due from him; and such Member shall not have the right to enjoy any of the privileges of Membership until his arrears be paid.

VI.—Honorary Members.

17. Every person eminent in Numismatic Science shall be eligible as an Honorary Member; but when proposed must be recommended by three or more Members, agreeably to the form No. 3, in the Appendix.

18. The mode of proposing and balloting for an Honorary Member shall be the same as that prescribed in the case of an ordinary Member; but no person shall be balloted for as an Honorary Member unless the Council shall have previously approved of him as a Candidate.

19. Whenever a person shall have been elected an Honorary Member, the Secretary shall inform him thereof, and forward to him his Diploma, drawn up agreeably to the form prescribed by the Council.

20. Honorary Members shall not have the right of holding any Office in the Society, but may receive the Publications of the Society.

VII.—Council.

21. The Council shall have the management and direction of all the affairs of the Society, subject to the control of the General Meetings.

22. The Council shall meet at the house or apartments of the Society, once at least, in every month during the Session; and due notice of each Meeting shall be sent, by one of the Secretaries, to every Member thereof, five of whom shall form a quorum.

23. All questions shall be decided in the Council by open vote.

24. The Council shall draw up a Report on the state of the affairs of the Society, to be presented at the Annual

General Meeting. In this **Report** shall be given an Abstract of their Proceedings during the year.

25. Minutes of the Proceedings of the Council **shall be** taken by one of the Secretaries, which shall **be afterwards** fairly entered into the Minute Book; and, having **been read** over at the **next** Meeting of the **Council, shall be signed by** the President, **or other Member then in the** chair.

VIII.—Ordinary Meetings.

26. The Ordinary Meetings of the **Society shall be held on the third Thursday in every month, from November to June, both inclusive.**

27. Business shall commence at **seven o'clock in the** evening precisely, **when** the Minutes **of** the preceding Ordinary Meeting shall be read.

28. The business at the Ordinary Meetings shall **be to** propose and ballot for Members; to announce such **Donations** as may have been made to the Society; to **read Communications** relating to **Numismatic Science, and the subjects** connected therewith; and to proceed upon any **other** subject which may have been authorised **by** the **Council.**

29. Every Member shall have the privilege of introducing a Visitor at any of the Ordinary Meetings, on writing the name of such **Visitor opposite to his own name, in a book** provided for that purpose.

IX.—Annual General Meeting.

30. A General Meeting **shall be** held annually, on the third Thursday in June, at 7 P.M., to receive the Report of the Council on **the state of the Society;** to determine such questions as may be proposed relative to the affairs of the Society; and to elect the Officers for the ensuing year.

31. The President, or other Member in the chair, shall appoint two or more Scrutineers from among the Members present, to superintend the Ballot during its progress, and to report the result to the Meeting.

32. The Ballot shall commence at 7 P.M. and close at 8 P.M.

X.—Alteration of Rules.

33. Whenever the Council may think it advisable to propose the enactment of any new Rule, or the alteration or repeal of any existing Rule, they shall recommend the same to the Society at the Annual General Meeting, or at an Ordinary Meeting, notice whereof shall have been sent to each Member one fortnight previously.

34. Any five Members may recommend any new Rule, or the alteration or repeal of any existing Rule, to the Council, by letter, the ultimate decision in all cases resting with the Society.

XI.—Special Committees.

35. Committees for forwarding specific objects connected with Numismatic Science may, from time to time, be appointed by the Council, to whom their Reports shall be submitted. In the formation of these Committees, the Council may request the assistance and advice of persons not Members of the Society.

XII.—President and Vice-Presidents.

36. The duty of the President shall be to take the chair at every Meeting of the Society and Council.

37. In the absence of the President, one of the Vice-Presidents, or, in their absence, the Treasurer, or one of the Members of the Council, shall take the chair, and

conduct the business of the Meeting; and in case of the absence of all those Officers, the Meeting may elect any other Member present to take the chair.

38. The President, or other Member in the chair, shall not vote on any question brought before the Meeting, except where a casting vote be necessary, in which case he shall be at liberty to give such casting vote.

XIII.—TREASURER.

39. The Treasurer shall receive and pay all sums of money due to and by the Society; and shall keep a regular account of receipts and payments in the mode which may seem most proper to the Council, who shall have the direction and control of the money in his hands.

40. No sum of money payable on account of the Society, amounting to five pounds and upwards, shall be paid, except by order of the Council, signed by the President, or other Member in the chair, and registered by one of the Secretaries.

41. The account of the Treasurer shall be audited annually by two or more auditors, chosen by the Society at one of the three Ordinary Meetings immediately preceding the Annual General Meeting, who shall report at such Annual General Meeting the particulars of the receipts and expenditure of the past year, the balance in hand, and the general state of the funds and property of the Society; and shall also lay on the table a list of the names of those Members who may be in arrear for sums due at the last Annual General Meeting, together with the amount of the same.

42. The Treasurer may, with the approbation of the Council, appoint a proper person to collect the annual contributions of the Members.

XIV.—The Secretaries.

43. The duties of the Secretaries shall be to attend all the Meetings of the Society and of the Council; to take Minutes of all their proceedings, and cause them to be entered as early as possible in the proper books provided for that purpose.

44. Their duty at the Ordinary Meetings shall also be to read the Minutes of the preceding Meeting; to announce the Donations made to the Society since the last Meeting; to give notice of any candidate proposed for admission, or to be balloted for; and to read the letters and papers presented to the Society; but, should any person be desirous of reading his own paper, he shall be at liberty so to do, with permission of the Council.

45. The Secretaries shall have the superintendence of all the persons employed by the Society (except the Collector), and the management of the correspondence of the Society, subject, however, to the direction and control of the Council.

46. The Secretaries shall have the charge (under the direction of the Council) of Printing and Publishing the Proceedings and other papers of the Society.

XV.—The Library and Museum.

47. The President, Secretaries, and Librarian, shall have the superintendence of the Library and Cabinets of Coins and Medals, Casts, and other like property, and be a permanent Committee for that purpose.

48. A Catalogue of the Books presented to, or purchased by, the Society; and of all Coins, Medals, Casts, and other like property, shall be kept under the superintendence of the above Committee, with the names of the respective Donors.

XVI.—The Common Seal and Deeds.

49. The common Seal of the Society shall be a representation of the Symbols of Metals and Mintage, surrounded by the words, *Sigillum Societatis Numismaticæ Londinensis.*

50. The Common Seal and Muniments of the Society shall be in the charge of the Library Committee.

51. The Common Seal shall not be affixed to any Deed or Writing except at a Meeting of the Council, and by their authority; and such Deed or Writing shall then be signed by the President, or other Member in the Chair, and by one of the Secretaries, and the particulars of the same entered in the Minute Book.

XVII.—The Property of the Society.

52. The Council shall appoint three Members of the Society to act as Trustees of the property of the Society, and may appoint others in their place on any vacancy occurring by resignation or otherwise. The Council shall, from time to time, decide on the mode of investing the property of the Society, which investment shall be made in the names of the Trustees for the time being.

53. Every Paper which may be presented to the Society shall, in consequence of such presentation, be considered as the property of the Society, unless there shall have been any previous engagement with its Author to the contrary; and the Council may publish the same in any way and at any time that they may think proper.

54. No Books, Papers, or other property belonging to the Society, shall be lent without leave of the Librarian;

but every Member shall be at liberty to inspect the Books, Coins, and Medals belonging to the Society; but no Moulds shall be taken without the consent of the Council.

XVIII.—DONATIONS AND BEQUESTS.

55. Every Person who shall contribute to the Collection, to the Library, or to the general Funds of the Society, shall be recorded as a Benefactor or Benefactress, and his or her name shall be read at the Annual General Meeting and be inserted in the next Report of the Proceedings.

RECOMMENDATIONS.

1. FORM FOR CHEQUE.

London, _____ _____ 18

Messrs. _____

I request that you will pay to the Numismatic Society *now* the sum of One Guinea, and that you will continue the payment thereof on each succeeding First of January, until further notice.

The above when filled up should be returned to the Treasurer or Collector.

2. Every person desirous of bequeathing to the Society any Money, Stock, Manuscripts, Books, Coins, or Medals, or other personal property, is requested to make use of the following form in his or her will; viz. :—

"I give to the Trustees for the time being of the Society formed in London under the name of the Numismatic Society, for the use of such Society,

[*Here specify the sum of Money, or Stock, or the other personal property intended to be given.*]

"And I direct that the same shall be delivered within six months after my decease. And I hereby declare that the receipt of such Trustees shall be an effectual discharge to my Executors for the said Legacy."

3. Every person desirous of giving to the Society any Land, Houses, or other real property, for the general purposes of the Society, is requested to take notice that any devise of real property to the Society would be void at Law under the Mortmain Act; and that the proper mode of proceeding in such a case is to convey the Land, Houses, or other real property to the Society by deed; which deed, to be effective, must be executed in the presence of two or more witnesses, twelve months before the death of the Donor, and enrolled in the Court of Chancery within six calendar months after its execution.

It may be proper, also, to add, for the information of every person desirous of conveying to the Society any Land or other real property, or any interest connected with Land, or Money to be laid out in land, or the proceeds of the sale of Land; that it is desirable that he should not proceed to carry his intention into execution without first consulting some professional person.

APPENDIX.

Form No. 1.

A.B. [*Here state the Christian Name, Surname, Rank, Profession, and usual place of Residence of the Candidate.*] being desirous of Admission into the Numismatic Society, we, the undersigned, propose and recommend him as a proper person to become a Member thereof.

Witness our hands this day of   18

_____ from Personal knowledge.

_____ from General knowledge.

_____

Form No. 2.

Sir,—I am directed by the Council of the Numismatic Society, to inform you that the sum of   was due on account of your annual contributions, on the first day of January last; the payment of which I earnestly request.

I am, Sir,
Your obedient Servant,

Treasurer.

FORM No. 3.

We, the undersigned, having a personal knowledge of, or being acquainted with the works of,

> [*Here state the* **Christian Name**, *Surname, Rank, Profession, usual place* **of** *Residence, and Title of one or more of* **the Works**, *of the* **person proposed.**]

propose and recommend him as a proper person to become an Honorary Member of the Numismatic Society.

Witness our hands this   day of
18

———————————————

———————————————

Approved by the Council.

Secretary.

———————————————

We, the Committee appointed to reconstruct the Rules of the Numismatic Society of London, have agreed to the accompanying Code, which we submit to the Council for their consideration.

(Signed)   W. S. W. VAUX
                JOHN EVANS
                F. MADDEN
                G. H. VIRTUE
                R. M. MURCHISON.

13, *Gate St., Lincoln's-Inn-Fields,*
     January 10, 1861.

LIST OF MEMBERS

OF THE

NUMISMATIC SOCIETY

OF LONDON,

DECEMBER, 1861.

LIST OF MEMBERS

OF THE

NUMISMATIC SOCIETY

OF LONDON,

DECEMBER 1861.

An Asterisk prefixed to a name indicates that the Member has compounded for his annual contribution.

*ALEXANDER, EDWARD NELSON, Esq., Halifax, Yorkshire.
ALLEN, WILLIAM, Esq., North Villa, Winchmore Hill, Southgate.
ANDERSON, COL. WILLIAM, C.B., 19, Gloucester Square.

*BABINGTON, REV. CHURCHILL, B.D., St. John's College, Cambridge.
BARTON, WILLIAM HENRY, Esq., Royal Mint, Tower Hill.
BAYLEY, E. CLIVE, Esq., H.E.I.C.S., India.
BERGNE, JOHN B., Esq., F.S.A., Foreign Office, Downing Street, *Vice-President.*
BIRCH, SAMUEL, Esq., F.S.A., British Museum.
BOTFIELD, BERIAH, Esq., M.P., F.R.S., F.S.A., F.G.S., 5, Grosvenor Square.
BOYNE, WILLIAM, Esq., F.S.A., 6, Moore Park Villas, Fulham.
BROWN, THOMAS, Esq., 39, Paternoster Row.
BUNBURY, EDWARD H., Esq., M.A., F.G.S., 15, Jermyn Street.
BURNEY, VENERABLE ARCHDEACON, D.D., F.R.S., F.S.A., Rectory, Sible Hedingham, Essex.
BUSH, COLONEL TOBIN, East Hill Place, Hastings.

CHAMBERS, MONTAGUE, Esq., Q.C., Child's Place, Temple Bar.
COXE, W. H., Esq., F.Z.S., British Museum.

DICKINSON, W. BINLEY, Esq., 5, Lansdowne Terrace, Leamington.
DRYDEN, SIR HENRY, BART., Canon's Ashby, Northamptonshire.

LIST OF MEMBERS.

ENNISKILLEN, RIGHT HON. THE EARL OF, HON. D.C.L., F.R.S., F.G.S., M.R.I.A., Florence Court, Feomanagh, Ireland.
EVANS, JOHN, ESQ., F.S.A., F.G.S., Nash Mills, Hemel Hempstead, *Secretary.*
EVANS, SEBASTIAN, ESQ., M.A., 145, Highgate, Birmingham.

FAIRHOLT, F. W., ESQ., F.S.A., 11, Montpelier Square, Brompton.
FARROW, MORLEY, ESQ., M.R.S.L., Bridgewick Hall, Chapel, near Halstead, Essex.
FOX, LIEUT.-GEN., Addison Road, Kensington.
FRANKS, AUGUSTUS WOLLASTON, ESQ., M.A., Dir. Soc. Ant., British Museum.
FREUDENTHAL, W., ESQ., 4, Newington Place, Kennington Road.

*GUEST, EDWIN, ESQ., LL.D., D.C.L., Master of Caius College, Cambridge.

HARDY, WILLIAM, ESQ., F.S.A., Duchy of Lancaster Office, Somerset House.
HARFORD, REV. F. K., F.S.A., 36, Cavendish Square.
HARTWRIGHT, JOHN HENRY, ESQ., Tarvin Road, Chester.
HAWKINS, EDWARD, ESQ., F.S.A., F.L.S., 6, Lower Berkeley Street, Portman Square, *Vice-President.*
HAWKINS, WALTER, ESQ., F.S.A., 5, Leonard Place, Kensington.
HAY, MAJOR, H.E.I.C.S., Linden Lodge, Loan Head, Edinburgh.

JONES, JAMES COVE, ESQ., F.S.A., Loxley, Wellesbourne, Warwick.
JOYCE, GEO. PRINCE, ESQ., F.S.A., Quay Street, Newport, Isle of Wight.

*LEE, JOHN, ESQ., LL.D., F.R.S., &c., 5, College, Doctors' Commons.
LOEWE, DR. L., M.R.A.S., 46, Buckingham Place, Brighton.

MADDEN, FREDERIC WILLIAM, ESQ., M.R.S.L., British Museum, *Secretary.*
MAYER, JOS., ESQ., F.S.A., Lord Street, Liverpool.
MOORE, GENERAL, 102, Piccadilly, and U.S. Club.
MURCHISON, CAPTAIN, R.M., 27, Milsom Street, Bath.
MUSGRAVE, SIR GEORGE, BART., F.S.A., Eden Hall, Penrith.

LIST OF MEMBERS.

NICHOLS, J. GOUGH, ESQ., F.S.A., 25, Parliament Street.
NICHOLSON, REV. HENRY J. BOONE, D.D., F.S.A., Rectory, St. Alban's.
NORRIS, EDWIN, ESQ., F.S.A., 6, St. Michael's Grove, Brompton.

OLDFIELD, EDMUND, ESQ., M.A., F.S.A., 61, Pall Mall.

PFISTER, JOHN GEORGE, ESQ., British Museum.
POLLEXFEN, REV. J. H., St. Mary's Terrace, Colchester.
POOLE, REGINALD STUART, ESQ., M.R.S.L., British Museum.
POWELL, EDWARD JOS., ESQ., 8, Gordon Street, Gordon Square.
POWNALL, REV. ASSHETON, M.A., South Kilworth, Rugby.

RAMSAY, PROF. W., The College, Glasgow.
RASHLEIGH, JONATHAN, ESQ., 3, Cumberland Terrace, Regent's Park.
RAWLINSON, SIR HENRY C., K.C.B., F.R.S., HON. D.C.L., 39, Hill Street, Berkeley Square.
*READE, REV. J. B., F.R.S., Vicarage, Ellesborough, Bucks.
ROLFE, H. W., ESQ., 3, Punderson Place, Bethnal Green Road.

SALIS, J. F. W. DE, Hillingdon Place, Uxbridge.
SHARP, SAMUEL, ESQ., Dallington Hall, Northampton.
SIM, GEORGE, ESQ., 40, Charlotte Square, Edinburgh.

TAYLOR, CHARLES R., ESQ., 2, Montague Street, Russell Square.
*THOMAS, EDWARD, ESQ., H.E.I.C.S., 2, Albert Place, Kensington.

VAUX, W. SANDYS WRIGHT, ESQ., M.A., F.S.A., F.R.A.S., British Museum, *President*.
VIRTUE, GEORGE HENRY, ESQ., F.S.A., 25, Paternoster Row, *Treasurer*.
VIRTUE, JAMES SPRENT, ESQ., City Road.

WARREN, HON. J. LEICESTER, M.A., 33, St. James's Square.
WEATHERLEY, REV. C., Hillingdon, Uxbridge.
WEBSTER, W., ESQ., 17, Great Russell Street, Covent Garden.
WHITBOURN, RICHARD, ESQ., F.S.A., Bank, Godalming.
*WHITE, JAMES, ESQ., Rochester House, Little Ealing.
WIGAN, EDWARD, ESQ., 17, Highbury Terrace.
WILKINSON, JOHN, ESQ., F.S.A., 3, Wellington Street, Strand.

WILLIAMS, JOHN, ESQ., F.S.A., Royal Astronomical Society, **Somerset House**, *Librarian*.
WINGROVE, DRUMMOND BOND, ESQ., 30, Wood Street, Cheapside.
*WOOD, SAMUEL, ESQ., F.S.A., Shrewsbury.
WORMS, GEORGE, ESQ., 27, Park Crescent, Regent's Park.

HONORARY MEMBERS.

ADRIAN, DR. J. D., **Giessen**.
AKERMAN, J. YONGE, ESQ., F.S.A., Abingdon, **Berkshire**.
ARNETH, PROF. JOSEPH, **Vienna**.

BEHR, THE BARON, Constantinople.

CADALVENE, THE CHEVALIER EDOUARD DE, Constantinople.
CARRARA, PROF. DR. FRANC, Spalatro, Dalmatia.
CASTELLANOS, SEÑOR DON BASILIO SEBASTIAN, **Madrid**.
CAVEDONI, M., Naples.
CHALON, M. RENIER, Brussels.
CLERCQ, M. J. LE, Brussels.
COCHET, M. L'ABBÉ, 128, Rue d'Ecosse, Dieppe.

DELGADO, DON ANTONIO.
DIETRICHSEN, COUNT, **Vienna**.
DORN, DR. BERNHARD, St. Petersburg.

GONZALES, M. CARLO, Rome.
GREVILLE, M. B. DE, Paris.
GROTE, DR. H., Hanover.
GROTEFEND, DR. C. L., **Hanover**.
GUIOTH, M. LEON, **Liége**.

HART, A. WELLINGTON, ESQ., 16, Ex Place, New York.
HILDEBRAND, M. EMIL BROR, Stockholm.
HOLMBOE, PROF., Christiania.

LIST OF MEMBERS.

IVANHOFF, THE CHEVALIER THEODORE, Smyrna.

KŒHNE, DR. BERNHARD DE, St. Petersburg.

LAPLANE, M. EDOUARD, St. Omer.
LEEMANS, DR. CONRAD, Leyden.
LIS Y RIVES, SEÑOR DON V. BERTRAN DE, Madrid.
LONGPÉRIER, M. ADRIEN DE, Musée du Louvre, Paris.
LORICHS, COUNT GUSTAVUS DAN., Madrid.

MELCHIORRI, IL MARCHESE GIUSEPPE DI, Rome.
MINERVINI, CAR. GIULIO, Rome.

NAMUR, DR. A., Luxembourg.
NORTHUMBERLAND, HIS GRACE THE DUKE OF, F.R.S., F.S.A., Northumberland House, Strand.

OSTEN, THE CHEVALIER PROKESCH D', Athens.

PERTHES, M. JACQUES BOUCHER DE CRÈVECŒUR DE, Abbeville.
PIETRASZEWSKI, DR. IGNATIUS, Berlin.
PIRCHE, BARON DE, Avranches, Normandy.

RICCIO, GENNARO, Naples.

SABATIER, M. J., 30, Rue Antoinette, Montmartre, Paris.
SANTAREM, VISCOUNT DE, Paris.
SAULCY, M. F. DE, 5, Rue du Cirque, Paris.
SAUSSAYE, M. DE LA, 38, Rue des Sts. Pères, Paris.
SMITH, DR. AQUILLA, M.R.I.A., Baggot Street, Dublin.
SMITH, C. ROACH, ESQ., F.S.A., Temple Place, Strood, Kent.

THOMSEN, HERR CHRISTIAN JURGENSEN, Copenhagen.

VALLERSANI, IL PROF., Florence.
VERACHTER, M. FREDERICK, Antwerp.

WITTE, M. LE BARON DE, Paris.

www.ingramcontent.com/pod-product-compliance
Lightning Source LLC
Chambersburg PA
CBHW021209230426
43667CB00006B/631